INTERCEPTION

History and Foundations of Information Science
Edited by Michael Buckland, Jonathan Furner, and Markus Krajewski

Human Information Retrieval by Julian Warner

Good Faith Collaboration: The Culture of Wikipedia by Joseph Michael Reagle Jr.

Paper Machines: About Cards & Catalogs, 1548–1929 by Markus Krajewski, translated by Peter Krapp

Information and Intrigue: From Index Cards to Dewey Decimals to Alger Hiss by Colin B. Burke

Indexing It All: The Subject in the Age of Documentation, Information, and Data by Ronald E. Day

Bibliometrics and Research Evaluation: The Good, the Bad, and the Ugly by Yves Gingras

Search Foundations: Toward a Science of Technology-Mediated Experience by Sachi Arafat and Elham Ashoori

The Information Manifold: Why Computers Can't Solve Algorithmic Bias and Fake News by Antonio Badia

Documentarity: Evidence, Ontology, and Inscription by Ronald E. Day

The Infographic: A History of Data Graphics in News and Communications by Murray Dick

The Typographic Medium by Kate Brideau

Power of Position: Classification and the Biodiversity Sciences by Robert D. Montoya

Picture-Work: How Libraries, Museums, and Stock Agencies Launched a New Image Economy by Diana Kamin

Cats, Carpenters, and Accountants: Bibliographical Foundations of Information Science by Wayne de Fremery

Interception: State Surveillance from Postal Systems to Global Networks by Bernard Keenan

INTERCEPTION

STATE SURVEILLANCE FROM POSTAL SYSTEMS
TO GLOBAL NETWORKS

BERNARD KEENAN

THE MIT PRESS   CAMBRIDGE, MASSACHUSETTS   LONDON, ENGLAND

The MIT Press
Massachusetts Institute of Technology
77 Massachusetts Avenue, Cambridge, MA 02139
mitpress.mit.edu

© 2025 Massachusetts Institute of Technology

This work is subject to a Creative Commons CC-BY-NC-ND license.

This license applies only to the work in full and not to any components included with permission. Subject to such license, all rights are reserved. No part of this book may be used to train artificial intelligence systems without permission in writing from the MIT Press.

The MIT Press would like to thank the anonymous peer reviewers who provided comments on drafts of this book. The generous work of academic experts is essential for establishing the authority and quality of our publications. We acknowledge with gratitude the contributions of these otherwise uncredited readers.

This book was set in Stone Serif and Avenir LT Std. by Westchester Publishing Services. Printed and bound in the United States of America.

Library of Congress Cataloging-in-Publication Data

Names: Keenan, Bernard, author.
Title: Interception : state surveillance from postal systems to global networks / Bernard Keenan.
Description: Cambridge, Massachusetts : The MIT Press, 2025. | Series: History and foundations of information science | Includes bibliographical references and index.
Identifiers: LCCN 2024035306 (print) | LCCN 2024035307 (ebook) | ISBN 9780262552578 (paperback) | ISBN 9780262383448 (epub) | ISBN 9780262383455 (pdf)
Subjects: LCSH: Domestic intelligence—Great Britain. | Domestic intelligence—United States. | Electronic surveillance—Great Britain. | Electronic surveillance—United States. | Privacy, Right of—Great Britain. | Privacy, Right of—United States. | Confidential communications—Government policy—Great Britain. | Confidential communications—Government policy—United States.
Classification: LCC JC596.2.G7 K44 2025 (print) | LCC JC596.2.G7 (ebook) | DDC 353.1/70941—dc23/eng/20241216
LC record available at https://lccn.loc.gov/2024035306
LC ebook record available at https://lccn.loc.gov/2024035307

10 9 8 7 6 5 4 3 2 1

EU product safety and compliance information contact is: mitp-eu-gpsr@mit.edu

For Bo

CONTENTS

ACKNOWLEDGMENTS ix
1   INTRODUCTION 1
2   INTERCEPTION AND SOVEREIGNTY 15
3   INTERCEPTION AND PUBLICITY 37
4   ELECTRICAL INTERCEPTION 71
5   PHONES, SPOOKS, AND THE LEGISLATIVE TURN 105
6   COMPUTATIONAL POWER AND THE RADIO EPOCH 141
7   ENVIRONMENTAL INTERCEPTION 173
8   INTERCEPTION AND INTEGRATION 203

NOTES 217
INDEX 259

ACKNOWLEDGMENTS

First, I thank everyone who has listened, counselled, and cajoled this book into existence over the years. To Alain Pottage and Conor Gearty, thank you for your guidance and belief in me. Thank you Conor for your incisive advice, generosity of spirit, and ongoing friendship. Alain, thank you for being a friend, mentor, and collaborator. No one else has so deeply influenced the way I see the world.

Thanks to Markus Krajewski and Tim Murphy for their lucid reading of the first version of this work. Special thanks to Markus for encouraging me to submit it to the History and Foundations of Information Science series at MIT. At MIT, thanks to Gita Devi Manaktala, Suraiya Jetha, Haley MacArthur, Sheena Meng, Emma Martin, Karen Brogno, and Katie Helke for your expertise and patience in seeing it through. Thanks to Dr Nicola Lennon for expertly indexing the book.

Daniella Lock was an intrepid fellow researcher in the IPT when I started this project. She and Eric Kind, Jude Bunting KC, and Ben Jaffey KC shared many insights into the evolution of the "elucidatory" power. Later, James Ball shared details of his experience working on the Snowden disclosures. To all I am grateful.

My understanding of the changing nature of British state power owes much to Tom Poole and Martin Loughlin, and my understanding of law and information systems is due in great part to Orla Lynskey and Andrew

Murray inviting me to teach on their courses. My interest in German media theory I owe to the intellectual generosity of Bernard Dionysius Geoghegan, who introduced me to the key tenets of Shannon's information theory one sunny afternoon in Görlitzer Park.

Thank you to Peter Goodrich, who shares a passion for the arcane documents of law and an interest in telephone tapping, and to Avery Gordon for her brilliant writing workshops and advice, which helped enormously at a critical moment. Thanks to the students in my Digital Surveillance and Critical Approaches to Technology courses at Birkbeck for their insights and engagement with this material in its various forms, and to Nathan Moore for all the conversations.

Thank you to John Melaugh, Ewan Smith, and Michael Veale for your generous reading and comments, and Paul F. Scott, from whose work I have learned an immense amount. Thank you to my friends who have helped more than you know over the years, especially David E. Sugar, Alicia Nunes, Connal Parsley, Hyo Yoon Kang, Luke McDonagh, Tatiana Flessas, Kei Yoshida, Insa Koch, Kate Leader, Signe Larsen, Irene Claeys, Ross McElwain, Priya Gupta, Natalie Hanman, Syma Tariq, Deborah Pearson, Douglas Murphy, Alex Damianos, and especially Prudence Ivey.

I am grateful for the patient assistance of the staff of the National Archives of the UK at Kew, the Postal Museum and Archive, the British Library, and the BT Archives in London, especially the former telephone engineer who explained to me, in impressive detail, how telephone tapping was carried out in the analog era.

Most of all, I thank my family. Roisin McAuley and Richard Lee offered a home away from home when I first moved to London. This book could not have happened without them. More recently, Keith and Julia Bottomley helped so much, especially during the final weeks of writing. I thank my parents, Brian and Anne, for always encouraging me to follow my interests wherever they took me, and my brother John and sister Rachel for your love. Finally, I could not have completed this book without the love, patience, and support of my wife and best friend, Bo Bottomley, and Oisín, the little deer who lights up our lives every day.

1
INTRODUCTION

This book relays the story of interception powers in Britain and their relationship to the law from the seventeenth century to the present. In every age, interception shadows communication. There can be no technical communication without the risk that a message will be interfered with, copied, delayed, or stolen. The history of interception is therefore a particular history of communication media and power; both the power to control media, and their role in the production of power.

This book links interception powers to the dominant mode of technical communication in each era. In the postal epoch, the control of the sorting room afforded sovereigns a panoptic view of letters and parcels. The media of the electrical epoch transformed perceptions of time and space in communication and were accompanied by new legal forms that maintained state access to and appropriation of communication power. In the twentieth century, the automation of electromechanical teletext led to typewriters with supposedly unbreakable encryption built in, until the analysts and engineers at Bletchley Park built the first computers that guessed the solutions millions of times faster than anyone in history. Digital interception now takes place as a function of computer networks, which have again transformed the meaning and sense of communication.

Law's history is usually told through a succession of proclamations, legislation, cases, and conventions. Legal history therefore occludes the law's intrinsic dependence on media. On one level, law depends on the media that communicate it, give it form, and allow it to circulate within a given territory, institution, or computer network. On another level, law is called on to shape what media are, how they operate, and who may control them. Media technology changes faster than law, without giving warnings or asking for permission. In this respect, law is always playing catch-up with its own conditions of possibility.[1]

The history of law and interception power in Britain renders this relationship visible for several reasons. First, because of the secrecy of interception powers, they came to occupy a peculiar non-place within the edifice of British public law, which developed without a written constitutional document. Since the seventeenth century, successive secretaries of state have issued warrants permitting the intelligence organs of the state to open letters, read telegrams, tap telephone calls, intercept radio signals, and gather bulk quantities of private data. Yet successive governments kept interception powers out of view of the legal system for as long as possible. In the postal epoch, the power was sometimes identified with the doctrines of *raison d'état* and the royal prerogative, but by the mid-twentieth century, when people expected a right to privacy in their communication, a judicial committee inquiring into the legality of tapping telephones was unable to articulate a coherent basis for it in the law. For 350 years following the foundation of the Post Office in 1635, the power to intercept private communication had been treated as an administrative capacity of the state, with no need of articulation in legislation or judicial authority, an inherent feature of any medium that the government arrogated.

The government retained and defended its power to intercept communications with no oversight until 1985, when legislation was passed in response to an adverse decision of the European Court of Human Rights. The Interception of Communications Act 1985 provided a legislative basis for the interception power and introduced some thin regulations on its use. With the rise of the internet and the increasing importance of human rights law, that legislation was revised by the Regulation of Investigatory Powers Act 2000. Although the act provided a more detailed legal framework for investigatory powers, including interception, it was deliberately opaque as to how the most secret powers worked in practice.

In 2013, the true extent of the surveillance programs carried out under the law's auspices was revealed by Edward Snowden, the National Security Agency (NSA) whistleblower. Following political outcry, the law was revised again by the Investigatory Powers Act 2016, which makes clear the nature and scope of the powers to intercept, acquire, interfere with, and otherwise gain access to private communications and data. After Snowden, the public was acutely aware of the scope of surveillance that our digital media environment has made possible, and the era of obfuscation was over. Today, the Investigatory Powers Act 2016 describes a full suite of powers over communication that the government can utilize, requires that they only be used when necessary and proportionate, and subjects the regime to independent yet semisecret oversight.

The aim of the current legal framework is to ensure an "appropriate balance" between privacy and security on a case-by-case basis, drawing on principles and norms imported from the transnational European Convention on Human Rights, particularly Article 8 (the right to private and family life) and Article 10 (freedom of expression). Yet, as this book shows, things may be changing yet again.

MEDIA THEORY AND INTERCEPTION

Rather than relaying a linear history of the law, this book adopts a media theoretical genealogical methodology. According to this approach, communication media play tricks on human perception. Advancing technical standards fundamentally transform the way that we perceive ourselves and the world around us, yet they always seem natural to us at the time. As Marshall McLuhan put it, we have a "rear-view mirror view of the world."[2] Because it conditions our perception, the effect of the media environment is invisible to us while we are experiencing it. We can properly understand it only in the abstract, and see it clearly only when one media epoch has been superseded by another.

According to Friedrich Kittler, drawing on the French psychoanalyst Jacques Lacan, media elude direct observation because cultural discourse operates at the level of the *imaginary*. Modern humanism, for instance, posits an idealized fantasy of the human as the constant universal feature of history, essentially unchanged in a changing world. But such illusions are always conditioned by the order of the *symbolic*. The symbolic is the field where language and the unconscious operate, preceding and conditioning the imaginary. In their physical, programmable operations, they communicate, store, and process our access to reality. The symbolic order is the condition of possibility of sensing and understanding ourselves and our environment. Underlying this is the *real*, which exists beyond language and symbolization, which resists capture and means knowledge is always incomplete. By denoting written symbols, recording sounds, or capturing visual images, media establish the hardware on which the human cultural imaginary operates.[3] And when media undergo revolutionary changes, so too does the human—or, in Kittler's refrain, "so-called Man."[4]

For most of human history, media operated purely in the realm of the symbolic—primarily alphabetic writing. Technical and electrical media of the nineteenth century, particularly phonographs and film, went beyond the symbolic. They captured time—in the shifting frequencies of audio recordings and the rapid sequencing of images that appeared to move—and thus aspects of the *real*, which had previously escaped symbolization, were brought into the imaginary as elements that could be experienced and even manipulated. The typewriter and the telegraph, meanwhile, converted handwriting into discrete blocks of text, uniformly spaced and sequenced in time, changing the alphabet from a carrier of human thought into an object of mathematical research. Codes and formulae emerged based on the differences, frequencies, and forms of its elements. Language became the subject matter of a new science that would eventually be named "information."[5]

Therefore, Kittler suggests, in each media epoch, the perception of the human is itself contingent on the standards of technical media. Every culture can be defined by its media standards. This in turn explains why digital media have, since the Second World War, caused so many crises in human culture: digital media can perfectly simulate all other media, as Alan Turing already understood when he proposed a hypothetical programmable computer, the "universal discrete machine," as a thought experiment in 1936.[6] Today, the smartphone screen presents users with all the processing capacities of past media: the notepad, the camera, the tape recorder, the telephone, the postal service, the book, the map, the oracle. But this is merely a surface effect of digital operations that link the device to global computational networks while remaining below the threshold of perception. Computers and humanity are inseparably linked in an accelerating feedback loop. To grasp our situation, we need an analysis of the commands, addresses, and data flows that now condition reality through their binary operations.[7]

Interception is a unique phenomenon in the history of media for several reasons. First, it disrupts the illusion of smooth communication and control that all media offer their users. As we shall see, the interceptors have always been technicians, from Sir Samuel Morland in the seventeenth century, whose essay on letter interception opens the next chapter of this book, to Edward Snowden in the twenty-first century, a systems analyst who decided to debug the legal system, as he saw it.[8] Interception means ignoring the imaginary illusion of interpersonal communication and coming to grips with the processing, storage, and transmission standards of technology.

The second reason is the secrecy factor. When we examine the possibilities of technical interception, we see that it is often a small inflection or variation on the "normal" transmission, storage, or processing operations carried out in everyday communication. Where and how such inflections can happen depend on spatial and temporal factors related to the design and operation of the medium itself. In the postal era, it was the sorting room; in the telegraphic era, it was the filing cabinets containing records of telegrams; and in the radio era, it concerned electromagnetic waves propagating around the globe. Today, it is in the codes, protocols, and infrastructure of the same digital networks that make up the internet. The book argues that gaining access to media-technical operations, controlling them, and using them secretly against others is one of the secret marks of sovereign power. Thus, to resist the power of a sovereign, or to wage war against a rival sovereign, is to be confronted with the problem of communication security. Cryptography is not only a key strategic aspect of every interception regime, it has historically stimulated the study and technical development of media, most famously the early computers built to crack German codes at Bletchley Park.

This leads to the third reason. Legal tools have been used to define the difference between interception and normal transmission from the beginning, even when no statutory law formally describing and authorizing the power existed. The key device is the interception warrant. By tracing the history of interception warrants, showing how they changed in form and content, and understanding how they were made and used in different media epochs, this book reveals a secret relationship between interception and legality that prefigures the turn to legislation in the 1980s. Law and legal technique have been there from the beginning, giving form to interception power, enabling it, and maintaining the sovereign state's ability to access and observe communication.

By foregrounding technical media as a condition of communication and interception power, the book also takes a cue from Michel Serres, a French philosopher of technology. In his book *The Parasite*, Serres played on a French word, *parasite*, which means both "noise" and "interference" in a communication channel and something that feeds from a host while offering nothing in return—an uninvited guest. According to information theory, the mathematical science that enabled technical media to advance to the digital age by compressing information to its informative elements, the goal of successful communication is to eliminate noise from the channel to get a clear, pure transmission of information from A to B. For Serres, this ideal form of communication is a modern fantasy, with parallels found in every philosophical, legal, and political idea of a purified order. Serres points out that the elimination of static—of *le parasite* as such—is not possible. The parasite is not an intruder upon otherwise pristine communication but an effect of the communication system itself. The parasite is present in all communication media, yet excluded from their description. The medium is a "quasi-object"—its meaning depends on how it is observed. Viewed from the outside, it simply enables communication, and the parasite is regarded as a problematic interference. For the parasite, however, the interior of the medium is its whole environment. The communication that it interferes with is its nourishment. The parasite is thus in the position of the excluded middle, the blind spot of observation.

Serres applies this parasitic structure to language, thermodynamics, and ultimately all objects in the universe. Even political sovereignty depends on a parasitic relationship. Sovereignty enables communication and community as such, yet at the same time impedes and frustrates their realization. Sovereign power depends in each system on attempts to introduce control and bring order to the chaos from which communication emerges. Yet in so doing, the interceptors only produce a new relation and are, in turn, confronted by the very same problems they try to eliminate: the intercepted system turns on the interceptors in turn and tries to eliminate them from the system by recourse to the law.[9] In other words, media set the stage for an irresolvable tension between order and noise, law and power, community and sovereign, privacy and secrecy, and so on. Interception—including the attempt to write its history—is marked by this permanent contestation of order and interference.

When Snowden was asked by journalists in 2013 what he aimed to achieve through his disclosures of top secret files from the NSA, he spoke about the need for greater "technical literacy," which in our society "is a rare and precious resource."[10] Through technical literacy, he implied, better laws will be made that will limit or prevent the mass surveillance programs that he uncovered. But if technical literacy is read back into the archives, it suggests that the idea that law could guarantee pure communication without parasitic interception is a fantasy, too. That doesn't mean that law isn't important, or that Snowden was wrong. Rather, it means that law is shaped by the technical a priori of media. Every legal relationship is structured by a third element, a medium, whose operations cannot be directly included in the law, and that cannot be suppressed or commanded by the law. To understand communication, media, information, and power, we must pay attention to the technical production of the relations that precondition the subjects and objects that law imagines. This is both an abstract proposition and a call to examine the immanent techniques and media that enable communication almost imperceptibly around us.[11]

GENEALOGY AND METHOD

While informed by media theory and history, this book primarily draws on Foucault's genealogy of the "arts of government" in its approach to interception, tracing the "rationalization of governmental practice in the exercise of political sovereignty."[12] The focus on practice is key. Instead of beginning with the legal form of the state, Foucault focuses on the strategies, procedures, techniques, and ideas that were practiced at times and places. In this way, the "state" emerges as an effect of practices and technologies but has no fixed essence beyond those practices.[13] Changes occur in the meaning and practice of power from the outside, from the environment of power where media prefigure all relations.

To get away from thinking with the well-established categories of "law," "state," and "power," which bring a lot of taken-for-granted analytic baggage with them, Foucault proposed outlining *dispositifs*, deployed here in the translated form of "apparatus."[14] Foucault described an apparatus as "an essentially heterogeneous ensemble, composed of discourses, institutions, architectural formation, regulatory decisions, laws, administrative measures, scientific statements, philosophical, moral, and philanthropic arguments."[15] Its elements are connected contingently and, as they are not produced by an exterior or abstract power, composed only of the things that the apparatus organizes.

Finally, in any historical moment, an apparatus emerges because it has a strategic and functional role to play in an urgent situation that rationalizes it and directs it. This means that an apparatus is contingent on the choices of the researcher who portrays it. On the other hand, it allows critical connections to be drawn across diverse places and situations and demonstrates the contingencies that have, over time, sedimented to produce the rational order of things that we live with today.

The book argues that each media epoch has a distinctive interception regime, each involving a different combination of legal texts, administrative techniques, and normative codes. These include governmental theories, techniques, and modes of resistance to interception, and all are defined in relation to the dominant communication technology. The book shows how law and legislation play key roles in each iteration of the interception apparatus. Law stabilizes its form; defines its permissible uses; regulates, limits, and directs its operations; and even sets its external targets. This is how state power was actively made and remade through communication media.

By beginning in the postal epoch, the book identifies interception as a specifically modern technique, arising from an attitude that "presupposes, and thrives on, contingency."[16] For Foucault, contingency clearly differentiates modernity from non-modernity. At stake in the difference is a transformation in attitudes to the future. Foucault captured the difference in his well-known distinction between "classical" sovereignty, characterized simply by the right "to take life or let live," and modern biopolitics, characterized by the right "to make live and to let die."[17] The classical sovereign had a simple power over its subjects. It could ignore them or, if they transgressed the law, put them to death. The modern government, by contrast, involves a complex set of concerns for life itself. It takes account of statistical regularities, different economies and economic effects, and scientific forms of knowledge. Law is no longer fixed and natural but something that is actively changed to produce better outcomes. In short, life itself became an object to work on, grow, discipline, and govern.

A key insight of Foucault's work is that this transformation in power happens in response to contingency. Contingency is not something outside the order of government; rather, government is constantly producing and consuming contingency, converting it into plans, programs, and justifications for "exceptional" action that is everywhere the norm. Premodern cosmologies had attributed unexpected events, failures, and uncertainties to the will of fate, God, or nature—that is, something outside the perceptible world. By contrast, modernity intervenes in nature and treats the future as a horizon of risk and opportunity. After this epistemic break, events are effects of decisions previously taken. The discourses of security and intelligence that open the era of letter interception in the Post Office were a direct response to this realization of contingency and risk. From there, the security and intelligence priorities of the state have taken many forms, but they are all characterized by attentiveness to risk and a desire to manage the future.

The operation of law is conditioned by the operations of the underlying technical environment. Privacy, the other side of legal discourse on interception, is just as much an affordance of communication technologies of a given era. And as with legislation, the configuration of the rules, design, and operations of digital media can always be revised. For the purposes of this study, attention is therefore paid not only to the way that the power was understood within the state, as a juridical matter, but to the media technical dimensions through which legal rules and devices took effect and the filing systems from which intercepted information were converted into intelligence. The book filters the history of British public law through the media-genealogical approach articulated by Cornelia Vismann.[18]

SOURCES

The material on which the book is based is necessarily varied and diverse. For the period prior to the Second World War, the National Archives of the UK at Kew reveal much about the materiality of interception and the way that it was understood within government, particularly as manifested in interception warrants, which are scattered throughout different files and folios. These materials are combined with historical accounts of the postal system and intelligence apparatus of the British state to contextualize and understand their significance. A partial and fragmented collection of warrants, documents, files, copybooks, case notes, intercepted letters and telegrams, and other material connected to interception powers has made it possible to build a media-focused account of the power prior to 1945. Yet only what is no longer considered volatile can become a public record, and many classified documents have not survived long enough to make it to the open archive.

For the period after the Second World War, the records containing warrants and other operational material remain closed, but a greater volume of historical research and journalistic sources is available. In recent decades, the British government reversed its policy of absolute secrecy and has now permitted authorized histories of its major intelligence services, which have added important context, especially the work of John Ferris in the Government Communication Headquarters (GCHQ) archives.[19] This book also draws on the excellent mapping and interpretation work already done in relation to the law's historical role around intelligence and interception, particularly that of Phil Glover, Paul F. Scott, Keith Ewing, Joan Mahoney, and Andrew Moretta. The technical side of interception was uncovered through historical accounts and archival work in the British Telecom Archives, where a helpful archivist explained how wiretapping was performed back when he was a telephone engineer, and in the Postal Museum and Archive in London.[20] On some issues, investigative journalism by Duncan Campbell, Mark Leopold, and Peter Fitzgerald, published in the 1970s and 1980s, remains the only source of insight.

Although British legislation said very little about interception powers for over 350 years, the administrative techniques through which they were described and controlled offer a partial media genealogy of state intelligence. As Cornelia Vismann put it in her study of the materiality of administrative bureaucracy, the "spirit of officialdom" is "materialized in files," which operate not at the level of legal or political theory but as mechanisms, techniques, and technologies that provide power with its infrastructure.[21] The processes by which such documents and files are created and operationalized normally remain beneath the threshold of legal and political discourse, although they are the material substrate on which law and administrative power are made possible.

The overriding aim is to offer a genealogical account of the techniques and juridical forms of interception as they exist today so as to critically understand the conditions by which the present situation was made possible. With digital communication and especially the internet, all previous forms of media coexist side by side. Digital media can simulate all other media and impose rules, norms, and restrictions mutably, contingently, but with perfect control. Law attempts to narrow the scope and regulate the application, but it is in effect already transformed into an element of the programs and interfaces of digital media.

OUTLINE OF THE CHAPTERS

Chapter 2 traces the birth of interception in England in the seventeenth century, outlining the formation of the postal service as a surveillance apparatus and a means of bringing order to the nascent territorial state. Interception was an operation carried out within the internal space of the sorting room, where a disciplinary structure ensured the constant flow and surveillance of letters. Absolute sovereignty and *raison d'état* justified the power, leaving no possibility of legal resistance. Instead, writers turned to ciphers and illegal postal networks. Interception techniques and codebreaking became *arcana imperii*, the highest secrets of the state.

Chapter 3 follows the development of the postal system in the eighteenth and nineteenth centuries. The General Post Office served as a key apparatus for the intelligence of the state as it became governmentalized. In other words, the problems of government no longer concerned preserving the rule of the sovereign over the territory but took a growing interest in the population rather than individual subjects.[22] By the middle of the nineteenth century, when a scandal over letter interception at the Post Office created a political controversy, a process of de-intensification of surveillance and espionage unfolded. In place of the police state, Britain developed a more reflexive rationality, putting greater value on the need to grow commerce and communication than to suppress opposition. At the same time, the arts of government became sensitized to their own publicity, at which point the modern logic of official secrecy set in, becoming an article of bureaucratic faith for the coming century.

Chapter 4 reviews the interception of new electrical media as they were developed and deployed in the late nineteenth century and up to the outbreak of the First World War. We consider the "chronopoetics" of electrical media,[23] which engendered a radical reconfiguration of power, time, and space. The chapter reviews electrical telegraphy, both domestically and internationally; telephony, which was legally classified as a species of telegraphy in Britain; and wireless telegraphy. These technologies were developed during a period of liberal biopolitical rationality in Britain. The potential scope of the surveillance power they enabled was understood, and they were not yet regarded as private media. The full scale of interception, however, would not be demonstrated until the First World War.

Interception in the twentieth century is divided across two chapters. Chapter 5 traces the development of telephone interception, commonly called "tapping," in the "internal" domestic realm of the UK. The focus is on the Security Service, which used tapping extensively and without oversight until 1989 in its self-directed mission to tackle "subversion." Although there was widespread knowledge and concern about the power of the state to tap telephones, it was politically accepted that regulating the power would risk diminishing its efficacy. From a legal perspective, however, it became increasingly impossible to rationalize how it could be used at all. When a police wiretap was accidentally exposed in court, a legal process was set in motion that finally introduced some legislative control over the power.

Chapter 6 traces the development of global interception in the twentieth century as an effect of the epoch of radio. If the First World War suggested the potential of radio to transform military power, the Second World War confirmed it. In between, improvements in wireless and cable media made it possible to send messages at ever-higher frequencies, while the same electromechanical developments made it possible to design and build seemingly unbreakable encryption systems. The era of human computing was superseded by the advent of digital computing at Bletchley Park, where Alan Turing and Tommy Flowers form to his universal discrete machine, the medium that can imitate any other. From that point on, Britain began integrating its interception apparatus with that of the US, exchanging territorial reach for technological power, setting the stage for a global interception apparatus that by the close of the century was absorbing, processing, and analyzing a significant proportion of the world's electronic communications at an industrial scale.

Chapter 7 turns to the internet and the documents that Edward Snowden disclosed from the NSA in 2013. It argues that Snowden had a media-technical epistemology of the law that motivated his actions. The chapter highlights three broad categories of interception and related techniques: the interception and collection of massive volumes of data in transit, the acquisition of bulk quantities of data at rest, and the covert hacking of computers and networks. It argues that the revelations ended an era of legalized obfuscation, ushering in a reflexive, adaptive legal regime in its place. Moreover, it reveals an elucidatory approach not only to the law but to the objects of surveillance generally. Threats, patterns, and surprises are constantly being *discovered* in data mining, drawing on diverse and contingent sources of information, leading to a form of power that closely resembles a system closely attuned to its environment. The law productively integrates the media-technical form of environmental power with society, carving out protected categories of rights that provide conditional and limited degrees of protection from otherwise ubiquitous surveillance powers.

The concluding chapter draws out developments since Snowden, focusing on the interrelated themes of privatization, encryption, and the growing importance of tapping into the abundance of data circulating through commercial networks. Having shown throughout the book that interception is a shadow of communication media, chapter 8 ends with an analysis of contemporary interception practices as they are integrated with global computational networks. Interception is here read through Benjamin Bratton's concept of the "stack,"[24] a heuristic model for understanding sovereignty's ongoing reconfiguration in the age of planetary computation and platform capitalism.

2

INTERCEPTION AND SOVEREIGNTY

This chapter traces the birth of organized postal interception in Britain during the seventeenth century, the period of the English Civil War, the Interregnum, and the Restoration of the monarchy. It demonstrates how the power to open, detain, or delay letters was understood as an element of *raison d'état*, the expression of the will of the absolute sovereign. The significance of the discourse of "reason of state" is that it places interception powers on the side of the police state and, in this way, exempts them from the law. For this reason, there was no question of a right to privacy in correspondence, and no such right was asserted. Without law, epistolary subjects instead used techniques of encipherment to protect their correspondence from the interceptors, with limited success. This chapter also describes the central importance of the inception warrant, which even in its nascent form was a device that organized, controlled, and directed the power, giving form to the authority claimed in the name of reason of state and exercised by the sovereign's most important minister, the secretary of state.

The chapter argues that in the seventeenth century, interception and the subjective interpretation of intercepted letters were elements in a wider security apparatus that depended not on political justification but on the consolidation and formation of a unitary postal service, a key element in the emergence of territorial sovereignty precipitated from the civil wars of the seventeenth century. The modern state "needed to be imagined and personified before it could exist," requiring a new "spatial demarcation of political authority,"[1] and postal monopolization was a practical necessity for that emergence to occur. Interception was an inflection on practical postal operations; in other words, the same processes necessary to produce and tax a unified flow of letters necessarily afforded the chance to intercept them. The postal service was as much an object of security rationality as it was of commerce and communication. The role of the warrant, as an administrative device within the apparatus, was to direct and limit the power, designate targets, and ensure that sovereign power was maintained over the growing flow of letters passing through the sorting room.

OF INTELLIGENCE

Late in his life, the seventeenth-century English polymath Samuel Morland wrote a short essay entitled *A Brief Discourse concerning the Nature and Reason of Intelligence*, offering advice to princes on letter interception:

> Now among many other expedients for carrying on and settling a universal correspondence, A skilful Prince ought to make watch towers of his General Post Office of all his kingdoms and there to place such careful Sentinels, as that by their gaze and diligence he may have a constant view of all of any moment throughout the universe: but more especially of the various tempers of his own subjects, and of the first ferments of all factions, without which it is morally impossible for him long to sit on his throne, or to manage successfully the topping men of so many different Parties, and the Heroes of the Populace who like the untamed horses have thrown their unskilful riders many times within these fifty years. . . . And for want of this art and good intelligence, a Prince may lose his Crown or life, witness Charles I and James II.[2]

The text is within the genre of essays on "advice to the prince" that gave intellectual form to early modern discourse about sovereignty and reason of state. At the outbreak of the Thirty Years' War in Europe in 1618, Europe was flooded with printed pamphlets, books, and newsletters detailing, criticizing, and promoting the "unscrupulous methods of political action" known as "reason of state."[3] Machiavelli's *The Prince* (1532) is foundational, alongside the late Roman writer Tacitus, although the phrase *"ragion di stato"* was first popularized by Botero (1589) who heard it openly discussed at different royal courts.[4] This mode of political thought concerns utility, calculation, the prudent exercise of power, the assertion of necessity over law, and the justification for deception and strategy in the preservation of absolute sovereignty. It gave not only advice but political content to the emergent form of the territorial state,[5] and it was read widely in Europe.

Morland's contribution derives from his experience as a skilled interceptor of letters, first for the Protectorate government of Oliver Cromwell between 1649 and 1660, then for the "restored" monarchy of King Charles II. By the time Morland wrote his essay in 1695, he had seen two kings deposed: Charles I, who was executed in 1649 when Cromwell took power; and Charles II's successor, James II, who was removed from the throne by Parliament in the "Glorious Revolution" of 1688 and replaced by his niece, Mary II. These machinations provide context for the fundamental problem Morland addressed. His skills during that period allowed the discovery of plots, the subversion of trust among enemies by censoring or altering their correspondence, and the monitoring of shifting allegiances at home and abroad. As he put it, princes "move in orbes excentrick" to their neighbors and allies in a chaotic, treacherous world, where no agreements outlast their utility. His philosophical anthropology is implicitly predicated on humans as fundamentally evil, corrupt, traitorous, and brutal. Politically wise rulers must "use all endeavours . . . to know what cards are in their neighbours' hands,"[6] using their postal system as a machine for discovering the true intentions of subjects, enemies, and allies.

The equivalence Morland draws in his essay between "Prince" and "state" mirrors the two forms of sovereign regime that he served: the Protectorate, which proclaimed sovereignty in the name of the body politic represented by Parliament, and the restored monarchy of Charles II, who, like the rest of the Stuart dynasty, claimed that the divine right of princes gave him absolute authority. By 1695, the balance of power between Crown and Parliament had settled on parliamentary sovereignty, decisively as it would prove, although that was not yet certain.[7]

Seventeenth-century European sovereigns asserted absolute legal authority because their power was anything but absolute, depending no longer on religious and moral right but on the skillful management of political contingency. The arts of government were ever more concerned with interest, risk, utility, and profit. In turn, the question of "interest" came to constitute a basis for acting. The instrumentalism exemplified by Tacitus and Machiavelli displaced Christian and Aristotelian morality as the foundation of governmental logic.[8] As Foucault observed, the reality of sovereignty required new techniques for mastering the practical knowledge of "things rather than knowledge of the law, and this knowledge of the things that comprise the very reality of the state is precisely what at the time was called "statistics.""[9]

Morland's technical interception skills are only indirectly documented today.[10] During the Protectorate (1649–1660), he and his assistant, Isaac Dorislaus, intercepted letters at the General Post Office. The intelligence gained was reported to John Thurloe, Cromwell's secretary of state. An account was later provided by John Wildman, a fellow republican who later became postmaster general. Each post night, at about eleven o'clock, Dorislaus went to a private room allocated to him next to the foreign letters sorting room, where he had

> all the letters brought and laid before him, to open any as he should see good, and close them up again, and there he remained in that room, usually till about three or four in the morning, which was the usual time of shutting up the mail. And in process of time the said Dorislaus had got such knowledge of all hands and seals, that scarcely could a letter be brought him but he knew the hand that wrote it.[11]

Morland joined Dorislaus in the General Letter Office after midnight. The pair were primarily concerned with diplomatic correspondence to and from foreign embassies, as ambassadors and foreign ministers "are for the most part but great spies."[12] Sometimes, certain postal routes were ordered to be searched through—for instance, all the letters from Paris—but they normally operated from a written list of named targets supplied by Thurloe. The list, as Cornelia Vismann emphasizes, is a form of purely functional writing used to "control transfer operations," "sort and engender circulations," and thus listing is the basic technique of all written administrative cultures.[13]

Dorislaus's technique for opening seals was crude: melting the underside of the wax with a hot knife while trying to keep the imprinted surface intact, which according to Wildman left clear traces of interference. Morland, by contrast, took plaster impressions of his targets' seals and made careful forgeries, allowing him to simply remove the original seal entirely and replace it. He was reported to have invented a mechanical device for perfectly opening, copying, and resealing letters by wetting the ink and taking an impression, but it was apparently destroyed in the Great Fire of London.[14] He could mimic handwriting and recall on sight the hand and seals of his regular targets. As addressee's names were pseudonymized, such knowledge of handwriting was vital. The form of early modern letters was significant to their readers. Many letters were produced by professional secretariats, with different individuals taking charge of different aspects of the letter, such as drafting, writing the main body text, the signature, the superscription, and the enciphering, while even autographic letters followed epistolary conventions and formal structures.[15]

Thurloe's intelligence successes from interception included the undoing of the Sealed Knot conspiracy, for which Morland did the work: his intercepts uncovered the plot, observed their plans, and allowed him to interject forged correspondence to sow paranoia, insinuating that the conspirators had betrayed one another.[16] The techniques that he deployed offer an anatomy of the technologies of letters. The "privacy" afforded by the capacity of paper to be folded and sealed by wax depended on the production and distribution of paper, which began in Europe around the mid-thirteenth century.[17] Until then, the relationship between power and writing was manifest through elaborate parchment documents and rolls recording singular events, writs, and payments. Kings were among the first consumers of paper, applying their signatures (or "sign manual") to folded letters that could bypass the machinery of seals, privy councillors, and the chancery. In short, paper letters were the material precondition for modern political secrecy and private writing.[18]

CIVIL WAR

The interception of letters during the seventeenth century was no great secret. It was known to be endemic in an environment of religious and political civil war. The notoriety of the interceptors served "to discourage conspirators from using such a reliable means of transmission of communication, for fear of the regime gaining the insight."[19] Foreign ambassadors took steps to avoid the office with their dispatches or delay submitting them until the last possible moment to minimize interception time.[20] Bribes were paid for conspirators' letters.[21]

Letter interception had antecedents, but none on the same scale or with the same level of intensity: documents ordering letters be stopped at ports in times of war survive from as early as the fourteenth century,[22] when royal writs were issued to "mayors, sheriffs and bailiffs for the apprehension and examination of travelers, who were suspected of conveying treasonable correspondence between England and the Continent."[23] The first English monarch to organize an intelligence networks of spies, informers, and letter interceptors was Elizabeth I (1533–1603). Deciphered letters were key to the "Babington Plot" uncovered in 1586 by Elizabeth's secretary of state, Sir Francis Walsingham, which led to the execution for treason of her cousin Mary, Queen of Scots.[24] But those events relied on interceptions carried out on the roads or stealing and bribing couriers and postal officials across Europe. They preceded the monopolization of the postal system, the precondition for giving effect to the kind of observation that Morland imagined.[25]

In the sixteenth century, bags of letters were distributed abroad and domestically, not only by royal messengers but more commonly by guilds of merchant traders and the universities of continental Europe, where a decentralized set of postal networks had been established.[26] In London, the continental merchants' mail was known as the Merchant Posts and Strangers' Posts.[27] Under threat of Spanish invasion,[28] Elizabeth banned all but the royal messengers from carrying mail in and out of England by proclamation in 1591,[29] the first assertion of the English state's obsessive monopoly over communication.[30] Earlier networks existed across the continent, but each tended to carry its own kinds of correspondence: the university handled letters and payments from students, the merchants sent bills and contracts, and the king's messengers dispatched warrants and commands.[31] Known as *nuncii et cursores*, the medieval messengers were "intimately connected with the person of the sovereign."[32] They carried letters abroad to foreign courts, assembled local assemblies in the shires, carried proclamations of new laws around the kingdom, summoned the nobility to appear before the monarch, and distributed papal decrees, but their main occupation was tethering the Chancery and Exchequer to the court as it moved around the country.[33]

The monopolization of letter carrying and the opening of the posts as a public communication service are therefore intimately linked to the differentiation of the modern nation-state as the locus of political authority. In England, the Letter Office was opened to public use in 1635 by Thomas Witherings, the first postmaster general.[34] The royal messengers had long carried official documents and dispatches along a set of postal roads, each with fixed "posts" where horses were stabled and riders could rest,[35] which were maintained at significant cost to the Exchequer by deputy postmasters.[36] Witherings's plan was to convert that expense into a source of revenue and eventually profit.[37]

As the political conflict between Charles I and Parliament intensified over the nature and form of legitimate political authority, control over the posts fragmented. By 1641, there were two postmasters general, one for the Crown and one for Parliament, each nominally controlling posts in their faction's territory while competing with one another.[38] Meanwhile, radical pamphleteers claimed the postal monopoly was itself a violation of the Magna Carta, as freeborn Englishmen had the right to carry letters.[39] A private network was the best defense against interception.

When the English Civil War began, anyone stopped by soldiers on the roads was searched for letters. Royalist letters discovered by the parliamentary forces were sent to a Committee of the Lords in London for inspection and were frequently read aloud in Parliament, sometimes for their political value, sometimes to approve prizes for the soldiers who found them.[40] Some captured letters were printed as propaganda, transforming them into matters for public consumption.[41] Some remained private. Letters addressed to women were generally forwarded intact. Letters addressed to Charles I's wife, Henrietta Maria, were respected at first, until one was found addressed to her from Lord George Digby, the secretary of state. The Commons voted to open it; the House of Lords abstained.[42]

In 1644, the imprisoned writer James Howell published anonymously an open letter that bemoaned the "barbarism" of interception, which left "quite bereft all ingenious Spirits of that correspondency and sweet communication of fancy, which hath been always esteemed the best fuel of affection, and the very marrow of friendship."[43] To refer to oneself in written communication, to risk sharing one's thoughts in correspondence, was to risk their interception. Not even the king's letters were sacred. On June 14, 1645, Charles escaped capture at the Battle of Naseby, but his cabinet of papers was captured. Like most men of letters, he used ciphers to guard his correspondence in case of interception, but the cabinet contained his cipher keys along with plaintext drafts and deciphered versions of letters received. Parliament put them all on public display at Westminster then translated and transcribed them for publication as *The King's Cabinet Opened*. The introductory gloss points out the "cabbalistic" ciphers, mobilizing the general aura of mysticism ascribed to coded writing.[44] The book not only exposed the king's political intentions, undermining any prospect of negotiated peace, but it also symbolized the exposure, profanation, and desecration of mythical *arcana imperii*.[45]

The assertion of the monopoly was deeply unpopular among merchants, evidenced by records of printed pamphlets demanding the freedom to carry letters for reasons of efficiency and principle.[46] In 1649, Edmund Prideaux, postmaster general of the Commonwealth, eliminated a rival merchant postal system established by the Common Council of London during the civil war. Prideaux's men attacked the rival messengers, killing at least one, raided their offices, and appropriated the letters.[47] Private initiatives were similarly suppressed and appropriated in the towns of Bury, Dover, Norwich, and Thetford, but illegal local networks persisted. They charged lower postage and were more popular.[48]

In 1654, Oliver Cromwell, as Lord Protector of the Commonwealth, issued an ordinance reestablishing a General Post Office (GPO), and in 1657, his Parliament confirmed it by legislation.[49] The preamble to the 1657 Act for Settling the Post recognizes the importance of correspondence to commerce and its value to the state in the form of postage as a kind of taxation. The preamble explicitly foregrounds the question of state security, holding that the GPO's purpose was "to discover and prevent many wicked designs, which have been and are daily contrived against the peace and welfare of the Commonwealth, the intelligence whereof cannot well be communicated except by letters of escript."[50]

Legislative preambles disclose the world as the legislator pictures it, therefore they "tell a story that law does not and cannot contain."[51] By indicating problems and purposes that the law aims at, they posit an outline of the world on which law is to act. The General Post Office was to secure, encourage, tax, and inspect the flow of discourse across the territory of the Commonwealth, as the state was then known. While nothing in the legislation itself explicitly authorized interception, we see here the prototype of Morland's "careful sentinel," with its inherent power to regulate, tax, read, and interfere with the flow of writing. The office was "regarded as the pulse of all political movements, the deputy postmasters in the country serving as a hydra-headed agency for the State—seeing, hearing, and reporting everything of importance that transpired in their districts; while the opening of letters in the Post afforded a means of securing evidence against the enemies of the ruling powers for the time being."[52] In August 1659, utilizing this capacity, Cromwell's Council ordered that all mail to Ireland was to be stopped and checked, "not knowing of how dangerous consequence some of the letters might be."[53]

Thurloe survived Charles II's revenge against his father's regicides on account of his "black book," feared to contain many treasonous words copied from the letters of supposedly loyal subjects of the Restoration regime. Thurloe's surviving papers contain many examples of intercepted and deciphered letters, including letters sent from France by the future Charles II while in exile.[54] Morland won favor by turning against the Protectorate and warning Charles of an assassination plot, for which he was rewarded with a knighthood.[55] The Restoration carried on spying on and bribing its opponents and reading their letters and intensified its postal surveillance.[56]

The intelligence produced by the postal system created an economy of secrets and information. Domestic and foreign informers reported on local unrest, foreign shipping news, trade movements, and military developments abroad. In exchange, this small group of informers received not only the government's official postal newsletter, the *London Gazette*, but an additional private newssheet that was handwritten, containing selections of intelligence that they could put to their own advantage.[57] A discourse network emerged based on asymmetries of information, in the process constituting a new modality of power and permanent observation between the apparatus loyal to the king and the growing public that he watched over. It was deeply unpopular. Society was riven by informers, suspicion, and spies. As one historian of espionage put it, "the extent to which society was infested by these pests . . . is difficult to realize at the present time. . . . Hated by all decent people, these parasites, living on the earnings of better subjects than themselves, were often mobbed in the streets."[58]

The postal system both produced and intercepted epistolary discourse. It offered a medium in which one could share individual reflections and risk having them exposed. According to Morland, it made people governable. It revealed political opinion, intentions, beliefs, and states of mind, matters that were not determined by the law but the interiority of subjects who dared commit themselves and their plans to writing.

CRYPTOGRAPHIA

Without recourse to legal protection from interception, resistance took the form of cryptography. The arts of secret writing have roots in classical and medieval practices, but the sixteenth and seventeenth centuries saw a rise in its popularity, for several reasons: the increasing circulation of paper and ink, the formation of stable postal services, and the emerging concept of subjective privacy. Printed "cryptographies," instruction manuals for devising and using codes, were published widely as early as the sixteenth century.[59] Codes, transformation ciphers, special signs, symbols, and shared secret languages were commonly employed. Relatively sophisticated manuscript cipher systems are found in thousands of surviving letters from the period, in which politics, religious dissent, and conspiracy were general.[60]

There were three methods used for disguising the meaning of text on paper and ink. The first is technical steganography, which conceals the presence of the secret message by physically disguising it in a medium contained within other decoy media. Such media include "invisible" ink (milk with onion juice is an ancient formula), writing secreted within folded paper, or letters contained in hidden compartments of other objects. The second approach is linguistic steganography, which hides the "plaintext" of a message by embedding it sequentially within a larger decoy text. The intended recipient must extract the distributed letters of the hidden plaintext by applying a key or an algorithm—for instance, taking every third letter of the fourth word of every fourth line and transposing them sequentially.[61] More simply, linguistic steganography includes the use of predetermined code words or phrases to signify specific concepts.[62] The third method is coding or enciphering. Whereas steganography's aim is to avoid recognition, enciphering anticipates and defies it.[63] Coded or enciphered text is overtly recognizable as such: it defiantly shows itself as code, intended to be comprehensible only to someone who holds the key.[64]

The Reverend Dr. John Wallis wrote of "cryptographia" in 1641 that "there is scarce a Person of Quality, but is more or less acquainted with it."[65] Wallis was the principal codebreaker for both the Interregnum and the Restoration governments and later a chaplain to Charles II.[66] In his surviving papers are hundreds of pages of coded letters, series and sequences of copied intercepted text alongside the transformation tables that he deduced to crack them, mostly "nomenclator" codebook systems and monoalphabetic transformation systems.[67] A nomenclator codebook is simply a list of words with a tabulated list of corresponding codewords or numbers next to it. The coded elements would ideally be disarrayed so as not to correspond in any way to the alphabetic order of the plaintext, otherwise one correctly guessed codeword helped to unravel the others. Irregular tables and tables containing nulls, decoy code terms with no corresponding meaning, helped to complicate the deciphering process.[68] A monoalphabetic transformation system, also known as a Vigenère system, translates the common alphabet into an alternative alphabet using a key of random letters, often based on a mnemonic poem, song, or prayer. Each letter is assigned a ciphered substitute, and the plaintext of the message is transcribed accordingly.[69] For the decipherers facing such techniques, the statistical frequencies of commonly used words provided the starting point for deducing the key: an educated guess applied to the targeted letter at hand, given what is known of the targeted recipient. Cryptology is an iterative process of abductive and deductive reasoning. To secretly break a code is to win not only information but time to act.[70]

THE POSTAL APPARATUS

Once the state imposed a postal system on letter-writing correspondents, letter writers became subjects of the Crown, even in their most private moments.[71] First, the GPO had to function effectively and regularly, which required a new set of protocols and statistics and modes of disciplining the workers and postmasters that comprised the early postal system, which in turn put new economies into circulation by allowing goods, bills, and plans to be exchanged across distance. Posts were first established along roads in England as early as the fifteenth century as places where messengers could rest and exchange horses while carrying their mail. The first institution to hold a monopoly over the carriage of mail and to hold the proceeds of letters for the state, rather than the deputy postmasters who collected and dispensed them, was called the Inland Letter Office, established in 1635.[72] The intention was, first, to grow and tax correspondence in letters and parcels so that the royal messengers might be turned from a drain on the Exchequer to a source of profit and, second, to make correspondence available for interception. Following the English Civil War and Restoration, the financial administration of the GPO came under control of the Treasury in 1685, as postage became an instrument of state taxation. The GPO remained unprofitable, yet this did not constrain growth in three dimensions: professionalization, institutionalization, and the iterative dissemination of the arts of private letter writing.

First, postal work was professionalized. Boys were sent up to London to train as apprentice clerks; a "good Post Office education" included learning postal geography and different postage rates by heart, which equipped a youth for a lifetime of postal employment.[73] In 1703, a solicitor was appointed to manage the growing need for legal decisions; managers were appointed to conduct uniform weekly audits, and an architect was permanently appointed, as were two bag-makers.[74] Second, new permanent postal offices were opened. By the middle of the eighteenth century, most market towns and manufacturing regions had daily delivery and collection services at designated locations. Regional sorting offices increased circulation speed and lowered postage costs locally, while the central office in London was no longer the radial hub of the network. As the speed and coverage of mail carriage increased, competing illegal networks were swallowed up. New roads, canals, and turnpikes enhanced postal range and efficiency. As the volume and value of the mail grew, the first armored coaches appeared in the 1780s. By the end of the century, overseas postage rates were standardized.[75]

Finally, and of most significance, the postal system iteratively expanded its own customer base. Nothing improved public literacy more than the sending and receiving of letters. The GPO provided the opportunity to invent oneself in epistolary communication. Simply through "reading, copying, adapting, and composing narratives about their lives,"[76] people gained the capacity to engage in written communication. New circuits of economic exchange, financial opportunity, news and political opinion, and other communicative transactions emerged. Labor mobility was encouraged by the capacity to communicate with family and friends at home and to send money. The GPO slowly became regarded as a necessary service, from which a new formation of opinion, the writing public, began to demand ever more improvements in speed, reliability, and cost.[77] The network recursively grew and expanded its own successful delivery operations. The aim was no longer to appropriate preexisting correspondence but to produce it.[78] To this end, the office's surveyors measured, assessed, and modified its operations, adopting disciplinary techniques and surveillance of its workers and postmasters. Postal statistics were gathered and deployed to refine management practices and grow the revenue.

The GPO was assessed in a 1682 report by the master of ordinances, Thomas Gardiner, who surveyed the system and provided a detailed anatomy of its operations.[79] What emerges is a set of disciplinary practices and surveillance routines by which bodies, time, and media were tightly orchestrated to produce a medium of communication.[80] The GPO centered on an enclosed and segmented sorting office where workers, furniture, weighing scales, preprinted dockets, ledgers, forms, and accounting books combined to convert an unsorted inward flow of letters and money into an ordered outward flow of deliveries and revenue. Work was divided functionally. On Mondays, Wednesdays, and Fridays, inbound letters arrived at the Inland Letter Office early in the morning from six mail roads. The mail roads were named according to either their termination point or compass direction: Chester, West, Bristol, North, Yarmouth, and Kent, each of which linked London to a port. All that was required for delivery of a letter at this time was a name and a location. The location was not a formal address: often a neighborhood or the nearest postmaster's location was sufficient. This points to a certain spatial imaginary at work within the organization. Everything was counted, inspected, ordered, tallied, and differentiated territorially.

The "clerks of the road" were each responsible for processing the incoming mail, one for each of the post roads, from which they derived their income. Some of the roads had more posts on them and thus received more mail than others. As letters were taxed with postage based on how far they traveled from sender to receiver, and as clerks were paid according to how much postage they brought into the office, some post roads were more valuable to the clerks than others. Elsewhere in the office, "window men" received letters from the public counter, sorting them directly into one of six large drawing boxes, one for each outbound road; "sorters" placed letters into the different delivery bags for the city; "letter carriers" took the bags out around London and delivered them; a "stamper" stamped letters once the postage had been calculated and logged; "porters" carried bags of mail and parcels between the different parts of the office; "return men" dealt with dead (undelivered) letters. Other than the clerks, the workers performed each of these different roles in a weekly cycle, according to the order of the day.

Supervising it all was an accountant, treasurer, and comptroller. The comptroller symbolized "the authority and Person of the Chief Governors," according to Gardiner, who imagined the apparatus as if it were a living organism, in which the comptroller's job was "to influence the whole body through all circumstances of their duty."[81]

All letters arriving in the GPO were stamped with the date on the sealed side; a total postage charge payable on delivery was calculated, then converted into a charge levied against the letter carriers who delivered them. In the reverse operation, bags of outcome letters came from fixed collection walks through the suburbs of London. Carriers collected sums for paid post and applied a personal stamp to each letter they handed in. "Return men" disciplined the letter carriers by making checks on any letters they returned undelivered, as dead letters meant unpaid bills. At midnight, the office gates were closed. The priority then was efficiency, the timing of the day rigidly enforced to "keep the Clerks in continual action," as Gardiner put. Occasionally, "little offices abroad . . . bring a glut of Letters at that unreasonable time, most prejudicial to us."[82] To prevent collaboration between clerks and deputy postmasters, clerks were randomly assigned incoming mailbags, and the prices, numbers, and weights of the tallies they arrived at were checked by the accountant against paper bills supplied from the postmasters. Porters guarded the sorting rooms so that no one could enter or leave until the sorting work was completed. The sorting desks had pigeonholes for each of the towns of the roads in sequential order; this way, the territory of the postal network was represented in the furnishing and fittings of the office. A bill made out to each town's postmaster on a preprinted form was attached to their mailbag before postboys took the bags on horseback to the first posts on each of the roads.

Resistance to the monopoly emerged again in 1670, when William Dockwra started the "penny post" system in the City of London. Backed by the liberal faction in Parliament known as Whigs, the penny post exchanged letters between 180 shops and coffeehouses in the city, organized through several small sorting rooms. The world's first stamp system provided proof of payment on sending, generating huge efficiencies over the GPO. Every letter cost just a penny to send, so none went unpaid. Because there was no need to collect postage on delivery, there was anonymity for both sender and receiver. The network was indifferent to the identities of its customers and therefore private.[83]

Dockwra's universal exchange network quickly generated profits and deprived the GPO of business in London.[84] It proved extremely popular, generating an unprecedented flow of information, news, and political opinion throughout London.[85] It was subversive not only because of the ideas it enabled, but because it was invisible. In response, the Duke of York, holder of the monopoly, brought a successful legal action for infringement of the royal prerogative, and the network was incorporated into the General Post Office in 1692.[86]

Where law did not work, other disciplinary tactics emerged. A large and ongoing problem was ensuring that postage was paid to the GPO and not withheld illicitly by postmasters outside the tightly controlled space of the central sorting room.[87] In the countryside, postmasters and mailriders of the early postal system profited from "bye-letters," letters sent to destinations along the road before they reached London. Postmasters in general were underpaid, incurring losses from operating posts, so the opportunity to profit from bye-letters without reporting them to the GPO was tempting. In response, Gardiner's report suggested deploying "riding surveyors" to travel the roads and make random inspections of riders' bags. Instead, economic surveillance proved more efficient than physical inspection. Printed bills were sent out to each postmaster, requiring them to report back the number of bye-letters they collected. Average figures were then calculated for each postmaster, producing an expected number of bye-letters.[88] Postmasters whose returns notably deviated from the anticipated flow were placed under investigation, using statistical techniques to put disciplinary pressure on the postmasters to maintain and grow their business.

Another growth strategy fed on public interest in the news, which was growing with the increasing reliability of the posts. The GPO began distributing copies of the government's newsletter, the *London Gazette*, to postmasters, who sold copies for a penny. It was so popular that some postmasters asked to be paid for their work entirely in newsletters. Postal clerks in London held franking privileges over newspapers, granting them the right to post things free of charge. The clerks supplemented their low wages by buying newspapers in bulk from printers in London and sending them on free of postage to postmasters, who sold them to readers in local taverns and coffeehouses and split the profits with the clerks. Much later, in 1764, a statute aimed at restricting the abuse of franking privileges created a loophole that let members of Parliament (MPs) allow others to sign their franks on their behalf. Printers, booksellers, and newspaper publishers flooded the post with new printed matter, signed on behalf of their politician patrons. Between 1764 and 1796, the number of newspapers franked by postal clerks in London rose from one million to over eight million.[89] Newspapers circulated free of charge throughout the country, carrying news, criticism, gossip, and open letters from anyone who wished to write them. The relatively rapid expansion in critical discourse and news reporting destabilized the existing monarchical order, which ultimately paid for the costs of its transmission through the losses that franking incurred. Thus, the internal economy of the postal apparatus, which sought to discipline, survey, and control bodies and letters, produced a discernible difference in the structure of the communication that it carried.

THE USE OF WARRANTS

The device that administered and controlled interception was, and remains, the interception warrant. It is difficult to say precisely when the interception warrant emerged as a technology of government. Charles II reestablished the General Post Office by proclamation in 1663, ordering that no letters were to be delayed, detained, or opened except under the authority of a warrant signed by the secretary of state.[90] No such warrants seem to have survived from before 1712.[91]

Warrants are a kind of mundane administrative document that predate modern government. The word "warrant" came to the English language from French, originally referring to a guarantee, protection, defense, place of refuge, or safeguard. The Oxford English Dictionary lists John de Trevisa's *Polychronicon Ranulphi Higden* of 1387 as an early example of the word "warrant" in use, here in reference to a documentary form of royal authorization, which proved a particular command even "in absens of þe kyng."[92] Another dictionary definition of warrant as "a writ or order issued by some executive authority, empowering a ministerial officer to make an arrest, a seizure, or a search, to execute a judicial sentence, or to do other acts," was in use by around 1490. By then, a "warrant" was a species of writ. But the distinction between "warrant" and "writ" is not easily discerned.

Medieval government was composed of circulating documents: rights and titles were manifested, awarded, and contested through them. Until the sixteenth century, the Chancery was the great secretariat, the only source of authentic documents in the nascent bureaucracy of England, a scriptorium generating charters, diplomas, certificates, and writs.[93] Chancery clerks were educated in rhetorical forms of writing in monasteries and universities elsewhere in Europe.[94] There was no privacy or confidentiality in their products.[95] Documents were impressed with wax to validate their authority under the great seal, the medieval "key to the kingdom." The application of the great seal to a document depended on the receipt of an authorizing warrant addressed from the king to the chancellor.

Typically, warrants for the great seal were impressed by the privy seal, the application of which depended on the making of a warrant under the king's signet seal, held by his secretary, or marked by the king's personal signature. The entire administration of medieval power was a chain of warranty, one seal authorizing the operations of another, generating a flow of documentary rights recorded in linear fashion on parchment rolls. To the extent they functioned as administrative documents, warrants stood "behind" the law, carrying no rights or claims but authentication and directing a command be executed. In that capacity, they were key elements in the protocols and routines by which government was lawfully enacted, forming a kind of paper chain linking all official administrative communication referable ultimately to the king and, beyond him, divine right.

The emergence of the secretary of state as the locus of administrative power in England followed the reforms made by Thomas Cromwell during his tenure as principal secretary to Henry VIII between 1534 and 1540. Abandoning medieval protocols in favor of a direct, centralizing, and flexible mode of decision-making, the "new moving spirit in the administration was the secretary of state, and he acted by personal letter—by 'state paper'—rather than by any formal document under any seal."[96] Cromwell placed his secretaryship at the heart of government, displacing the traditional role of the chancellor—thereby sidelining the church—and undermining the privy council, a group of feudal lords and barons that had traditionally limited and advised the king. Cromwell's private office became the most effective element of government in England, overseeing changes in finances, policing, religion, legislation, economic policy, and foreign affairs,[97] with the secretarial warrant serving as a suitably adaptable form of command. He was appointed in the same year that Henry VIII obtained from Parliament the Act of Supremacy, awarding himself supreme headship of the newly formed Church of England and immunity from all "foreign laws."[98] Cromwell's centralization and elevation of the secretaryship marks a key moment in the formation of an apparatus of government referable to English territorial sovereignty alone, centered on the figure of the Crown.[99] The idea of the territorial state eventually displaced feudalism, empire, and the church, three key elements in the complex assemblage of overlapping authorities and nonterritorial jurisdictions that ruled medieval Europe.[100]

A warrant functions by enacting a limited transfer of power from its author to its addressee. It carries its authority with it as a written form. Authority is transferred to its executor, while the author in turn assumes legal liability. Yet this does not, and cannot, be traced backward to the original source of authority, the sovereign. As the ultimate source of law, the sovereign is theoretically beyond the question of liability. Sovereign exceptionalism was illustrated in December 1676, when Charles II commanded Henry Coventry, his secretary of state, to have the postmaster general intercept the letters of Edward Coleman. Coleman was a Catholic convert and courtier in contact with France on behalf of the future King James II, Charles's brother and then Duke of York, an initiative for which he was eventually executed.[101] Coventry asked the king to put his command in writing, so as "to justify myself to himself . . . in case of [Charles's] forgetting." But Charles refused, saying "he would remember it well enough." Coventry therefore instructed the deputy postmaster to intercept and copy Coleman's letters, with the important exception of any letter to or from James, who might have later taken exception.[102]

Liability lies with the one who signs the warrant but does not pass further up the chain to the king. As a matter of law, the "king can do no wrong."[103] Where the king makes an unlawful command, his minister might be tried for "deceiving" the king, inducing him to commit a "temporary injustice."[104] For instance, on November 18, 1678, Joseph Williamson, a secretary of state, was sent to the Tower of London by Parliament for illegally signing commissions in favor of "Popish recusants." Williamson's defense that he was merely countersigning orders from the king was no excuse, following from the fact that the king is the ultimate source of justice, including decisions about whether his government has acted unlawfully.[105]

In September 1677, Coventry outlined the interception power in a letter to the postmaster general. He wrote,

A Secretary of State may demand an account of any letters that come to the Posthouse from anybody employed there. . . . [Secretaries] have not . . . to ask anybody's leave but the King's, but to all inferiors their order is sufficient or else our Warrants to the postmasters are illegal, they not being our servants. The opening of letters is what no man can justify but from reason of state or the King's particular Command.[106]

In short, the secretary had authority to determine "reason of state" and issue warrants accordingly. Sovereign power—the king's particular command—is delegated. The sovereign is an absent presence standing behind the secretary's decision, a symbolic reference point irreducible to the person of the monarch. The king disappears behind a set of routine administrative orders, formalized documents, and contingent strategies and policies.[107] As Carl Schmitt observed, the minister who informs the sovereign of the situation and who signs on their behalf plays a crucial part in sovereign power. "Even the most absolute prince is reliant on reports and information," such that "every direct power is promptly subordinated to indirect influences."[108] Power is not located in the splendor of the court but in the secret antechambers, corridors, and back entrances where indirect influences gather and secrets are shared, unseen and unrecorded, to inform their decisions.

REASON OF STATE AND LEVIATHAN

Despite its arcane character, Coventry's invocation of reason of state drew on a "distinctly modern language of political action."[109] Although formally secret, everyone knew and speculated openly about reason of state and the "interests" of the sovereign, knowing also that certain aspects of government were not to be questioned in public. Accordingly, the "mysteries of state," *arcana imperii*, were nothing mysterious; they were political strategies that sought to impose limits on the law in a period when the political order was rapidly changing.[110]

In the war between king and parliament, common law had provided a language of resistance to the invocation of reason of state. Where reason of state asserted for the prince an essentially unlimited zone of decision-making outside and above the law, an "absolute prerogative" linked to the personal power of the monarch, its opponents deployed the discourse of law, claiming the prerogative of the monarch was an "ordinary" part of law and therefore limited by law. Such limits were rarely expressed in any detail or specificity.[111] They instead emerged as a set of singular principles slowly developed by the courts.

Thomas Hobbes successfully reconciled the concept of reason of state with the ordinary exercise of public power by law. Much like Samuel Morland, his political philosophy rested on a fundamentally pessimistic view of humanity cultivated by the turbulence of the seventeenth century.[112] In Hobbes's fictive state of nature, humanity is driven by passion, fear of death, and the right to appropriate everything in nature. The result is the war of all against all. Hobbes recognized that any coherent theory of modern power would necessarily be distinctly impersonal: the state as Leviathan required that the "sovereign" be defined not by a particular form or inheritance and not as something outside the legal order, but as an artificial creator of the law itself. Sovereignty is an artificial construction, legitimately exercised only when a sovereign, whether king or representative assembly, is authorized by the members of a given political community to speak on behalf of the unified Commonwealth, and only for as long as they aim to preserve the state and the ongoing common good of its subjects.[113]

In Hobbes's schema, sovereigns are representatives of the broader unity called the state. Only by occupying offices with duties attached to them do they enjoy the irresistible power and "halo of authority" once claimed by kings.[114] This is a vision of the state as a political technology, a construction differentiated from nature as the only source of order.[115] Beyond the state is nature, which has no order, only contingency. Hobbes thus neutralizes the difference between the sovereign prince and the legal order. But in the same move, he argues that the formerly subversive concepts of personal liberty and political self-interest must find expression within the law of the state. Hobbes proposed transferring them, in theory contractually, from individuals to the state for rational reasons. Outside the terms of this hypothetical contract between subject and sovereign, the exercise of coercive powers was illegitimate.[116]

The Commonwealth was thus an imaginary vehicle through which law is made by established processes, allowing subjects to pursue their interests freely where the law is silent, provided they obey where the law commands. The sovereign has unlimited public powers, provided they are exercised through law and on advice, including the power to judge what doctrines and opinions are threats to peace, who should be permitted to express them, and what should be allowed to be printed and published. The power of the state is thereby differentiated from the private opinions of subjects only insofar as opinions are an object of governance. One may privately disagree with the sovereign, provided one does not act against it publicly. The sovereign alone has the exclusive right to determine and decide on the necessity of public action. While subjects have a right to private morality and property, they have no right to take public action unsanctioned by the sovereign, who alone is the final arbiter on matters of controversy.[117] The sovereign reserves the power to override or dispense with ordinary laws where the safety and well-being of the Commonwealth is at stake. Exceptional powers were not abolished, but were absorbed by the state.[118]

CONCLUSION

In practice and theory, interception in the early modern state serves as a kind of cipher or model of state power. The absolute power of the sovereign necessitated and authorized absolute access to information carried through the public postal system, which was central to the emergence of secret intelligence. The unified postal monopoly on which it depended arose from the turmoil of civil war as a constative capacity of the modern territorial state. Interception was not invented in that moment, but through the General Post Office, it became institutionalized as both a political tactic and a juridical right, justified by reason of state and exercised through secretarial warrants. From the beginning, the postal system presented both the possibility of communication and the threat of interception as a feature of modern state power.

Reason of state was a justificatory strategy that claimed for the monarch the absolute prerogative power to act beyond the law if necessary. In practice, it authorized the growing management and development of bureaucratic protocols and practices. Postal interception involved specialized techniques, protocols, and media, organized and directed around the administrative device of the warrant. But the postal service as a whole, conditional as it was on the assertion by force of a monopoly and the suppression of alternative communication networks, exemplified emerging "police" powers—the power of the early-modern state to make policy and implement it.[119]

Absolute sovereignty and reason of state authorized the emergence of practices and techniques that first linked intelligence powers to the authority or will of the king and that materially took shape in processes, struggles, payments, sorting operations, inspections, seizures, interruptions, and cipher games, all of which were immanent to the new postal epoch's media of paper, ink, wax, and seals. Chapter 3 traces how this inherent power developed and was tempered by changing administrative practices and theories of political power.

3

INTERCEPTION AND PUBLICITY

This chapter outlines key changes in the tactics and justifications of postal interception that occurred in the eighteenth and nineteenth centuries in England. During the eighteenth century, interception was constantly practiced at varying degrees of intensity depending on the exigencies of the political situation. Primarily, it occurred in the "secret room," Britain's analogue to the Black Chambers of European states, where a skilled team of interceptors worked daily to discover the secrets of foreign diplomats, rival sovereigns, and domestic rebels. But postal surveillance extended also into the streets, where senders and receivers of letters were known and watched by letter carriers. The eighteenth-century General Post Office (GPO) was a central element in a wider police apparatus organized under the legal authority of the royal prerogative, the name given in the common law to the constrained powers of the sovereign that was exercised increasingly through ministerial warrants.

By the early nineteenth century, the interception apparatus was deeply unpopular. As utilitarian and reformist politics developed, a reformed postal economy emerged that no longer required the close observation of customers and postmasters. Just as the postal system ceased the close surveillance of its customers, letter interception became a public scandal, with outcry following the targeting of a political refugee's letters. This gave occasion for the abolition of Britain's foreign interception apparatus in the name of liberal restraint. The shift from an overbearing surveillance system to a liberal technology of communication reflects Foucault's description of a transition from strict disciplinary "governmentality" to a "biopolitical" diagram of power, where power is applied at a remove to contain its undesirable second-order impacts according to a new rationality of political economy. The "balance" of power between liberty and security in relation to economy became the key consideration of government.

In this respect, the work of Jeremy Bentham is illustrative. Our interest is not the panopticon, an idea of Bentham's frequently applied to the study of surveillance since Foucault used it as the paradigm model of the *dispositif* of disciplinary power.[1] Rather, we are concerned with Bentham's essay on publicity and its relationship to political legitimacy, first published in France in the revolutionary period. It offers a strategy for governing through transparent decision-making, in contrast to the *arcana imperii* and reason of state that had prevailed until then. To be effective, power must become cognizant of its own limits in response of the governed. The elite must believe that power is being exercised rationally in their interests, and the masses who are unequipped to understand politics must at least believe that the elite understands and is satisfied.

Thus, modern government must learn to rationally strategize, and publicity is the most effective and simple strategy for a political assembly to adopt. But total transparency gives too much away to enemies of the state, so government must selectively and strategically limit it, keeping its most sensitive secrets from view. This strategy underpinned the rise of a liberal model of governmental power in which secrecy was no longer a normative presupposition in government but a selectively applied tactic.

POSTAL SURVEILLANCE

By the eighteenth century the GPO was the primary intelligence apparatus of the state. All postal workers were expected to record and relay any "remarkable occurrences" in local areas by writing and sending reports through the post.[2] Surveyors and spies reported via the post office on crime, disorder, economic conditions, and local elections, while postmasters and secretaries in Ireland, Scotland, and the overseas colonies reported privately on civil and military issues, port officers provided news of enemy ship movements and copied passenger lists, and foreign spies wrote letters supplying Britain with oversees intelligence.[3]

The scope and capacity of postal surveillance was demonstrated incidentally during the case of *R. v. Doctor Hensey* (1758).[4] The case was included in the *State Trials*, an edited compendium of notorious cases concerning offenses against the state, first compiled anonymously in 1719 as a critique of the repressive use of law.[5] Compromising letters sent from France had been found in Dr. Hensey's bureau, alongside draft copies of letters he had sent in return detailing British forces and naval squadrons. To prove the drafts were Hensey's, a post office "bellman" from the City of London appeared as one of four prosecution witnesses, testifying that he regularly rang his bell and collected letters from the accused on Arundel Street. He said,

I observed that the letters I received of Dr. Hensey were generally directed abroad and to foreigners; and knowing the doctor to be a Roman Catholic, and as I imagined in the interest of the Pretender,[6] I advised the examining clerk at the office to inspect his letters, telling him that I had some suspicion that the writer of those letters was a spy.
Did you open any one of these letters yourself?
No; but I happened to challenge the letter about the Secret Expedition; and when it was opened at the post-office and found to be what it is, after that I received directions to bring every letter I received from the doctor's own hand, or from that house, directly to the office that it might be opened.[7]

The next witness was a postal clerk, Thomas Matthews, who explained that "when war is declared against any nation, immediate orders are given out by the Post Master General to stop all suspected letters, in order to prevent intelligence being given the enemy of our transactions at home. These orders are given to all the clerks of the said office, and to every servant carrying letters."[8] Hensey was convicted and eventually transported to Australia.

Here, one glimpses the scope of postal surveillance extending beyond targeted interception and encompassing a general capacity to intercept or censor entire postal routes and to conduct direct surveillance of the public by letter carriers. The postal apparatus gave form to the abstractly defined political right of the state. It operated according to its own governmentality, which "resides in the things it manages and in the pursuit of the perfection and intensification of the processes it directs."[9] In other words, it was power only formally described by the law. Rather than being determined by the juridical right, it was driven and developed through the immanent techniques, discourses, disciplinary institutions, economies, and objects that allow the population and territory to be apprehended and governed through the knowledge it produced. The same processes that generated and developed the postal system intensified its powers of surveillance over the population.

During the period that postal interception became organized and professionalized, formal sovereign powers changed hands several times. England was under the reign of Queen Mary and her Dutch husband King William III, whom Parliament invited to ascend the thrones of England, Scotland, and Ireland in 1688, deposing her father, James II (1633–1701), who had continued to practice the family tradition of asserting absolute monarchy and reason of state. Parliament ruled that he had "abandoned" his throne, overthrowing him in the so-called Glorious Revolution that marked the advent of parliamentary sovereignty as the highest source of law.

On James II's death in 1701, his son, James Francis Edward Stuart (1688–1766), claimed the English, Scottish, and Irish thrones from exile; his claim was recognized by France and Spain. The English response was the Act of Settlement 1701, by which any Catholic or anyone married to a Catholic was disqualified from the British thrones. Thus, on Queen Anne's death in 1714, the crown passed to the first Hanoverian king of England, George I. James Stuart became known as the "Old Pretender" and his supporters as the Jacobites. They twice tried to install him in violent risings of 1715 and 1745, and their plans were a constant source of concern for the eighteenth-century intelligence system.

The point is not to rehearse or labor the complex crises of succession but to situate the practice of interception in a political environment of contingency, crises, and opportunistic rivalry between European powers engaged in colonial appropriation.[10] The Jacobites engaged in plots, assassination attempts, foreign liaisons, and open rebellions, producing "an almost pathological fear" of rebellion until the middle of the century, their cause serving to rally other politically disaffected groups, making it a "force that seemed to assume infinite proportions the less visible it was to the eye."[11] The Post Office accordingly received a stream of warrants from the secretaries of state to detain, open, search, and copy mail while seeking to detect what could not be seen.

The interception regime primarily targeted foreign diplomats and domestic political opponents. Diplomatic post sent through the "Foreign Office" arrived in bags received at a public window from each foreign embassy. This made it easy to differentiate and intercept. A deciphered diplomatic post was the most important form of intelligence available to the state. It was the principal method of devising foreign policy and politics and the means by which foreign views and plans were understood, closing the gap "between real and professed views."[12] Domestically, intelligence gathering depended on a list of targets, formally supplied to the postmaster general in the form of warrants from the secretary of state. Targets were copied and distributed to the sorting clerks from warrants sent by the secretaries of state to the postmaster general.[13] As the sorting and delivery process of the post required the visual inspection of each letter to determine its address and postage, the name of each addressee was noted as a matter of routine. Other observations were possible using visual identifiers other than a target's name: their seal, signature, handwriting, code name, or destination all served as potential selection criteria. Where interception concerned a domestic criminal investigation, letters were intercepted in local sorting rooms, sometimes by inspectors dispatched from the GPO. Letters intercepted for political reasons, however, were forwarded unopened to the private office or "Secret Office" located next to the sorting room of the GPO in London, where a team of skilled interceptors opened them undetected.[14]

SECRET OFFICE

The Secret Office was the main site of interception, the British instantiation of the so-called Black Chambers that emerged during the eighteenth century. Intercepts were "part of a system of multiple inputs to ministers," a part of the accepted political process, and a "cat and mouse game played by all European governments with varying degrees of technical skill."[15] As a matter of routine, the Foreign Office clerks processed four inbound posts from overseas a week. The head of the office, the foreign secretary, removed diplomatic, warranted, and suspicious letters for inspection in the Secret Office, returning them within a few hours for onward processing. To give the appearance that diplomatic mail was not intercepted, they prioritized the rapid delivery of diplomatic bags to foreign embassies.[16] In the evenings, when outgoing post arrived from the embassies to be sent overseas, the foreign secretary again took possession of the diplomatic bags and any targeted letters.

The interceptors slept in two apartments adjoining the office and worked by candlelight in dark and cramped conditions. A fire was kept lit for warmth and the disposal of warrants. The staff came and went through a private entrance located on Abchurch Lane, avoiding the main entrance on Lombard Street. Admission to the Secret Office was restricted to the postmaster general. Only the salary of the foreign secretary, who was also head of the Secret Office, was listed in official GPO accounts. Otherwise, the existence of the department and the names of the trained professional interceptors were kept secret, with their salaries paid anonymously from a general pot of secret service money allocated to the GPO by Parliament.[17]

Anthony Todd (1717–1802) was a farmer's son who entered the GPO as a boy and eventually rose to the position of postmaster general. He became foreign secretary in 1752. Todd recorded of his time in the Secret Office that he was always first in to the office, at about 8 a.m. and 10 p.m. on post days, when he selected mail for opening, marked passages for copying, and noted the "connexion of hand, address, and seal" revealed in each letter.[18] He helped the chief clerk with letter opening, supervised the copying clerks making copies at dictation speed, then put the interceptions in the distinctive envelopes known as "long packets" that were used to securely transmit intelligence and dispatched them by messenger to addressees on the distribution list.[19] Everything intercepted in plaintext and deemed to be of potential use went directly to the king while enciphered messages were sent by courier to members of the Deciphering Branch and from there to the king, then to his secretary of state for circulation to select ministers, who received them in a long packet marked with their initials. The long packet was returned to the secretaries' office for storage under the category of "private" papers, not yet in any systemically organized way.[20]

Todd took responsibility for improving the interception operation. Fearing that potential intelligence was lost because of complex seals, diplomatic cipher changes, and foreign clerks taking greater care to courier their letters to avoid the office, he arranged for the chief clerk's son, John Bode, to go to Hanover to train in the arts of interception. Once the clerks had finished with a letter, the precise color and type of wax used on the original letter was selected, melted, applied, and stamped with a precise forgery of the original seal. Where a seal had changed or a new target was selected, a clerk immediately set about carefully engraving a forgery. Supplies of ink and wax were procured across Europe to disguise the work. Aside from engraving, copying, and translating, other techniques and skills were applied. Where the use of invisible ink was suspected, special liquors were used to reveal them. Translators were on hand for letters penned in other languages. All letters had to be returned to their original packets intact and in the original order. Interception was an organized flow of paper, ink, and wax media.[21]

The Deciphering Branch was formally funded at a rate of £100 per year beginning in 1701 under the mathematician John Wallis, a founder of the Royal Society, who had been solving ciphers for bounty since the Civil War era.[22] On his death in 1703, it passed to his grandson, William Blencowe, then aged 20, and then Dr John Keill, an astronomer. From 1716, the role of decipherer was held by the then 22-year-old Edward Willes, who continued in the role into his seventies, by which time he had ascended to the rank of bishop.[23] Thereafter, his descendants inherited the office until it was abolished in 1844.[24] Clerks of the Secret Office were trained to recognize information in intercepted letters that could be useful as "cribs"—that is, any information that gives a contextual clue as to words or letters that may have been substituted or enciphered in a message. Cribs could precede or follow the coded text that they refer to; in principle, everything that a target sends or receives by post is a potential crib. A common source of cribs came from diplomatic staff of foreign embassies encoding the contents of documents that their ambassador had obtained from the British government. Provided the decipherers kept note who wrote to whom and when, they could simply look up possible solutions to coded terms in plaintext, accessing stored records of older elements in an ongoing chain of correspondence.

The techniques occasionally came to public attention. In 1723, intercepted enciphered letters formed part of the evidence against the Jacobite Bishop Atterbury, with evidence from the decipherers Edward Willes and Anthony Corbiere presented to the House of Lords by the head of the private office, known as the Foreign Secretary of the Post Office.[25] Convicted on the evidence of his correspondence, Atterbury was banished from Britain, living his remaining years in France with the Pretender.[26] During the trial, two decipherers were called to testify that they had deciphered the intercepted letters shown in evidence. The defense challenged them to demonstrate how they had done it. However, the Lords intervened, ruling that they should not explain their methods or say anything that might reveal "the Art or Mystery of deciphering."[27]

WARRANTS AND LEGISLATION

The secretarial authority to make warrants was nowhere positively stated, but it was recognized by section 40 of the Post Office (Revenues) Act 1710, which provided that

no person or persons shall presume wittingly, willingly, or knowingly, to open, detain, or cause, procure, permit, or suffer to be opened, detained, or delayed, any letter or letters, packet or packets . . . except by an express warrant in writing under the hand of one of the principal secretaries of state for every such opening, detaining, or delaying.[28]

Under section 41, all postal workers swore an oath upon their employment that was administered in the following words:

I do swear, That I will not wittingly, willingly, or knowingly open, detain, or delay, or cause, procure, permit, or suffer to be opened, detained, or delayed any letter or letters, packet or packets, which shall come into my hands, power, or custody, by reason of my employment in or relating to the post office; except by the consent of the person or persons to whom the same is or shall be directed, or by an express warrant in writing under the hand of one of the principal Secretaries of State for that purpose.[29]

The sequence was frequently reversed in practice: a postal clerk or inspector would identify and intercept a potentially interesting source of intelligence and notify the secretary of state, and then the warrant would follow.[30] Nevertheless, by legislating for these provisions, Parliament had clearly recognized that the power to direct the interception of letters existed. Similarly, in 1735, a complaint was made in the House of Commons that letters from members of Parliament (MPs) were intercepted and opened. The secretary of state, Sir Robert Walpole, informed the House that in times of danger, a discretionary power of ordering letters to be opened at the Post Office was needed to discover "bad practices" against the government. Parliament resolved that a secretarial warrant was the only lawful means of authorizing letter interception.[31]

The earliest surviving interception warrant identified in the report commissioned from a Secret Committee investigation in 1844 was made in 1712, two years after the introduction of legislation prohibiting interception without a warrant. The only earlier example of interception that the Secret Committee specifically mentioned was that of Edward Coleman, who was the target of Charles II's 1676 oral command to his secretary of state Coventry. They also noted that until 1799. "it was not the practice to record such Warrants regularly in any official book."[32]

For this reason, interception warrants and the intelligence that they produced are difficult to locate and reconcile, as those that survive from the eighteenth century are scattered throughout the archival collections known as "state papers."[33] There, we can locate examples of warrants of enormous breadth and scope, composed on sheets of paper of varying sizes and shapes, written in copperplate cursive. For instance, in 1722 and 1731, warrants were issued to the postmasters general to detain and forward all letters in the French and Flanders mails. Others were targeted at named specific individuals.

From the year 1726, we find a hybrid, a warrant that states, "Whereas it is apprehended that there is a correspondence carried on to the prejudice of the King and Government by letters sent, directed, and under cover, to the persons following, vz, the Emperor," then lists a further ninety-five named targets, including kings of France and Sweden.[34] The warrant is "to authorize and direct you from time to time and until you shall receive orders to the contrary, to open and detain all letters and packets that shall come to your office, directed to any of the persons afore named, or under cover to them or any or every of them, and to cause the same to be copied. . . . And for doing this shall be your sufficient warrant. Given under my hand at the Cockpit, Whitehall, this third first day of August 1726" (see figures 3.1 and 3.2).

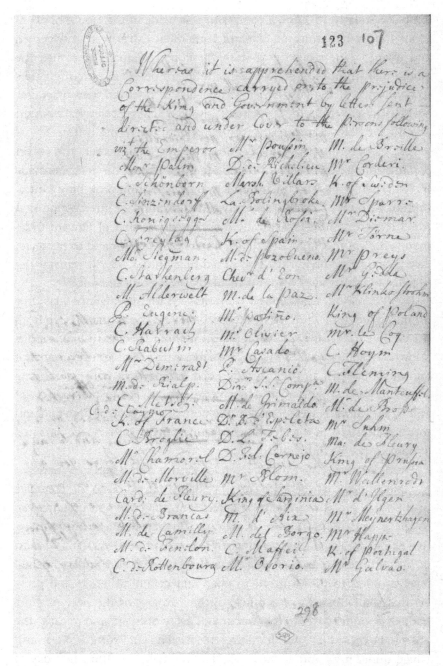

3.1 & 3.2 A two-sided warrant dated August 31, 1726, for the interception of letters of around ninety different people, the first one being "the Emperor." *Source*: The National Archives SP 35/62 f. 289.

Mr de Mendonza	D. of Modena
States Generall	Mr Riva
Mr Hop	Mr Vicetti
Mr Fagel	Mr Pucci
Mr Vandermeer	Mr Fiorelli
Mr Borcel	Mr Hernd Lewis
Mr Bruynincx	Pr. Hsse Cassel
D. of Parma	Mr Morosini
~~Claudio Re~~	Mr Piridolfi
Mr Scotti	~~C. d. Cayns~~
Mr St Severini	Card. Bentivoglio
Mr Landi	

These are therefore to authorize and direct you from time to time; and untill you shall receive Orders to the contrary, to open and detain all letters and packets that shall come, directed to your Office to any of the persons before named, or under Cover to them, or any, or every of them, and to cause the same to be copyed, which Copys you are immediately to transmitt to me, or one of his Maty's principal Secretarys of State. And for so doing this shall be your sufficient Warrant. Given under my hand & Seal at the Cockpit Whitehall this thirty first day of Augst 1726

To Edward Cartret and Edward
Harrison Esqrs, Post Master General.

3.1 & 3.2 *(Continued)*

General warrants were issued during the Jacobite rebellion of 1745, ordering the postmaster general to detain letters "suspected to contain matter of a dangerous tendency," and these warrants required the assistants of the Yarmouth and Chester roads to detain letters "suspected to contain treasonable correspondence."[35] When the French occupied the United Provinces in 1795, all mail to those countries was stopped but not opened. Legislation was passed that allowed letters to be opened and returned to the senders.[36]

The materiality of surviving warrants retained in the National Archives reveals differences and continuities in the form of the warrant over time. For instance, a warrant dated April 28, 1792, contained in a book of copied "Out letters" reveals similarities and discontinuities.[37] The copied document loosely resembles a letter (see figure 3.3).

It begins: "To His Majesty's Post Master General, This is to authorize and direct you to open and take copies of all letters which pass through the Post Office directed to any of the following persons." There follows a list of eleven names, headed by two notable entries, Thomas Paine and John Horne Tooke, who were prosecuted for seditious libel and treason, along with Thomas Hardy and others, for supporting the ideals of the French Revolution.[38] No reasons are provided in the warrant as to why they are targets. To direct interceptors to the relevant mailbags, some of the targets are in named cities: Bruxelles, Rotterdam, The Hague. The warrant's authority is confirmed with the phrase, "And for so doing this shall be Your Warrant. Given under my hand and Seal at Whitehall, the 28th day of April 1792."

The key element in all the warrants is the performative one: "this shall be your (sufficient) warrant." This formulation, which varies over time, as we shall see later, is the constitutive ingredient that converts the documents from mere vehicles for sending information—the list of targets—into authoritative administrative agents within the governmental apparatus.

For the interceptors in the Post Office, the list of targets of course provided them with the information required to discriminate between the letters that they searched. The cities mentioned would direct the sorting clerks to provide the relevant foreign mailbags for searching, and the names would allow them to identify individual letters, seals, and handwriting to recursively include in their search operations. Interception

INTERCEPTION AND PUBLICITY

> To His Majesty's
> Post Master General
>
> This is to ~~authorize and~~ direct You to open and take copies of all Letters which pass through the Post Office directed to any of the following persons
>
> Mr Thomas Paine
> Mr John Horne Tooke
> Mr Isaac Blydestyn of Harp Lane
> Mr Dilly
> Mr J. S. Jordan
> Mr Syder of Rotterdam
> Mr Bennet — Ditto
> Dr Aickma — Ditto
> Dr Atkinson
> Messrs Frederick Romberg & Son at Bruxelles
> Mr Short — at the Hague
>
> And for so doing this shall be Your Warrant. Given under my hand and Seal at Whitehall this 28th day of April 1792.

3.3 Warrant for the interception of letters of eleven individuals, including Thomas Paine and John Horn Tooke, April 28, 1792. *Source:* The National Archives HO 42/208.

warrants existed as elements in an information exchange, a two-way transfer operation by which the secretary of state transferred lists of selected targets to the Post Office, which performed the technical operations of searching, selecting, and copying, then returning intercepted material. General warrants aimed at territorial zones defined by postal routes. For instance, all letters on the Chester Road effectively meant all letters in and out of Ireland, as Chester was the primary port on the Irish Sea.

Warrants of both kinds highlight not only the spatiality of the postal apparatus of the eighteenth century but also the functionality of lists. Lists are an elementary form of legal writing, giving organizational structure to communication. They "do not communicate, they control transfer operations. . . . Lists sort and engender circulations."[39] A list is a simple technology with no functional equivalent in purely oral communication. Because they can record information intended for use in a different time and place, lists abstract and order the world. Warrants, like all legal and administrative documents, did not merely symbolize a preexisting political power. They organized, precipitated, and anticipated action, and they retroactively served to record the legitimacy of its execution.[40] Their agency was a key element in the functioning of the apparatus.

PROHIBITION ON GENERAL WARRANTS

Interception warrants were not challenged in court until 1979, but this was not the case with search warrants, which were issued on similar grounds but produced more tangible effects. In 1765, the use of general warrants for searching premises and detaining individuals was ruled unlawful in the case of *Entick v. Carrington*.[41] The case arose from the search and seizure of property and the arrest of writers and printers who had satirized the king and mocked his government.[42] General warrants authorized the arrest of anyone connected to the so-called seditious libel.[43] On that authority, the king's messengers searched premises, seized personal papers, and arrested several men. The primary goal was intimidation.[44] The crime of seditious libel was broadly constructed and oppressive. The truth of the alleged libel against the sovereign was irrelevant to the crime; one could seditiously libel a dead king; and seditious libel did not even require publication: merely passing an unfavorable opinion on the sovereign to a third party sufficed.[45] It was therefore useful to the regime and deeply unpopular with its opponents.

A series of cases challenging the general searches and arrests culminated on 27 November 1765 in *Entick v. Carrington*. The ruling may be summarized in three points: the absolute protection of private property from trespass without lawful justification; a specific rejection of state necessity, or reason of state, as a justification for trespass; and the finding that state authority be grounded in positive law found "in our books."[46] The key legal point is the rejection of the Crown's case that general warrants could override the rights of individual subjects. A warrant would only be recognized as valid where there was a lawful reason for its issuance. A *general* warrant, aimed only at a purpose but not a particular individual or case, could not give lawful authorization to its addressee to interfere with the legal rights of others. The case is, strictly speaking, a ruling on the relationship between the authority of the Crown and common law. Yet it was, and is, celebrated as a shorthand refutation on the parasitism of the state. The key point is the break from the era of reason of state as the assertion of necessity over law. To obtain a search warrant, some grounds justifying a particular search must be shown.

The idea that all warrants should be issued by a court and only based on what is now called reasonable grounds for suspicion, or probable cause, is still key to legal arguments about the legitimacy and lawfulness of interception powers today. Yet the analogy was not applied to the interception of the post. Even if one could prove interception of one's correspondence under general warrant, trespassing on private property and seizing one's confidential papers were not obviously equivalent in law. As long as the law remained silent, the practice could continue. General warrants for letter interception continued to be issued secretly in times of civil unrest and war.

POSTAL GOVERNMENTALITY

The development of the interception apparatus took place without legal sanction. It was instead a development of governmental rationality whereby "the instruments of government, instead of being laws, now come to be a range of multiform tactics."[47] The distinction between the administrative powers practiced in the name of governmental rationality and the legal form of sovereignty that justifies it corresponds to the distinction between power as *potentia* and power as *potestas*, where the former is the *capacity* to act and the latter is the *right* to command it.[48] In Adam Smith's writing, the distinction is rendered as one of "justice" and "police," and in William Blackstone's *Commentaries on the Laws of England* (1765), the jurist wrote that the king alone enjoys the lawful right to police and manage the "economy" using prerogative powers, where police means "the due regulation and domestic order of the kingdom: whereby the individuals of the state, like members of a well-governed family, are bound to conform their general behaviour to the rules of propriety, good neighbourhood, and good manners."[49] Blackstone noted that the seventeenth-century prerogative counted among the *arcana imperii*,[50] and although the Crown was made subordinate to Parliament in the Glorious Revolution of 1688–89, the interests of Parliament and the Crown—the "common good"—were assumed to align as a matter of law. Prerogative power, according to Blackstone, had a legal basis. It "must be in its nature singular and eccentrical; that it can only be applied to those rights and capacities which the King enjoys alone, in contradistinction to others."[51] In the eighteenth century, questions of authority and liberty were settled, replaced by questions of how state power should be best utilized.

The rise of the police state inaugurated a new order of rationality that focused not only on external enemies, rival princes, and sedition but on the idea of the population as an object to be developed, cultivated, and nurtured. Only where prerogative conflicted with established legal rights did the courts step in, as in *Entick v. Carrington*. Otherwise, the administrative state grew its internal complexity without any categorical definition of public power, which thanks to Britain's "unwritten constitution" remains ambiguous today.[52] The governmental machine operated and developed under its own logic and precedents. In so doing, the postal apparatus delivered the conditions for epistolary literacy and, with it, the normative claim that private communication is a right. This interior space of the epistolary subject, opposed to the "artificial man" of the Hobbesian state, is the political counterweight to the interception power. The challenge would be articulated first through Parliament, not the courts.

EPISTOLARY SUBJECTIVITY

The seventeenth and eighteenth centuries saw the emergence of a distinctly modern form of subjectivity that found its truest expression in private correspondence. The communion of the self and other through private letters was both a new form of self-reference and a new mode of sociality.[53] As John Donne wrote in the seventeenth century, "This writing of letters, when it is with any seriousness, is a kind of extasie, and a departure and secession and suspension of the soul, which doth then communicate itself to two bodies."[54] Susan Whyman has shown in detail that the rise of modern epistolary literacy was an iterative process enabled by the postal service. Over the course of the seventeenth and eighteen centuries, the Post Office had a great effect on the rise of literacy. It "created a mass of new writers engaged in private writing, unsupervised reading, and independent judgements."[55] Those who learned the techniques of reading and writing acquired "all the tools they needed to criticize their society."[56] The security of correspondence soon became a political topic conceived as one of public right.[57] Epistolary literacy involved learning and reiteratively practicing techniques that unfolded in private settings away from the state's right of interception and supervision, producing the conditions for a new normative relationship to society and authority.

In this mode, Michel de Servan (1737–1807), French lawyer and exemplar of the emergent *Republic de lettres*, addressed an open letter to the *cabinet noir* that claimed private letters constituted a form of private property. As property, they belonged equally to the sender and the intended receiver; interception is, then, trespass. Servan argued that letter writers attained an otherwise unattainable level of freedom of thought and expression that united them in space and time. It allowed new, tentative, half-formed ideas to be suggested and developed, abandoned without consequence, or successfully developed and published as pamphlets or essays. Privacy reduced the risk of misunderstanding and encouraged experimentation, affording thought a new space in which the "republic of letters" took shape. Author and addressee are morally bound to each other to keep their shared property private.[58] The seal was the mark of private confidence, the breaking of the seal its violation.[59]

This appears now as an intersubjective claim, a relational form expressed in the semantics of property. To write an open letter criticizing it was risky.

Servan argued that interception was ultimately good for nothing, not even the state, because it diminishes the confidence that the public can place in their rulers and the freedom of thought they can exercise in letters.[60] He protested a condition that affected everyone who engaged in the new discourse networks of the postal epoch. Through writing as the materialization and transmission of thought, the individual subject challenges the sovereign state as the organizing principle of political order and public morality. Subjects have the right to private communication and to share ideas in the exchange of letters. In this sense, the Enlightenment was as much a new media epoch as a philosophical break, the rise of the modern individual epiphenomenal to the distribution of postal correspondence.

In Britain too, letter interception was challenged by the discourse of political freedom. In 1818, for instance, the political radical and nonconformist preacher, publisher, pornographer, and pamphleteer William Benbow published "Censorship Exposed," accusing Home Secretary Henry Addington, also known as Viscount Sidmouth, of intercepting and withholding a letter Benbow sent his wife (see figure 3.4).[61] The previous year, Sidmouth had introduced the Habeas Corpus Suspension Act 1817 in response to political unrest. The following year, he presided over the Peterloo Massacre in Manchester, when a rally calling for parliamentary reform was met with violence by the yeomanry and eighteen people were killed. Political corruption, the demand for universal suffrage, and prolonged economic depression had radicalized extra-parliamentary domestic unrest. The response from the established ruling class was to intensify police strategies of suppression.[62]

The Post Office acted as a conduit for both radical political communication and government espionage networks. Reports, pamphlets, and posters documenting the meetings and rhetoric of the emergent labor and reform movements poured into post offices from spies and informers. General interception warrants for the domestic mail were issued in 1780 during the Gordon Riots and again in 1799, 1809, and 1812. Between 1799 and 1844, to intercept the correspondence of 724 named individuals, 372 warrants were issued alongside a host of general warrants. Of these, 77 warrants concerned "political" crimes of radicals who were tried and executed for treason between 1817 and 1820 under Sidmouth's espionage rings, and the Chartist strikes and riots of 1842 to 1843, the

Censorship Exposed;

OR,

LETTERS

ADDRESSED

To the R. H. V. SIDMOUTH,

AND

To Mrs. BENBOW,

In which the the Business of the Cowardly Oligarchy is brought to Light, and Exposed to the Execretion of all who admire

The cause of FREE *and* EQUAL REPRESENTATION,

By W. Benbow,

Lately confined by Virtue of a Lettre de Cachet in the Bastile, But who eventually defeated the whole Posse of Borough Mongering Tyrants.

" The brave meet danger, and the coward flies;
" To die, or conquer, proves a hero's part."

HOMER.

" Tyranny, I say will not always be hid, even to the lowest capacities; and the next truth they will discover afterwards is, that a whole PEOPLE can never have THE WILL, without having, at the same time, power to redeem themselves."

COWLEY.

Manchester.

Printed for the Author, by W. Ogden, and may be had of all the Booksellers, and of Mr. Benbow, Pump-street, Bank Top.

Price THREEPENCE, or 2s, 3d. per Dozen.

3.4 Pamphlet titled "Censorship Exposed" by W. Benbow, March 7, 1818, complaining of letters intercepted by the secretary of state. *Source*: The National Archives HO 33/2/13.

first working-class mass movement in Britain that demanded democratic reform and seemed to threaten the established order of power and property.[63] In 1844, the Mazzini scandal prompted the first historical account of interception practices and led to a transformation in their use.

MAZZINI

Giuseppe Mazzini, an Italian revolutionary living in exile in London, realized that his letters were being intercepted when comrades in Bari were arrested and executed by the Neapolitan government of the Austro-Hungarian Empire. How he detected the interception is unclear. One account claims he posted letters to himself containing poppy seeds, which were conspicuously missing when the letters were delivered.[64] Another claims that he sent two letters to his address on the same day, one addressed with his own name, the other with a pseudonym, and observed that the first arrived later than the second.[65] Either way, Mazzini deduced that someone was reading his letters and was passing intelligence to the Austrian ambassador.

He recruited the support of the Chartist MP Thomas Duncombe, who raised the case in Parliament and the press.[66] An outcry followed. The diarist Charles Greville recorded, "It lit up a flame throughout the country. Every foolish person who spoils papers and pens fancied his nonsense was read at the Home Office."[67] The philosopher Thomas Carlyle wrote a public response, declaring that it is "vital to us that sealed letters in an English post-office be, as we all fancied they were, respected as things sacred,"[68] while an editorial in *The Times* of June 17, 1844 said:

> We want facts and circumstances. We want such evidence as would satisfy any reasonable man or any set of men that the Home Secretary was morally justified in the course which he pursued. The whole question is one of constitutional rights, and nothing else. Mr. Mazzini's character and habits and society are nothing to the point, unless connected with some certain or probable evidence of evil intentions or treasonable plots. We know nothing, and care nothing about him. He may be the most worthless and the most vicious creature in the world. But this is no reason of itself why his letters should be detained and opened.[69]

In response, the Home Secretary, Sir James Graham, commissioned two Secret Committees of Parliament, one from the Commons, one from the

Lords, to investigate postal interception and prepare reports.[70] These are partial and politicized histories, as was already clear at the time, and only the Commons report was published. The committees were viewed with suspicion by opposition MPs, who objected to the departure from normal procedure and the absence of legally qualified MPs from the House of Commons on the committee; by contrast, the unelected chamber, the House of Lords, contributed three ex-ministers and two ex-chancellors who were loyal to the government and "accustomed to the most skilful mode of examination either for suppressing or for eliciting information."[71] Duncombe claimed to have witnesses willing to testify about the details of interception practices who were willfully excluded from the investigation, raising an unsuccessful motion in the Commons on July 18, 1844 for a vote to alter the constitution of the committees. He also asked in the House of Commons if his letters had been targeted by the Post Office. Home Secretary Sir James Graham said he was unable to answer publicly:

[Duncombe] has put to me a question to which he knows it is not consistent with my own sense of duty to attempt an answer. I have already stated to the House, respectfully and firmly, that consistently with my sense of duty, and bound by the obligation by which I am bound—and I am the judge of that sense of duty—I cannot answer, and will not answer this question.[72]

To neither confirm nor deny a question is not to refuse to answer it as much as to refuse its premise. It maintains an existing information asymmetry while implicitly defending the ambiguity that begged the question. In short, it delegitimizes some questions as outside the range of democratic politics. As a blanket policy for dealing with matters of state secrecy, it has pragmatic value because it avoids the need to assess making potentially sensitive disclosures on a case-by-case basis or creating a potentially unhelpful precedent.

Formally, it allows ministers sworn to secrecy not to contravene their duty to speak truthfully and sincerely to the legislature and broadly remains government policy on such questions today.[73] The acronym "NCND," neither confirm nor deny, is now the standard response to public queries about official secrets. The exchange between Graham and Duncombe may be the first time it was deployed in Parliament, illustrating the role that radical politicians and news media played in altering the conditions of political discourse.

The Secret Committees' reports offer the first historiographical account of interception in Britain. They found that no records had been kept of interception warrants until 1712, two years after the Post Office (Revenues) Act of 1710, and that the few warrants that had survived were vague in detail. Some were said to clearly represent an abuse of patronage, being used to spy on family members within the nobility. To give one example, in 1741, on the request of Mr. "A," his eldest son was granted a warrant to open and inspect any letters that A's youngest son should write to two named women, "one of whom that youngest son had imprudently married."[74] This warrant was selected as an exemplar to indicate triviality in the corrupt age of grace and favor, when matchmaking within the nobility was a critical element of patronage and wealth. The report makes the point that in the nineteenth century, these abuses had ended.

In 1782, the offices of the secretaries of state ceased to be sinecures and were institutionalized as the Home Office and the Foreign Office. This not only changed the political and financial structure of power, but it also marked a shift in the management and purpose of documents in government. Records were from then on kept in an organized manner intended to create a lasting archival resource. Clerks were no longer personal servants of the secretary of the day but employees of a permanent bureaucracy, administering to programs and policies rather than serving a patron, although patronage continued to dominate recruitment until 1870.[75] A new kind of historic accountability became possible on this basis. Between 1799 and 1805, a registry was kept of all interception warrants issued by the Home Office. From 1806 until 1844,

the practice was introduced at the Home Office of recording the issuing of every [interception] Warrant in a private book belonging, not to the head of the department, but to the Office, and always accessible to the two Under Secretaries of State and the Chief Clerk of the Domestic Department.[76]

From 1822 onward, "original warrants [were] preserved at the Post Office; the earlier warrants having been destroyed."[77] By recording and storing the interception warrants that were generated, each warrant became a temporal marker of a decision with two dimensions: an authorization, recorded in the Home Office register, and an executive action, carried out by interceptors in the Post Office.[78] As Foucault conceptualized it, the shift from a sovereign power concerned purely with order began to give way to more complex forces, producing "a sort of double system. On the one hand will be a whole series of mechanisms that fall within the province of the economy and the management of the population with the function of increasing the forces of the state. Then, on the other hand, there will be an apparatus or instruments for ensuring the prevention or repression of disorder, irregularity, illegality, and delinquency."[79] The function of increasing the economic circulation of goods, money, and communication is thus in tension with the security function of postal interception. The latter, the police function in the modern sense, "is entirely overturned, marginalized, and takes on the purely negative meaning familiar to us."[80]

The practice of interception had by 1844 been divided into two classes: criminal cases and political cases, the latter of which were then almost all concerned with Irish nationalism.[81] Domestic labor unrest was the current cause for criminal concern. In August 1842, a clerk was sent to "the manufacturing and mining districts . . . in the week of the greatest anxiety" with a warrant to open letters of named persons, certainly from the Chartist movement. Most of the targets were subsequently convicted before a special commission. Two clerks were sent to other towns with interception warrants but found no letters to open and returned to their "ordinary business" soon after.[82]

Tabulated statistics in the report demonstrate the decline in the number of interception events while representing interception as a well-organized, carefully controlled practice.[83] Subjecting the question of interception to a utilitarian moral calculus, they calculated the mean number of warrants per year; it was eight since the start of the nineteenth century. Each warrant had an average of two names per warrant and no defined limits in time. The committee concluded that selective interception minimizes intrusions into the "liberty" of correspondents because it produces useful intelligence leading to measured responses, thereby preempting the need for more intrusive overreactions that could in turn lead to violent popular reactions. By this logic, interception was used judiciously toward the end of securing order. At the population level, then, privacy and freedom in the post were found by the Secret Committees to have increased since the eighteenth century, thanks in part to the selective use of interception.[84]

For a criminal investigation warrant, the procedure governing the making of interception warrants in 1844 was as follows:

> The application is made, in the first instance, to that one of the two Under Secretaries of State who is of the legal profession; and the usual course is for the applicant to state the circumstances in writing; but if the case be very urgent, owing to the time being too short, before the departure of the post, to draw out a written statement, that condition is sometimes dispensed with. . . . If the Under Secretary accedes to the application, he submits the case to the Principal Secretary of State; with whose approval, a Warrant is drawn by the head clerk of the Domestic Department, under the instructions of the Under Secretary, and is then signed by the Principal Secretary of State. A record of the date of the Warrant is kept under lock and key, in a private book, to which the two Under Secretaries and the above-mentioned head clerk have access.[85]

If approved, the secretary's staff transposed the list of targets to a draft warrant, entered a copy in the records, and presented it for the secretary's signature. The will of the secretary to authorize the request was manifested by the signature and, for a while at least, wax impressed with the signet seal. This way, all operations passed through the bottleneck of the Home Office warrant, even if the ends were not Home Office business. In relation to criminal matters, the home secretary was an administrative element in an investigation process that began and concluded elsewhere.[86]

For political warrants, by contrast, the warrant came from the top down, initiated by the home secretary's office:

> The Principal Secretary of State, of his own discretion, determines when to issue them, and gives instructions accordingly to the Under Secretary, whose office is then purely ministerial. The mode of preparing them, and keeping record of them in a private book, is the same as in the case of Criminal Warrants. There is no record kept of the grounds on which they are issued, except so far as correspondence preserved at the Home-office may lead to infer them.[87]

In practice, the home secretary issued warrants based on information received from spies, informers, and information returned from the Post Office, filtered through their undersecretaries. Dividing the purpose of interception into the categories of criminal investigation and political surveillance was not new, but the procedural differentiation reflected a more complex bureaucracy and filing system. When files are relied on to give evidence of past practices, "administrative acts reveal themselves to be historical anticipations."[88]

The queen, who enjoyed reading intercepted material, favored its continuation, particularly with respect to the European revolutionaries and rebels like Mazzini who found asylum in Britain.[89] Yet she did not make policy. Power had decisively shifted from the classical model of sovereignty to a model of executive management and cabinet secrecy. While the figure of the Crown remained the symbol of authority, it had been thoroughly displaced by a system composed of ministers, policies, and files and a new economy of publicity and secrecy.[90]

SECRECY AS POLICY

When the Mazzini scandal erupted, the Post Office monitored the scandal unfolding in the press. An entry book in the postal archives shows records of news reports, commentaries, magazine articles, and letters to the editors, all cut out and collected over a period of ten months between June 14, 1844, and April 4, 1845. The use is unclear, but the Post Office was certainly attuned to its own publicity, an intelligence organization observing itself being publicly criticized in the press.[91] The cartoon figure of "Paul Pry" was depicted snooping on mail, and the association with immoral snooping lasted for the rest of the Home Secretary's life.[92] The fantasies circulating about letter espionage at the Post Office sparked by the press and the political accusation in Parliament far outstripped the reality. The control over this new factor, the impressions and experiences of politics experienced by the "public," which was not yet a democratic public, played a decisive role in the decision not to pass legislation in response to the Mazzini scandal but instead to adopt a policy of secrecy.

The Secret Committees reported that letter interception had been recognized as a prerogative power of the Crown by successive statutes, although it lacked a positive legal basis.[93] The committees considered whether the government should legislate on the topic. The key question was publicity. Legislation might help because the public would better tolerate letter interception if they knew it was permitted only under a warrant rather than through the use of "extraordinary powers."[94] But while the public would probably tolerate interception for policing purposes, the political use of interception risked inducing a strong "moral feeling which exists against the practice of opening of letters, with its accompaniments of mystery and concealment."[95] Ultimately, legislation would therefore attract unwanted attention:

> It must not be forgotten that, after the publicity given to the fact, that the Secretary of State has occasionally recourse to the opening of letters as a means of defence in dangerous and difficult times, few who hereafter may engage in dangerous designs, will venture to communicate their intentions by the medium of the Post; and the importance of retaining the power, as a measure of detective police, will consequently be greatly diminished.[96]

Hence, "it may appear to some that to leave it a mystery whether or not this power is ever exercised is the way best calculated to deter the evil-minded," and in the final analysis, the committee recommended maintaining the status quo.[97] The issue of whether or not to clarify the law was not decided by reference to justice or legal coherence but by anticipating the public response to law as a mode of publicity.[98]

On February 18, 1845, when the affair was no longer a pressing news story, Home Secretary Sir James Graham, "telling the truth in carefully chosen words,"[99] announced that the department maintained by the foreign secretary of the Post Office had been abolished. The Post Office continued collecting news clippings on the issue for two more months until satisfied that press attention had moved on. Parliament was satisfied by the reports of the committees and rejected calls for any further inquiry.[100]

Between 1845 and the Boer War of 1899, the British state had no permanent interception agency targeting foreign communications. Ad hoc projects for intercepting and deciphering foreign communication were arranged when deemed necessary, such as an 1892 order to intercept foreign carrier pigeons.[101] Similar economic logic led to the decline of most of the other Black Chambers across Europe in the nineteenth century, when securing the growth of commercial correspondence and postal revenues was prioritized over the security of the political state.

Domestic letter interception quietly continued. According to Postmaster General Rowland Hill, it was used in relation "exclusively to burglars, and others of that stamp."[102] In practice, however, it found new purposes. Of particular concern was the use of the postal system to deliver advertisements for illegal lottery competitions, fraudulently inviting people to send money in the hope of winning a fortune. There was at the same time a growth in the circulation of pornographic material of the kind Benbow promoted, contrary to Victorian sexual morality. The task of the interceptors expanded to censorship in the name of the moral health of the nation. Immoral material had to be intercepted, blocked, and eliminated from the network.[103] But political monitoring stopped. The last substantial use of domestic espionage took place in 1848 in relation to the Chartist movement. Thereafter, Britain was governed without secret intelligence agencies for around thirty years. British government espionage and political interception effectively ceased between 1850 and 1880 simply because it "did not square with the way things would be."[104]

POSTAL TECHNOLOGY

Spying has been described as incompatible with Victorian liberalism, a political ideology that *"depended* on not having political spies."[105] On this account, it was counterproductive to good government; a political police force would only provoke the kind of subversion it was intended to suppress. Political policing ended after the 1840s until the creation of the Metropolitan Police's "Special Branch" in 1883, in response to an Irish republican bombing campaign.[106] But this straightforward story of liberal ideological restraint was also, in a different register a refinement in the techniques of governmentality. The strategies that had prevailed when sovereignty was the central preoccupation were ineffective at achieving the ends of a government that was increasingly concerned with political economy.[107]

On Foucault's account, liberalism marks a reflexive rationality of government that reflects on governmental practices themselves and subjects them to an economic rationality. Government became cognizant of its own effects, asking not what grants the *right* to the government to do something—raise taxes, intercept letters—but what the *effects* will be.[108] The overarching problem is the management of power as an "art of contingency."[109] Liberalism rested on ideas of a "natural" order of things that emerged not because of governmental power but as a limit to its power. The risk of governing "too much" is that this natural harmony will be disrupted by the unlimited power of the police state; the risk of governing not enough is that it will be neglected and fail to prosper. The question is one of striking and maintaining a balance that reflects the true rather than the good. Governmental rationality thus adopted a second-order attitude to government and normativity, one that incorporated the contingency of its own operations and anticipated "action upon actions," with communication taking precedence over the application of disciplinary force. If the "defining component of sovereignty as a political code was a claim to occupy a privileged position of observation and intervention . . . as the ultimate master of events within its territory," then the defining feature of what Foucault labelled "biopower" is an understanding of life as a complex social fabric where none "has any privileged claim to a position of observation or intervention."[110]

This was perhaps reflected in the recognition in 1844 that the question of whether to explicitly legalize interception was ultimately resolved according to the effect it would have on the public's perception of security, rather than by any legal or constitutional principle. While the government continued to use communication technologies to suppress the revolutionary potential embedded in political reformist movements, it increasingly adopted a multiplicity of techniques and knowledges to do so, always in carefully limited ways, such as extending the franchise to vote to a portion of the urban, male working class in the Representation of the People Act of 1867.

By the mid-nineteenth century, this reformist attitude had begun to reshape the postal system, which had long been regarded as inefficient and uneconomical. Perennially high postage and the abuse of the franking privileges that allowed MPs and members of the nobility to send mail free of charge were increasingly condemned as corrupt and counterproductive to the ideal of social progress. A parliamentary committee that convened in 1837 on the matter heard the following complaints:

Bills for small amounts were not drawn, commercial travellers did not write until several orders could be sent on one sheet of paper, samples were not sent by post, communication between banks and branches was restricted, statistical information was denied, social correspondence restricted especially among the poor, working men were ignorant of the rates of wages in other parts of the country, and the high postage was a bad means of raising revenue.[111]

In 1840, Rowland Hill, a schoolmaster inspired by Bentham's utilitarianism, was appointed postmaster general.[112] Despite having no experience in postal work, he devised a schema by which postage would be paid in advance of posting a letter at a fixed uniform rate of one penny per letter, regardless of the distance it traveled from sender to receiver. Losses incurred on long-distance letters would be more than offset by the increased profits from local deliveries. The key was to ensure prepayment at an affordable price. The immediate response was a surge in postal revenues. Under the uniform "penny post" system, anyone could afford to send a letter anywhere in the country. At the same time, franking privileges were abolished, making the postal system indifferent not just to spatial distance but to social class.[113] Postage stamps were manufactured for the first time, separating the cash economy from postal operations. Letter carriers and postmasters no longer had to take time to give out bills and collect cash with each delivery. Postal carriers could move from house to house, rapidly dropping off letters that had been paid for before they were sent. So immediately successful was this plan that the supply of adhesive stamps, introduced in May 1840, could not keep pace with demand.[114]

Collection boxes were installed in cities, towns, and villages, and letter boxes appeared on front doors.[115] In 1856, the GPO began the process of affixing street names and street numbers to all addressable sites in the country. Codes and street names were slowly introduced in other large towns and cities. Idiosyncratic descriptions of addressees and their homes fell out of use for good. The unified postal address system transformed and differentiated urban space by fixing in place both "souls and houses."[116] Without such an index of addresses, there had been only an indistinct "*sea* of houses,"[117] which required local knowledge to navigate. A postal address allowed anyone to navigate the territory. In turn, it became a way of fixing and identifying individuals and families, becoming the precondition of access to other services.

The postal system thus rationalized cartographic geography, ultimately indexing all delivery points addressable according to a single master index, a coding of space, indifferent to the particular people located there.[118] From then on, letter writers had to adjust their mode of address to match the one applied by the Post Office. The implementation of the address system was a corollary of the liberalization of labor in the mid-nineteenth century, when workers began to be encouraged to save money and enjoy leisure time, thus channeling time into economies of exchange and political power that connected workers as addressable consumers in need of links to banks, advertisers, and commodity producers.[119]

In adopting a universal operational protocol in place of outmoded and complex couplings with class and money, the postal system became functionally differentiated from territory, politics, and the economy and standardized in its own internal media and operations. At this point, according to Bernhard Siegert, postal communication became an operationally closed machine.[120] Siegert borrows the concept of operational closure from systems theory, where it indicates the self-referential quality of differentiated systems of communication.[121] Systems are sense-making epistemic filters that contingently condition how reality is understood, apprehended, and reproduced, not merely as an organizational or institutional achievement but as an effect of communication itself.

The differentiation and "closure" of postal communication as a system has at least three dimensions: the material, the social, and the temporal. The material dimension concerns territory, the social dimension concerns class, and the temporal dimension concerns the relation to the economy. Materially, the postal system was no longer "coupled" to territorial space. After 1840, it no longer mattered how far a letter traveled along the post roads from sender to addressee; the only question was whether or not an item had a valid stamp. If it did, it was to be delivered regardless of distance. Conversely, the universal address system meant that postal workers no longer needed local knowledge of individuals or urban spaces. Socially, postage was decoupled from social class. The upper classes had long enjoyed, expected, and abused franking privileges as a matter of course, profiting from allowing others to use their privileges, enhancing their own social capital at the expense of those below them in the social order who paid punitively high postage rates. When franking was abolished, the system became universally open. When everyone has an address and anyone can use a public postbox, the system became formally indifferent to the particularities of the people it served.

Temporally, postal communication was decoupled from the moment of payment as individuals were no longer required to pay postage on receipt for letters and parcels. Letter carriers, in turn, were no longer revenue collectors but could post a letter in a box and move on. After 1840, all that mattered was the affixing of a stamp applied before sending. Indeed, the very indifference to temporality of stamps gave rise to an inversion: old unused stamps turned into collector's items, recursively finding new economic value depending on the age and relative scarcity of items created for purely functional reasons.

In other words, the technical dimensions of the postal network were removed from the direct experience of the user. Conversely, users of the postal service no longer had to consider distance, class, or money when using the system. Hence, the "materiality of the postal service could remain beneath the threshold of consciousness."[122] From then on, "communication" grew in the popular imagination as an abstract function, with normative, economic, governmental, and material dimensions that intensified with the introduction of electrical media.[123] Discourse about communication proceeded independently of its media. The Mazzini scandal, coming just four years after these reforms, was scandalous precisely because it infringed on the normative expectations of privacy in a public communication system. Communication became operationally independent of state security. What counted, then, was "not so much the immediate impact of new communications systems as the vision of their future."[124] From then on, the most secret security techniques of the state required techniques of publicity and secrecy management.[125]

Governmental secrecy had long been "embedded in administrative structures, regulations, and *mentalités*."[126] In other words, discretion was expected of a gentlemanly civil servant. As government increasingly became a matter of maintaining a constant flow of updated registries, memos, and files, ever more clerks and officials were required, opening up government to people of lower social standing who senior civil servants believed were susceptible to the temptation of selling secrets.[127] Criminalization was the inevitable outcome after a series of high-profile leaks during the second half of the nineteenth century, as secrecy was turned into legal rules, most notably the series of Official Secrets Acts, which were first passed in 1889.

In media-technical terms, secrecy management was a procedural inflection on file management and classification. The circulation of information to and from files could only be permitted using closed, secure channels that corresponded to the classification of the information within. Policies on secrecy became indexed as "precedents" that could be stored and recalled as needed: files governed their own circulation, instructing users how to treat them. Today, there are relatively few examples of files and materials concerning interception in the National Archives, a consequence of the excision of files on the topic. Indeed in 1957, when a retired judge, Lord Birkett, led a parliamentary committee investigation into the interception power, the Home Office and Security Service, MI5, reported that they could not provide comprehensive records of interception practices as they had destroyed them, the simplest approach to maintaining the secrecy of documents.[128]

CONCLUSION

The birth of interception depended on three preconditions: first, a monopoly over communication; second, a physically segregated space for inspecting letters selected from sorting operations or relay points; third, sufficient time in which to operate. Interception was materially constrained by the number of disciplined inspectors that could be effectively deployed at once in relation to the flow of correspondence. Everything not selected proceeded to delivery, constituting the norm. The delivery of an untouched letter was a consequence of its non-interception and referable to the legislative prohibitions against interference with the post. Interception was always an irreducible potentiality inherent in the system itself. What matters is the application and description of these powers.

The second-order consideration of how this potential was to be constrained and applied reveals the shift in the self-description of state power that had occurred by the nineteenth century, and the growing importance of publicity in relation to power. It is common to refer to Foucault's famous reading of Bentham's "panopticon" as a prototypical model of disciplinary surveillance power. But a better reference, for our purposes, might be the second part of Bentham's *Essay on Political Tactics*, entitled *Of Publicity*. Bentham differentiates the public into classes—those educated enough to know and judge the facts well and those who are ignorant and must judge based on their belief in the good judgments of others.[129] Publicity serves to allow the elites to know and to judge and, at the same time, for the middle classes and masses to *believe* that the elites are judging well. This in turn allows the masses and middle classes to amuse themselves with the frivolous entertainment value of publicity. Government by secret tribunal, by contrast, cannot be accurately judged by the elites, nor can it benefit from their wisdom. It fails to secure the faith of the middle classes and the masses. Secrets generate suspicion, while publicity engenders healthy distrust—we should distrust those empowered to make decisions, and for this we require publicity, without which "no good is permanent," under which "no evil can continue."[130]

Bentham's argument for an informed public nevertheless remains a form of advice to elites, a political tactic that has the informed public as its object of governance. This is demonstrated by Bentham's three exceptions to the general principle of publicity: publicity is to be limited where it might "favour the projects of an enemy," "injure innocent persons," or "inflict too severe a punishment upon the guilty."[131] Secrecy should not be the "instrument of regular government," but it must remain an essential component of the state. Power, in short, had become reflexive—a matter of tactical publicity and exceptional secrecy. Interception powers had been reconfigured accordingly.

4
ELECTRICAL INTERCEPTION

This chapter frames interception in respect of three new electrical communication media of the late nineteenth century: the telegraph, the telephone, and wireless. Taking each in turn, the chapter explores the relationship between the materiality of the transmission, storage, and information-processing features of each medium, highlighting the technical inflections that differentiated transmission and interception, then connects each to the juridical category of interception as mediated by the secretarial warrant. As we shall see, the juridical form of the warrant was neither appropriate nor necessary in each instance and was thus combined with the disciplinary techniques of licensing where necessary to manage, control, and suppress interception. In short, the administrative apparatus of the British state responded in different ways to the spatial, technical, and temporal properties of each medium.

As established in chapter 3, these parallel developments in relation to each medium unfolded during a period in which Britain did not operate an organized foreign intelligence service or a domestic secret police force. Interception powers were used by the Victorians with relatively low intensity when compared to the preceding and subsequent periods. This reflected a concern for an economic rationality of power, whereby the task of governing was to allow a natural order of things to emerge, to foster its growth, and to stimulate its productivity.

The application of interception power, however, radically changed with the censorship regime of the First World War, where all media were collectively subjected to open and total surveillance. That event marks the end of this chapter and the beginning of the following chapters. The guiding thread here, then, is simply the media-technical and juridical development of interception in the epoch of electrical media, which prefigures contemporary questions about the materiality of media and the political power and epistemic possibilities that they produce.

ELECTRICAL TELEGRAPHY

The material labor and sorting operations that allowed the spatial bridging of the post to generate a "communion of souls" remained largely imperceptible to readers and writers of letters. The technical complexity of electrical media, by contrast, was apparent from the beginning. The telegraph was commonly imagined as having "annihilated time and space."[1] By 1889, the prime minister could remark that the British imperial network of undersea cables had "assembled all mankind upon one great plane, where they can see everything that is done, and hear everything that is said."[2] But rather than annihilating time, telegraphy intensified it, standardized it, and turned it into an active element critical to technical communication. As Wolfgang Ernst puts it, the "act of transmission becomes time-critical when its temporal form is just as crucial as its bridging of space."[3] Morse code is the most famous and most simple example, as the communication of a message depends on its encoding using binary units—discrete, individual signs composed of electrical pulses of varying lengths—as "electromagnetically induced time events."[4]

The patent granted by George IV to William Fothergill Cooke and Charles Wheatstone in 1837 referred to an assemblage of widely available materials and equipment: the "electromagnets, the galvanometer needles, the voltaic batteries that made up an electrician's working equipment" arranged in a rudimentary communication apparatus.[5] Through a combination of public exhibitions celebrating scientific and industrial progress and investment from railway companies seeking a means to provide time-critical signaling, they succeeded in building the first commercial telegraphy business in Britain. By 1838, their telegraph was integrated with the development of new railways.[6] As Cooke pointed out, telegraphy's utility derived from its surveillance capacity, which afforded a "bird's-eye view" of the railway network at any moment in time. Without knowledge of where trains were, planners had to rely on rigid and fixed timetables and statistical regularities. Electrical telegraphy made the contingent state of the system knowable within a short time period. Crucially, messages could travel much faster than trains. This improved the flexibility, safety, and efficiency of the network while negating the spatial and temporal barriers that had previously constrained it.[7]

Cooke emphasized that telegraphy also imposed on railway workers "unremitting vigilance and alertness," creating a kind of remote panopticon for "instant and infallible detection at headquarters of individual remissness."[8] When commercial messaging services began, similar disciplinary rules were imposed on the telegraphers themselves. Cooke's 1836 prospectus for telegraphic communication promised privacy and confidentiality, with subscribers alone having access to the "confidential clerks" who would handle and transmit their messages.[9] On the other hand, the surveillant power of the telegraph could be made available to the authorities, "in case of dangerous riots or popular excitement, the earliest intimation thereof should be conveyed to the ear of Government alone, and a check put to the circulation of unnecessary alarm."[10]

The Electric Telegraph Company was granted a charter by an act of Parliament in 1846, with a clause allowing the home secretary to declare an emergency and take possession of the company's apparatus where "expedient for the public service." A warrant was duly signed on April 10, 1848, the day of a grand demonstration by the Chartists on Kennington Common in London. The warrant required the company to suppress Chartist messages and allow officials to coordinate the responses across England and Ireland by local magistrates.[11] The Telegraph Act 1863 renewed the preemptive emergency power.[12] Telegraphy offered not only discipline, but time—the opportunity of receiving fresh information. The political imperative was to take advantage of the temporal differential the telegraph afforded and "maintain its mastery by manipulating time to outmanoeuvre the machinations of the deviant or subversive."[13]

The temporal revolution that telegraphy caused in the Victorian imagination was profound, not least because it standardized time itself. In

1852, an electric clock was installed at Greenwich and connected by telegraph cable, first to the switching room at London Bridge station and from there to the Electric Telegraph Company's offices, where a time signal was distributed across the network. From then on, telegraphy not only collapsed space and time in the illusion of instantaneous transmission, it also provided "a universal grid against which that instantaneity could be measured."[14] The temporal advantages this offered to economic communication cannot be overstated. Alongside messaging services, telegraph companies also offered the first collecting services for financial news. Newspaper production was similarly transformed as stories were syndicated among regional publications. "Telegraph" became synonymous with newspapers, which rented private lines to ensure the security and confidentiality of the valuable news they relayed.[15] Once it became possible to assume the same knowledge was generally known throughout the territory and updated daily, a new sense of social reality emerged, as news and current affairs came to form the common horizon of shared understanding.[16]

The financial impact of telegraphic time is most obviously represented in the stock ticker, developed in 1867 by Edward Calahan as a solution to the "noise and confusion" of price fluctuations on the floor of the New York Stock Exchange.[17] Calahan sold the patent to Western Union, which began distributing stock quotations over its private telegraph network across the United States. Only one telegrapher was required to input the name of the security, the price quote, and later the volume traded, distributing it to all subscribers. Banks were also early adopters of private telegraph lines that allowed secure peer-to-peer transactional information to be sent instantaneously.[18] The movement of the tape moved the market.[19]

The London Stock Exchange permitted only one company, Extel, to operate telegraph lines for ticker tape machines from 1872. The license issued by the GPO permitted Extel to circulate prices only within nine hundred yards of the stock exchange, barring Extel from competing with post office telegrams and preventing Extel subscribers from transmitting onward telegrams containing advance price information.[20] The stock exchange joined gambling as a mode of telegraphic speculation on contingency.[21] Access to advance information moved from the realm of government strategy and security to a means of beating the house. By 1890, the stock exchanges of New York and London learned of one another's prices within minutes by ticket. This led to international arbitrage, with buyers purchasing stock on one market and instantly selling it on another to take advantage of the differential.[22] Framed as an inherently "masculine" medium, the curt efficiency of telegrams lacked the soul expected of "feminine" forms of letter writing, which became increasingly indexed to slower concerns, like love and gossip.[23]

After twenty years of telegraphic communication dominated by three companies operating as an effective cartel, the quality of service, the geography of the networks, and the high price of telegrams in the UK led to growing political support for nationalization.[24] Subscribers complained that telegraph companies promoted some messages over others and sometimes appropriated information.[25] When government announced plans for the compulsory purchase of the telegraphs, the companies objected, with the Electric Telegraph Company invoking interception in a pamphlet:

What is a telegram? Practically it is an open letter, the contents of which is known to and is capable of being used by everyone through whose hands it passes. Is it desirable that the most important part of correspondence of the country should pass through the hands and be subject to the surveillance of government officials?[26]

The specter of interception and snooping had little impact. The Telegraph Act 1868 granted the government power to compulsorily purchase "telegraphs, wires, posts, pipes, tubes, and other works, materials, lands" and other property" from "any Company, Corporation, or Persons now engaged in the United Kingdom of Great Britain and Ireland in transmitting, or authorized to transmit, Messages for Money or other Consideration, by means of Electric or other Telegraphs, or mechanical Agencies, and each and every of those Companies."[27] The following year, further legislation granted the General Post Office (GPO) a monopoly over telegraphic communication services in order to provide, as the preamble put it, "a cheaper, more widely extended, and more expeditious System of Telegraphy." The distribution of Greenwich Mean Time became the distribution of government time,[28] and from there, it became world time.[29]

TAPPING THE LINE

The most direct form of intercepting telegraphy involves "tapping" the current on the line. Popular public accounts of wiretapping emerged during the American Civil War (1861–1865). Both Confederate and Union armies recognized the value of telegraphic communication in organizing a war, and both employed signal clerks to tap into enemy lines to intercept signals.[30] The earliest accounts date from 1862, with an early visual representation of the technique appearing in *Frank Leslie's Illustrated Newspaper* in 1865: in this illustration, a clerk calmly sits on the ground beneath telegraph lines and, with one hand, makes notes in a book resting against his thigh while holding a pocket sounder in the other hand; nearby, a rider waits.[31] Such stories tended to circulate in postwar literature aiming to romanticize the conflict as a noble struggle between equal and just white Americans, thereby diverting attention from the political question of slavery at its heart.[32]

In England, people speculated in the letter sections of newspapers about the technicalities of trying to "tap telegraph lines without discovery." Some thought the line would have to be cut to insert a receiver, alerting the line operators. Others pointed out that electrical connections can be attached to a line before it is intercepted "so that the electric fluid passes along without the slightest break in the continuity of the wire." The only trace of the tapper might be a slight change in the electrical impedance of the line, which would be nearly impossible to detect without a sensitive galvanometer. As such, "a skilful operator could, with some trouble, intercept important government messages," but it would be much easier to offer the operators "the temptation of heavy bribe [to] reveal the secrets of the telegraph."[33]

It seems the first governmental use of wiretapping in Britain was conducted against the telegraphers themselves. Shortly after the GPO assumed control over telegraphy in 1870, the newly nationalized telegraph clerks found their ordinary working hours extended, conditions of employment reduced, and long-term remuneration frozen.[34] In 1871, a group of telegraphers attempted to form a union and organize a strike. As one telegraphist wrote in a letter to the press that November, the new regime undervalued their skills, "setting in motion all the irritating machinery of official routine with a view of reducing us to mere human machines."[35] As there was no right to unionize in Britain, the telegraphers used the network itself to plan a collective walkout at multiple offices, intending to bring about a sudden and unexpected nationwide disruption to economic and news communication.

An internal report to the postmaster general, Frank Ives Scudamore,[36] explained that the strike's leaders were suspected to be based in the Liverpool and Bristol offices, but that they could not be precisely identified as they were careful to check the identity of the operator on the other end of the line before signaling any sensitive information. A memo on file notes that "a combination of Telegraph Clerks" can form more easily than postal workers, as they "can communicate with each other so freely on a wire, no matter what its length may be, as if they were sitting face to face in the same room."[37] During working hours, the lines were too busy to organize, so the telegraphers communicated only at night. Spies working on behalf of Scudamore went to work tapping the lines. Where and how they did it was not explained; the only observation was that

they can be watched in a manner which I need not specify at intermediate points on the wires, those whom I have reason to speak of being watched at this moment, and it is from the conversation which has gone on between them, and which is reported to be by the watchers at intermediate points, that I am enabled to state that I know the full extent of the movement.[38]

Handwritten notes taken at the interception site record the telegraphic circuits targeted, the dates and times of intercepted exchanges, and summaries of the conversations. When the strike went ahead in December 1871, signaling clerks from the army were standing by to take over the network. To ensure this preemptive strike-break succeeded, Scudamore ordered all press telegrams be delayed for several hours on the day the strike began. This delay in reporting the news caused outcry, with the Manchester Chamber of Commerce denouncing the "tyranny" and abuse of the new monopoly. A subsequent letter to the postmaster general confirmed that the leaders of the planned union had been identified and dismissed. The wiretapping of the workers was not mentioned in the press or in subsequent histories of the GPO.[39] Here are the dimensions of telegraphic interception: a conflict determined by better access to the wire; the wiretap gaining a temporal advantage of preemption; and the political power to suspend the network's normal operations, granting the

Post Office the capacity to delay, prohibit, or otherwise interfere with messages. Again, time was the critical factor in the telegraphic economy.

Wiretap fraud was a commonly charged criminal offense, with bookmakers commonly the victims. News from horse races was a lucrative early source of telegraphic business. In 1870, for instance, the Newmarket race meetings produced around 20,000 telegraphic messages in two weeks, growing to 34,500 eight years later.[40] Gamblers frequently tried to bribe telegraph workers to give them the results of races before the bookies, while tappers connected telegraphic sounders on the wires between the racetracks and the betting rooms. Some were so bold as to rent rooms directly above the targeted bookmaker's shop and cut the line to the shop, placing themselves in the middle as a hidden relay point. The interceptors received all transmissions and relayed the information to the unwitting target as if from the track, letting the bookmaker know the results only after betting on the correct outcome.[41] Reporting on a wiretapping trial in 1895, the *Globe* newspaper commented, "Of course but little moral is to be drawn, except that it is exceedingly difficult to baffle the skill of the man who means winning without minding how."[42] In both war and gambling, time is a resource. The more you have, the greater the advantage.

Thus, wiretapping attained a reputation as "the domain of criminals, cheats, and con artists."[43] But these examples demonstrate that telegraphic wiretapping was conditioned by time and target. Tapping a line made sense only if one knew in advance which line to tap and when to tap it. It was a means of gaining a time advantage over one's opponent, whether politically or financially, provided one had advance knowledge and skill. The metaphor of the "tap" confirms the temporal flow integral to telegraphic coding. To read and write code, time is required. The discrete binary elements of a code can be depicted together on a page, but it is their temporal distribution that enables telegraphic transmission as a flow of information that can be "tapped." Interception is easier once the flow has stopped, captured in the form of a telegram.

TELEGRAM ACQUISITION

Just as electrical transmission collapsed the time of communication between relay points to near-zero, the public telegram delivery service extended the life of transmissions in the opposite direction, giving the network a paper memory function. Telegraphic transmissions were decoded into alphabetic script and transcribed or printed onto paper. All post office telegrams remained available for three months in the offices that sent and received them, a kind of distributed archive. This service allowed transmission errors to be identified and corrected, old messages retrieved, and messages relayed to several addressees. At the same time, storage provided a window of time for the reconstruction of the content and addressees of the messages, extending the temporal possibilities of interception, which became differentiated from the transmission process and instead took the form of access to stored information.

Telegrams were accordingly understood to be "open" to the services that handled them. Furthermore, their prices were calculated by the number of signs a message contained, which determined the time a message took in transmission. Privacy and efficiency generated a new market in codebooks containing ciphering techniques and abbreviations to reduce messages to maximum efficiency. At that point, the measure of communication changed: "minimum signs release maximum energy..... Once there are telegrams and postcards, style is no longer the man, but an economy of signs."[44]

Telegraphic codes and ciphers were popular not only for reasons of efficiency but out of concern for privacy.[45] Telegrams were calibrated for short, inexpensive, and unconcealed communication. Like postcards (although preceding them), they could be posted with an appropriate prepaid stamp at any street corner pillar box to be collected, sorted, and sent to the nearest telegraphy station for transmission to the recipient's local station, where a copy was delivered to its destination as part of the normal mail delivery routine or urgently hand-delivered by a post office messenger. Customers could simultaneously send multiple copies of a single message to several receivers simply by listing them and their local offices on the form and affixing the correct number of stamps.[46] Errors were a constant problem. As compression and codes were common, and as telegraphers used Morse code for transmission, all messages were repeated by the receiver back to the sender for accuracy.[47] Paper telegrams provided the network with memory to ensure that signals had the necessary redundancy required to be useful.

This may be the reason why the Telegraph Act 1868 contained a clause on "Punishment for disclosing or intercepting Messages" at section 20:

Any Person having official Duties connected with the Post Office, or acting on behalf of the Postmaster General, who shall, contrary to his Duty, disclose or in any way make known or intercept the Contents or any Part of the Contents of any Telegraphic Messages or any Messages intrusted to the Postmaster General for the Purpose of Transmission, shall, in England and in Ireland, be guilty of a Misdemeanor, and in Scotland of a Crime and Offence, and shall upon Conviction be subject to Imprisonment for a Term not exceeding Twelve Calendar Months; and the Postmaster General shall make Regulations to carry out the Intentions of this Section; and to prevent the improper Use by any Person in his Employment or acting on his Behalf of any Knowledge he may acquire of the Contents of any Telegraphic Message.

This rule differs from provisions in earlier Post Office acts that prohibited the delay or opening of letters unless pursuant to a secretarial warrant. The Telegraph Act makes no mention of warrants, nor does it criminalize interference with or interception of telegraphic messages in general. Rather, the legislation refers to the duties of post office operators and employees who had direct access to telegraphs and telegrams and empowers the postmaster general to arbitrarily set regulations under which telegrams could be intercepted or disclosed.[48] The risk of disclosure or interception was a tempting possibility inherent to a telegrapher's powers and duties,[49] such that "interception" refers to the unauthorized disclosure of a message and "improper use" of knowledge gained in the course of employment. Further, any private operators of telegraphic messaging services are not bound by this provision.

Most of the telegraphic intermediaries exposed to confidential information were women.[50] Henry James captured the particularity of telegraphic memory in his 1898 novella *In the Cage*.[51] The story is a meditation on the materiality of telegraphy, contrasting the simple life of a telegrapher girl trapped in her job with her impression of life among the wealthier classes whose messages she processes. Our unnamed telegrapher works alone, enclosed in a glass dome within a wire cage in a telegraph office located at the back of a grocery shop. There, she receives and sends telegrams, exchanging messages for money.

The drama arises when she finds herself serving as the medium for correspondence in a love affair unfolding between a wealthy married man,

Captain Everard, and Lady Bradeen, both of whom belonged "supremely to the class that wired everything, even their expensive feelings." They send telegrams to arrange meetings, exchange cryptic comments, and send fond wishes. The telegrapher's imagination exploits the latent ambiguity of their abbreviated exchanges as she pictures their affair unfolding. After engineering an encounter with Captain Everard near his home, she is pleased that he does not try to seduce her, preserving her good image of him. When a few weeks later, he rushes into her office demanding a copy of a telegram Lady Bradeen previously sent him, she provides him the message from memory. She then discovers from a friend that there is gossip that the pair are to be married, Lady Bradeen's husband having suddenly died, with the penniless scoundrel Captain Everard reprieved from disaster by a telegram.

As James noted, the drama of the story involves observing an unobserved observer. What does it mean, James asked, "for confined and cramped and yet considerably tutored young officials of either sex to be made so free, intellectually, of a range of experience otherwise quite closed to them"?[52] In cybernetic terms, the telegrapher is a nontrivial component of the telegraphic machinery.[53] She is not merely part of the apparatus, although that is how the proponents of telegraphy as an "electric Ariel" sending pure information from one point to another would have it. Understood that way, electric telegraphy appeared to some as indistinguishable from occult spiritualist practices—a pure "medium."[54] The telegrapher is invisible, merged with the wires, incorporating their nervous system into an artificial nervous system of society.[55] In practice, however, the labor of transposing messages from alphabetic form to binary code on the wires introduces an irreducible element, a conscious observer who understands the message for themselves and has the capacity to transform it into something surprising, a contingency entirely unrelated to the intentions of the nominal sender or receiver. In practice, telegraphers always occupied a privileged point of unseen second-order observation—much like an interceptor, or an author.[56]

TELEGRAPHIC WARRANTS

In 1886, the Home Office obtained a legal officer's opinion on the legality of the interception of letters and telegrams. In approving the practice, subject to the provision of an interception warrant from the secretary of state, the legal officer observed that telegrams

do not merely multiply communications but remain for some time as a record in the Post Office which, if necessary can be collected during that time without the person whose telegrams are examined finding it out and taking alarm, as is the case where letters are detained or appear to have been opened. Again, telegrams can be identified more easily than letters—a certain man is known to have gone to a certain post office, it will be easy to find out the telegram he has read without disturbing other telegrams or even delaying the delivery of the message. It is obvious therefore that these telegrams in the Post Office constitute an immense resource for police investigation only if it is proper they should be used for this purpose.[57]

An example of a telegram interception warrant prepared on January 12, 1888, gives a sense of the scope of search that the memory system afforded. The warrant was a command and authorization

to forward to this office copies of any telegrams which may during the last three months have been sent by Major Teufler to a person of the name of Lane, or to a person of the name of Edward, at Birmingham, London, or old Charlton; or to any person at Birmingham from the following telegraph offices:

New Brompton, Kent
Old Brompton, Kent
Brompton Barracks, Chatham,
Chatham,
Rainham.[58]

Telegrams were standardized forms. Nothing differentiated one telegram from another, unlike the traces of personal identity observable in letters: paper, signatures, seals, inks, and handwriting. With a telegram, content, sender, and addressee are the only variables. Selection criteria referred to the addressing options used by the telegraph network: names, dates, addresses, and local telegraph offices. Warrants listed targeted names and listed the local telegraph offices where stored telegrams were to be checked for matches.

Telegraphic storage and retransmission meant that interception became a matter of relaying targeted messages back to the GPO from branch offices. Designated clerks at headquarters received interception warrants from the Home Office and arranged for any relevant telegrams to be forwarded on to them. Clerks signed their name on a cover letter, added the date and reference of the relevant warrant, and sent the information to the Home Office. Telegrams were copied by hand at the Home Office onto standard preprinted post office telegram forms,[59] and a copy was filed at the GPO alongside the warrant.[60] Warrants no longer only directed operations in postal sorting rooms. Now, they were both the condition under which telegrams could be accessed and the organizing element in a circuit of information and material between files—a new organizational technology that materially reconfigured the capacity to process and use intelligence.

FILES AND COPIES

Files offered a flexibility and flow to information that mirrored the circuits of the telegraph system. In 1848, the reformist spirit saw the development of new organizational policies in the Home Office, such that for the first time a single register was kept of all letters received each day. The undifferentiated mass of loose records that had previously been accumulated and retained was sifted through, and papers deemed redundant were disposed of. Those selected for retention were categorized into one of four numbered series that loosely overlapped in subject matter,[61] and a new inspectorate was created to further reduce waste by assessing the utility of retained material going forward.[62] The complexity of the new file referencing system grew, with a numerical file reference system introduced in 1871 and updated in 1880 with an alphanumerical system.[63]

The next step was taken in 1887, when the Home Office acquired copying presses, eliminating the need for clerks to work as scriveners.[64] Copy presses and letter copying books vastly reduced the time required to duplicate items,[65] thanks to the invention of quick-drying aniline ink. They were sold as blank bound entry books containing sheets of tough tissue paper. Dampers, sheets of oiled paper, and blotting material were also required. An office boy counted the number of outgoing letters of the day and prepared the corresponding number of pages in the copybook by dampening them with a sponge. Taking the first available blank page in the book and putting a fresh outgoing letter face up beneath it, they placed an oiled sheet on either side to prevent water and ink from soaking through, then closed the book and compressed it in the copy press for about two minutes. When all the letters had been copied, they took them to be posted while the book was left to dry by the fireplace. The method gives the entries a distinctive blotted appearance, a consequence of a relatively short-lived cultural technique bracketed by handwriting and typing (see figure 4.1).[66]

One such book containing copies of outgoing letters and interception warrants sent from the Home Office to the Post Office survives today.[67] Its position in the National Archives' catalog suggests that similar records have since been destroyed. The book prefigures files in a few dimensions. First, warrants copied into the entry book did not merely register and store copies of warrants sent out but served as a place to record further details, including the cancellation of warrants by overwriting the copy.

The practice of overwriting copies of warrants persisted until 1933, by which point it had become an inherited practice, carried on even after the use of typed cancellation notices had allowed carbon copy "flimsies" to be put on files. Placing a copy of a cancellation letter on file negated the purpose of overwriting, so the cancellation practice was itself canceled in 1933.[68] Reforms to cancellation practices were driven by pressure from the Post Office. The postmaster general wrote to the home secretary at various stages with lists of names subject to warrants that had returned no intercepted material, asking that their names be formally canceled from the list of active warrants. While the Home Office could issue warrants and simply forgot about them, at the Post Office, each warrant was an additional selector element in the ongoing processes of interception. The development of efficient file-checks to ensure timely cancellations thus began as a matter of administrative efficiency rather than protection of privacy.[69]

Entries in the copybook, which begin in 1876, reveal the growing importance of file reference numbers. On the earlier entries, alphanumeric references are overwritten in pencil after the warrant was initially issued and copied. From around 1890 onward, file references were included on the face of the original letters. In the book, copies of warrants are preceded by copies of covering letters addressed to the postmaster general stating the purpose and target of the warrant. Warrants merely repeat the information stated in the covering letter, distinguished only by the targets and by variations on the phrase found in precedent examples:

4.1 A warrant in a blotted copybook, dated August 29, 1894, and signed by then Home Secretary (later Prime Minister) H. H. Asquith. *Source*: The National Archives HO 151/7, 193.

And for so doing this shall be your sufficient warrant, followed by the signature of a secretary of state. This indicates the symbolic difference between a letter and a warrant. The difference mattered; a warrant is not just writing but has its own protocols. By the nineteenth century, there are no references to seals, only signatures. Instead of seals, a different system for guaranteeing authenticity had developed in the file reference number.

Entries in the book end abruptly, thanks to another innovation in filing technology. The Home Office acquired two typewriters in 1890, initially with reluctance because typing was considered a feminine job and the subject matter that the Home Office dealt with was considered too vulgar for feminine sensibilities.[70] Thereafter, typed warrants began to supersede handwritten warrants. The final letter impressed into the copybook is dated March 22, 1899. Fittingly, it was typed.

At that point, files of papers replaced books. Whereas the copybook stored copies of outgoing letters arranged by topic, the file and the filing cabinet brought all elements in each case together as particularized matters of concern.[71] From then on, the signature would only be applied to the version that was posted. A case file concerning correspondence on the interception of telegrams in relation to a murder suspect in 1901 contains a copy of a letter received from the postmaster general, illustrating the difference between a typed carbon copy slip and an outgoing pressed copy. With the typewriter, "original" documents are differentiated from identical file copies by their materiality. The latter are flimsy and unadorned, whereas posted copies go under printed letterheads on embossed paper authenticated by handwritten signatures.[72]

With the shift from entry books to individual files, collected case material was bound together with a lace tag and kept in a single uniform cardboard file. Files contain instructions as to their own procedures. Many files can be operated by one administrator, who can universally distribute matters of concern and cases of interest among bureaucrats who each add their own memos and amend one another's draft letters before they are typed and dispatched. Files thus became the active agents in bureaucracies.[73] As with telegraphic communication, knowledge was superseded by information, hermeneutics by pragmatics, and the arts of script by mechanical technologies of cataloging, storage, and retrieval. The sovereign decision-maker of *raison d'etat* no longer fit in a bureaucracy growing under its own complexity, a set of self-referential closed circuits developing their own logics and priorities.

Large-scale strategic observation for intelligence purposes, then, depended on access to messages in plain language, archived and ordered. Only then could one reconstruct a full mosaic of meaning and a fuller "environment" of intercepted material. Now, however, what was intercepted was no longer the full self-referential knowledge composed by an author of a letter but a series of short, sharp, encoded exchanges in a new economy of information. The capacity to access and copy sent telegrams solved the problem of maintaining the sovereign position in the network. As before, the warrant represented sovereign power in its position as the unseen observer with access to the interior operations of the network.

TELEPHONY

In 1876, a year after Alexander Graham Bell's first call and just a few years after the nationalization of the telegraph networks, Sir William Thompson (later Lord Kelvin) demonstrated the Bell telephone in Glasgow, calling it "the greatest by far of all the marvels of the electric telegraph," and reportedly adding that "before long, friends will whisper their secrets over the electric wire."[74] In 1878, the status and originality of Bell's patent was challenged in the US by Western Union, which relied on the patent filed the same day by Bell's assistant. Bell argued that the originality of his method lay in its specific application to "transmitting vocal or other sounds."[75] The technical insight was that to transmit sounds over wire, a constant undulating current is required, unlike the on/off switching of telegraphic transmission. But the specific inventiveness, Bell's lawyers insisted, was in linking this engineering achievement to the sensibility of the voice. In late 1879, Western Union settled its case by consent, but others pursued the matter until, in 1881, a court finally confirmed that Bell's patent constituted a "new art." By linking undulating current to speech transmission, the court granted Bell the "exclusive right of talking over a wire by electricity," as *Scientific American* magazine reported it, which included rights over superior telephones that had followed his own.[76] In the meantime, a different legal definition of telephony prevailed in England.

The Post Office began planning to allow subscribers to equip private subscription telegraph circuits with rudimentary telephones as early as 1877. Private telephone networks started operating to provide exclusive telephonic services in 1879, including the Edison Telephone Company, which offered Thomas Edison's patented American telephone receivers. As there was still substantial public debt attached to the nationalization of the telegraph network, there was little political appetite for another round of compulsory purchases. Instead, the postmaster general adopted the policy in 1879 of asserting that telephones were telegraphs for the purpose of section 3 of the Telegraph Act 1869 (which amended the Telegraph Act 1868)—namely, "any apparatus for transmitting messages or other communications by means of electric signals." Therefore, the monopoly the Post Office held over the transmission of telegraphic messages automatically applied, and the new companies were required to apply and pay for licenses to operate.[77] In *Attorney-General v. Edison Telephone Co of London Ltd* (1880) LR 6 QBD 244, this argument was upheld. The court ruled that the monopoly

was intended to confer powers and to impose duties upon companies established for the purpose of communicating information by the action of electricity upon wires, and absurd consequences would follow if the nature and extent of those powers and duties were made dependent upon the means employed for the purpose of giving the information.[78]

Information, electricity, wire. Medium and message coincided in the law. Telephone lines and networks were thus subject to Post Office licensing requirements until they were all eventually nationalized in 1910.[79]

Early telephone networks depended on the "psychotechnical discipline" of operators,[80] the impersonal proto-cybernetic figures that made and broke the connections. Female voices were naturally preferred for the depersonalization required to speak on behalf of the switching equipment: "Operator. Number please."[81] New norms of conversational etiquette emerged and ways of managing the absence of presence; the simultaneous intimacy of hearing another's voice was coupled to the uncertainty of the forced intrusion of a stranger's voice in one's home.[82] Operators were there not to partake in the exchange. The depersonalized voice spoke from the same position of the phone tapper, intercepting, permitting, and ultimately breaking the connection.

Telephone tapping, like telegraphic line-tapping, was an obvious technical possibility, and again the structure of the network determined where interception could take place. In January 1900, the *Mirror of Life* magazine carried an illustrated story of an unfaithful wife caught cheating by her husband, his solicitor, an electrician, and a stenographer. As the magazine's headline announced, "They Tapped the Telephone Wire." The telephone "has its advantages for the businessman, but beware he who switches it on to the lady of his affections." By the 1920s, telephone tapping was frequently conducted by the secret Security Service, known as MI5, which was formed in anticipation of the First World War. An MI5 officer, Frederick Booth, recalled that early telephone tapping was hard work: "The only method of recording the conversation was by handwriting. The results were not accurate or useful and the written returns showed increasingly the remark 'Conversation in a foreign language—not understood.'"[83]

As Marshall McLuhan put it, "The telephone demands complete participation, unlike the written and printed page."[84] Within the secret space of the local telephone exchange, the same techniques used by telephone engineers to check problems on a subscribers' line enabled interception. Tapping a call as it occurs demands constant and careful listening, even before anything interesting has occurred. Bell's patent argument was perceptive: the capture of the reality of the voice in a symbolic aural medium transformed psychic life.[85]

Yet in the eyes of the law, it was nothing but a new form of telegraphy. Moreover, as no telegram was produced, the legislative prohibition on unwarranted disclosure did not apply. The telephonic system entirely belonged by statute to the state, which could tap it freely. As such, no telephonic warrants were thought necessary until 1937, when they were secretly introduced as a matter of internal administrative policy.[86]

SUBMARINE TELEGRAPHY

The first international undersea cable between France and England was laid in 1851, and soon after, it was dredged up and broken by a trawler. It took time to develop reliable undersea telegraphy. When the Crimean War broke out in 1855, France and Britain constructed overland cables to communicate with their armies. In 1865, a telegraphic connection was made to India, Britain's most important colony, but it required that telegrams be relayed over land to Constantinople, then to Al-Faw in Iraq, and from there by submarine cable to Karachi. Lines passing over foreign territory were vulnerable to being tapped, cut, or appropriated, and indeed the International Telegraph Conventions, first organized and agreed among European land-bound states, gave states the right to censor communications on lines within their jurisdiction in case of emergency, provided they first notified the other contracting parties through the International Telegraph Bureau in Berne.[87] The first convention, signed in 1865, promised protection for the secrecy of correspondence but allowed for the power "to stop the transmission of any private telegram which may appear dangerous to the security of the State, or which may be contrary to the laws of the country, to public order or decency."

The British imperial order was built on free trade backed by naval supremacy. Colonial control over the jungles of Sumatra, Malaya, and Borneo gave Britain a monopoly over the production of gutta-percha, a natural tree sap rubber and the only available waterproof insulator of the time.[88] Gutta-percha transformed the ocean from an obstacle into an asset. Freeing messages from the risk of overland line-tapping, it furthered British imperial dominance over maritime communication. From the 1870s, the British government invested heavily in international telegraph companies and regulated their operations through licensing conditions, quickly succeeding Belgium as the hegemonic state in the International Telegraph Union.[89] The wealth of the industrial empire afforded British firms the capital needed to manufacture and lay enormous long-distance cables, while the reach and distribution of the ports of the empire allowed the construction of world communication networks, mostly aligned with their existing imperial nodes and routes of sea communication.[90] The desire to securely connect sites of colonial rule with the metropolitan center in London led to a remapping of the empire,[91] with cable landing stations constructed at remote sites, like Ascension Island or St. Helena, as well as major ports, balancing the social requirements of "existing populations and infrastructure" against the geographic "affordances of an area's natural and social topography."[92] The "Empire Cables" became "the cerebrospinal axis of our political system . . . through which would freely pass the sensory impressions and the motor impulses of the British people."[93]

Physical threats to undersea cables took many forms: underwater topography, erosion, sea animals, earthquakes, ships' anchors, and deliberate dragging and dredging by enemy vessels. Cable landings were fortified and defended on several fronts, including the markets. The Committee on Telegraphic Communication with India in 1891 contemplated the risk that a syndicate of foreign state powers could, under cover of commercial aliases, buy the shares of the Eastern Telegraph Company and thereby "alienate" it from the British Empire.[94] In response to this financial threat, an "all-red line" was devised and built, a submarine telegraph network controlled by government, landing only on British shores.[95] Its realization became a "virtual fetish" for the colonial defense committee, counteracted by the recognition that connections to foreign states served as an investment that allowed money and communication to flow into London's international finance system.[96]

Royal Navy patrols were aligned along cable routes, and some stations were fortified with wire and naval guns. Cable huts were situated to be invisible from the sea, ideally in sheltered harbors or otherwise "where there is a possibility for guns or rifles alone to make it defensible."[97] Redundancy was added to the network by triangulating links between stations so that the loss of no one station would disrupt the global imperial network. Licensing conditions ensured that private cable operators complied with the requirements set by the Cables (Landing Rights) Committee of the Board of Trade. For the first generation of cable landing stations, geographical isolation was threatening because the station would be sited far from local garrisons and sources of food and water in case of attack or blockade. Following decolonization, the inverse logic would apply. Local populations became part of the threat, and relative isolation was considered a source of security.[98]

At the same time, the internationalization of communication that submarine telegraphy permitted gave rise to a new epistemic imaginary of an interconnected world and liberal peace. One of the key figures behind the laying of the first transatlantic cable, Cyrus Field, was the brother of David Field, a key figure in the Euro-American movement to codify positive international law.[99] The undersea cables became objects of international law. Communication was ideologically equated with understanding. The 1884 Convention for the Protection of Submarine Telegraph Cables required all ships to remain at least one nautical mile from cable-laying ships, while fishing vessels that hooked a cable were to cut away their nets and seek compensation rather than risking the line. Yet, at Britain's insistence, the convention contained a provision recognizing the right to cut the enemy's cables in times of war—a power that, in practice, was unilaterally in their favor. British companies had laid most submarine cables, so they knew exactly where to find them, while by far the greatest number of ships capable of dredging, cutting, or repairing undersea lines were British owned and operated.[100]

Human-operated relays and junctions allowed the undersea network to function. Telegraphers were posted at key points around the network to relay messages at locations determined, in part, by the maximum distance a clear signal could travel without being lost in the entropic noise of electrical resistance and interference from the earth's magnetic field. Known as "cablemen" they were typically drawn from the metropolitan British middle classes and were trained at a specialized school in Porthcurno, Cornwall.[101] Whereas domestic telegraphy was conducted by women and men, long-distance cable work was male dominated, and understood as a kind of imperial duty. As the Cornish locals provided the telegraphers with servants at Porthcurno, so the cablemen overseas lived apart from indigenous communities where they were based, typically feeling more connected "to a distant homeland and other cablemen." They inhabited "a social structure that kept the men from becoming attached to specific locations; stabilized flows within the network; and prevented information, expertise, or resources from diffusing to individuals outside the cable colony."[102] Cablemen were discouraged from marrying, drinking alcohol was disapproved of, and "improper language" or "quarrelling on the instrument" was strictly forbidden. Magazines and newsletters circulated to produce an "imagined cable community." Through the apparatus itself, individual errors in transmission were remotely tracked and recorded to evaluate telegraphers' reliability as they passed cablegram messages from station to station, servicing different circuits.[103] Securing submarine cables from breaches, interception, and noise required a complex set of governmental strategies.[104] The cables—critical elements in the production of globalized society—in turn produced the fear of globalized threats.

CABLE CENSORSHIP

The evolution of undersea cable communication occurred during a period when Britain had no permanent foreign intelligence and codebreaking apparatus.[105] With respect to the imperial cable network, it appears that interception was not considered legally possible except in times of war. For instance, in 1892, the British government sought confidential legal advice on whether Britain, as a neutral party in a war between two other belligerents, would be obliged to stop or pass on cable messages being transmitted through British relay stations. The advice notes that in English law, a telegram is equivalent to a "post letter" once it is handled by the Post Office, at which point the "interception clauses" of the International Telegraph Convention 1875 would apply to allow the government to inspect the correspondence or stop it. But as the international commercial telegraphy cables were operated by private companies, messages passing through British cable stations in Cornwall to destinations not in Britain would at no time come under Post Office control, leaving their legal status uncertain. Moreover, as it would be easy for warring parties to use codes and keywords to communicate by telegraph without being noticed, any state that tried to selectively filter and detain cable messages in times of war would be unable to do it. In practice, they would need to stop and inspect all telegrams and remove any that appeared to use coded language. In other words, full and total censorship would have to be imposed. But this, the advice stresses, was a matter of fact, not law.[106]

The advice prefigured what followed in 1898, when the intelligence department of the War Office began concretely planning the steps necessary for controlling and filtering submarine communications in time of war.[107] A year later, the plan was enacted during the Boer War of 1899–1902. All messages by cable to or from the Boer republics, the South African Republic and the Orange Free State, were necessarily transmitted through Cape Town, Durban, or Aden; so, those were the locations of the censors. From September 1899, the restrictions aimed at preventing military news of the Boer successes and British defeats from reaching the

London newspapers.[108] On October 7, 1899, the secretary of state for the colonies issued regulations requiring the censorship of military information transmitted from Natal and requiring all coded or ciphered messages to be presented in plaintext for inspection. On October 11, 1899, the war began. On November 17, 1899, the postmaster general, at the behest of the War Office, formally notified the International Telegraph Bureau in Berne that all coded transmissions were prohibited on British lines south of Aden, and all telegrams were sent subject to censorship and at the sender's risk.[109]

In practice, Boer War censorship amounted to a prohibition on the use of ciphers and codes. This created diplomatic and commercial problems, leading to some relaxation of the censorship regime to allow the use of "secret language" by the Portuguese and German governments, which were unwilling to hand over their codebooks to cable their colonies in southern Africa, and by banks, which relied on coded communication to authenticate remittance payments. Otherwise, messages written in any code not provided to the censors were not transmitted.[110]

The question of applying censorship within the domestic network was considered but rejected by the War Office as unnecessary and not worth the controversy it would cause. However, in late 1899, when the War Office learned that "telegrams of a suspicious character were being exchanged between persons acting as Boer agents in this country and others in South Africa and Europe," it decided "to keep a watch on them."[111] For this reason, the War Office obtained a warrant from the home secretary on January 6, 1900, requiring the Post Office

to produce, for the information of the Intelligence Department of the War Office, until further notice, any telegrams passing through the Central Telegraph Office, which there is reason to believe are sent with the object of aiding, abetting, or assisting the South African Republic and the Orange Free State.'[112]

General interception continued at the Central Telegraph Office in London until July 1900.

Censorship was primarily a question of controlling and suppressing coded transmissions. The aim was not simply to gain intelligence from the information of others but, more importantly, to suppress communication that could not be viewed by the censor. The British thus gained control over information being sent from the conflict zone to the press or foreign governments while cutting off the Boers from seeking foreign support or intelligence on British military planning. It was conducted in accordance with, and by explicit reference to, the internationally agreed rules of the International Telegraph Bureau in Berne, which governed conventions agreed among colonial powers. In short, it was understood as a juridically distinct practice from interception.

When Boer prisoners were interned on the island of St. Helena, cable censorship was extended there, too.[113] But the Boer War was not won by censorship or secret intelligence. The decisive innovation was a different tool of biopolitical warfare that prefigured the twentieth century: burning farms and villages and forcing the civilian population into concentration camps.[114] Nevertheless the conflict marked the first time since 1844 that Britain deployed cryptanalysis against foreign traffic.[115]

It may seem counterintuitive that prior to 1914, sitting in the middle of a worldwide web of cables that carried global traffic in telegraphic communications, Britain did not invest in developing a permanent bureau of cryptanalysis. The exception was the colonial government in India, where the general staff created in a permanent cipher bureau with a view to intercepting and deciphering Russian telegrams, with some success.[116] Historian of intelligence John Ferris blames a combination of "technical circumstances and of attitudes."[117]

First, the government had no legal power to acquire telegrams in peacetime from private cable companies, unlike the governments of France and India, and no political interest in repeating the public outcry of 1844 should such legislation be proposed.

Moreover, there had been no reason to invest in attacking foreign government codes. Britain's strength was its navy. Undersea cables could be cut or appropriated should war come, and it was unlikely that Britain would have the opportunity to tap enemy cables directly. This meant that there was an insufficient supply of intercepted material on which to build up samples of foreign coded messages. Codebreaking from first principles requires a sustained source of encoded messages that can be subject to statistical analysis, which was not readily available despite the monopoly over the infrastructure. Yet this cryptographic principle was not widely understood, and many officials simply assumed codes were effectively unbreakable. Unless one could successfully steal and copy a codebook undetected, there was little expectation of breaking a code.[118] It was assumed that the practice of codebreaking would take too long, cost too much, and produce very little valuable intelligence.

The strategic value of the international telegraph network, in other words, was initially conceived in terms of access, control, and suppression. Interception was an inherent capacity of the network, but codes made it too costly to pursue. As in the postal epoch, the social utility of encryption was again indexed to the enemy's capacity and determination to attempt breaking it.

WIRELESS MESSAGING

Wireless media began as a physics experiment. Heinrich Hertz's discovery of controllable electromagnetic waves, using a linear spark-gap oscillator in the laboratory in late 1887,[119] was primarily an attempt to produce and observe electromagnetic waves, as theorized by James Clerk Maxwell several years before.

The same year, Royal Navy experiments with fast torpedo boats had identified a problem of distinguishing friendly vessels from enemies, especially at night. By 1891, Commander Henry Jackson, a torpedo officer, suggested the use of "Hertzian waves."[120] He led preliminary experiments successfully transmitting Morse code twenty-five yards from *HMS Defiance* in August 1896. He met Guglielmo Marconi that autumn. Marconi was working on a beamed wireless system for the Post Office. Successful demonstrations of the apparatus followed at Salisbury Plain and the Bristol Channel in 1897, when the Royal Navy formally adopted the technology and the Wireless Telegraph and Signal Company was formed, acquiring Marconi's patents in exchange for a controlling interest.[121]

The successful patent of Marconi's "black box" put electromagnetic waves to work as a transmission medium.[122] Patterned pulses joined the undifferentiated noise of the universe under the legal form of intellectual property. Wireless telegraphy initially used spark-gap transmitters and vertical antennae connected to basic "coherer" receivers. Each spark across the transmitter's capacitor generated electromagnetic waves with a broad bandwidth. The transmitter was used to broadcast damped radio waves in discrete bursts, reproducing the on/off patterns of telegraphic codes. The potential advantages of wireless for maritime safety were obvious. It enabled communication from ship to shore, in night or fog, without automatically revealing the transmitter's position, and it enabled a single message to be sent simultaneously from the Admiralty to all units in range, implying the concept of broadcasting. Conversely, distress signals could be broadcast and picked up by every other ship in range.

Against this backdrop was the lack of secrecy in transmission. It was not clear to the experimental pioneers of radio that transmissions were necessarily open to all receivers.[123] Moreover, the early wireless system was not tuned, creating a problem of noise pollution. Superpositioning of radio waves produced interference, limiting the effective transmission range, and just as an untuned receiver could pick up the signal, anyone with an equally primitive transmitter could create interference, later known as "signal jamming." Only inside knowledge of Marconi's secret experiments with syntonic tuning maintained the confidence of the Royal Navy in radio during the late 1890s, the point when the US Navy rejected the technology.[124] Syntony refers to the harmonic resonance achieved when the sending and receiving sets operate on the same wavelength. Tuning was initially developed with the intention of eliminating not only the interference of other transmitters but also the risk of interception.[125] When there were relatively few receiving sets available in the world, two sets tuned to a predetermined frequency would effectively produce a secret channel. Later, a series of public demonstrations of Marconi's syntonic technology suggested the opposite, with dramatic interruptions staged by rival radio entrepreneur Nevil Maskelyne, who tried to embarrass Marconi by beaming in a series of Morse code insults during a public event. Maskelyne set up a receiving aerial at Porthcurnow, Cornwall, the cable hub of the British Empire, where the state telegraphers were grateful to receive updates on the progress of Marconi's experimental transmitter a few miles up the Cornish coast.[126] Maskelyne proved that the airwaves were open, and that even syntonic messages were easy to intercept or jam.[127]

Nevertheless by 1899, Marconi's company was offering to equip Royal Navy vessels for £100 per ship per annum. The Admiralty, with detailed knowledge of the technology, initially invoked the power of the Crown granted in the Patents, Designs and Trade Marks Act 1883 to manufacture patented technologies on its own terms, but it failed to achieve the same results and, by the following year, had agreed to the contract.[128] By 1901, the year of Marconi's first confirmed transatlantic broadcast, the Royal Navy had thirty-one Marconi sets, sixty-three of its own sets, and around two hundred ships worldwide were communicating with one another and around one hundred shore stations, the ships with a range of around fifty miles.[129] The first military radio interception occurred in 1904 on board *HMS Diana* at Suez. The ship produced an intelligence report, critical of the slow rate of transmission and poor spelling of Russian naval radio operators, who were by then at war with Japan.[130]

Wireless interception and wireless reception were materially identical. Moreover, interference was potentially as problematic. On the one hand, noise pollution obscures the signal; on the other hand, a silent receiver secretly observes it. With the advent of electronic valves around 1910, cheaper receivers were designed to serve as both amplifiers and tuning oscillators. The problem of open reception became a virtue: the mass audience was invented when wireless telegraphy became broadcast radio, an entirely new kind of psychopolitical technology.[131] From then on, "power is only a variety of din."[132]

DIVIDING THE ETHER

In 1904, the British Parliament passed the Wireless Telegraph Act 1904, establishing the first juridical regulation over wireless technology on land or sea. All transmitters and receivers, including those on British-registered ships and ships in territorial waters, required a GPO license to operate. Wireless telegraphy companies were licensed to operate subject to the familiar proviso that stations could be commandeered by the government in case of emergencies. Communications security was indexed to colonial supremacy: only British subjects were permitted to be employed at radio stations in British dominions. Section 5 of the act empowered the government "to obtain information as to the contents, sender or addressee or any message (whether sent by means of wireless telegraphy or not)" and to prosecute anyone else who obtained such information without the authority of the postmaster general or "in the course of their duty as a servant of the Crown." This created a dichotomy between the regulation of media: telephones could be intercepted without reference to statutory powers, while wireless interception of messages was expressly reserved to the government.[133] Whereas telegraphic regulation revolved around the object of the telegram, with wireless being a cognitively "open" receiving system, the technology itself was the object of regulation.[134]

By 1906, the growing number of private wireless sets in use prompted concern in the GPO about the enforcement of license provisions. All licensed wireless operators were obliged to make a "declaration of secrecy" not to divulge or to make use of any message they received that was not intended for them. Yet the limits and effect were unclear. Passenger ship wireless operators, for instance, received news agency messages transmitted wirelessly and posted the information on ships' noticeboards for passengers to read; in the US, this kind of interception was expressly prohibited by law. Lawyers for the GPO reflected on the meaning of the Post Office (Protection) Act 1884, which forbade post office employees from divulging the content of telegrams. The law would not apply to telephone conversations, and with respect to wireless, it only applied to "a written or printed message or communication" handled by a telecommunications company. It would not apply to "a private owner" of "an experimental installation," and it would only apply to the "improper" use of intercepted messages, as distress calls are intended to be "picked up by anybody with the appropriate apparatus." As such, in law, wireless interception turned on whether the "character of the message indicated that it should be divulged or not." Overall, legislation was not thought necessary for an essentially academic problem.[135]

The juridical problem of interception applied by extension to international transmission. Ships had sufficient electrical power for short-range transmissions only. Therefore, transoceanic vessels had to cooperate to relay messages to shore, which meant that rudimentary rules and protocols were required to produce a network, eliminate interference, and bring about the "common use of the ether."[136] At the third international radio conference in London in 1913, state parties to the first radiotelegraphic convention agreed that the wavelengths of 300 meters and 600 meters would be reserved for ship-to-shore and ship-to-ship communications for passing along "public correspondence."[137] All ships and all shore stations would be constantly ready to receive and relay transmissions on these wavelengths and would ensure their shore stations were connected to landline telegraph networks for onward transmission, regardless of the commercial company that initiated the transmission.[138] Standard lists of stations, universal Morse call signs, worldwide hours of operation, and financial arrangements for the costs of transmission were agreed on. Wireless operators were placed on "listening watch," transforming sea traffic into a distributed network of moving relay points in a global commercial transmission system. Ships hosting radiotelegraph operators from private communications companies became mobile telegram stations for passengers and police to communicate while in transit. The protocols enabled a rapid growth in the volume of traffic; by the 1930s, radiotelegraph operators on different ships had to "queue up" on their shared wavelengths, which constituted channels, waiting for the chance to jump into the stream of traffic to transmit or receive their passengers' correspondence to shore stations.

In other words, establishing a functional wireless network relied as much on protocols as it did on transmission hardware—protocols established by international legal conventions. Transmission wavelengths were reserved and registered for different purposes.[139] Technical standards were promulgated.[140] The law could not determine the status of the ether, so it instead determined juridical rules for operators. Only licensed operators could participate in radio discourse and only on the wavelength settings assigned to them. Licenses distributed virtual addresses that referred not to any specified location or territory, but to the call-sign identity of the ship or station on the airwaves. In effect, all licensed wireless users were included in a ring of disciplinary confidentiality, with the license a certificate of systemic trust and obligation to the law. The right to receive information was coupled to a duty not to misuse it.

While the GPO policed the licensing system, violations seem mainly to have concerned the salvage vessels, penalized for offering unsolicited assistance to ships that reported mechanical difficulties back to their owners. The complaints were usually received from insurance firms querying the salvage costs.[141] Only a ship's master, usually the captain, could authorize a radio operator to disclose signals against the obligation not to, with the master liable should the infringement later be held unlawful. Absent such authority, every message received but not specifically addressed to the ship had to be ignored. The exception was the emergency transmission, prefixed with the Morse code for SOS. The urgency of the repeated sequence *dot-dot-dot, dash-dash-dash, dot-dot-dot* has the juridical function of authorizing the reception and disclosure of a message, suspending the interception norm by marking out universal emergency conditions.

The invention of wireless communication produced another epistemic novelty for state intelligence in the form of the second-order observation of the materiality of radio waves. Although the principle underlying directional detection had been discovered by Hertz, functional "direction finding" techniques (typically abbreviated to RDF or D/F) emerged as a beneficial side effect of attempts to build directive transmitters that would produce a radio beam in a particular direction rather than as radial emanations. Long-wave radio transmitters of the time scattered their signals in all directions; to create a focusing device would have required an impossibly large reflector. The aim was to enhance the secrecy of transmissions while reducing noise and interference from nearby transmitters. In 1905, the Post Office began conducting experiments with the Bellini-Tosi directive device. While the principle worked, it was not nearly effective enough to realize the fantasy of making a radio wave that could function like a wire. In 1907, it was discovered that an inverted Bellini-Tosi device coupled to a receiver could accurately pinpoint to within a couple of degrees the vector of an incoming radio transmission. Previously, rudimentary direction-finding equipment had relied on massive fixed-aerial devices. As a small, portable D/F apparatus, the Bellini-Tosi device could be easily deployed at sea, allowing ships' navigators to precisely fix their location relative to fixed D/F transmitters located at ports, lighthouses, and along shorelines through geometric triangulation. From then on, ships could fix their geographical location, even in heavy fog. Naval navigation became indexed to artificially generated geographical referents. Radio waves became a medium for geometrically remapping the world and finding one's place in it.[142]

Meanwhile, direction finders on land went to work detecting irregular wireless installations. As early as 1903, there had been concerns about the use of private radio transmitters by foreign spies.[143] When the First World War began, the Defence of the Realm Act 1914 made it illegal to possess any wireless apparatus without express permission of the postmaster general.[144] Police confiscated or sealed up 2,500 licensed sets and 750 unlicensed sets, using Bellini-Tosi D/F finders mounted on vans to locate transmitters.[145] But they missed some, and soon, amateur enthusiasts who had managed to keep hold of their sets came forward to alert the Admiralty to the prevalence of openly available German naval transmissions, enthusiastically passing on the streams of coded messages they received.[146]

Although navies in the First World War used sophisticated and specialized codebooks to transmit in Morse code, the capacity to spatially locate transmissions made them vulnerable to over-the-horizon observation.[147] The British military began the war with only one official interception station at Stockton. By the end of 1914, the military had embarked on building a chain of direction-finding B stations along the coast from Shetland to Kent, in Ireland and Gibraltar, and were sending rudimentary mobile stations to the frontline trenches. The purpose of each station was not only to intercept communicative messages but also to triangulate, using D/F techniques, the location of enemy forces. Individual German ships and submarines were pinpointed as soon as they broke radio silence and sometimes identified by their operators' characteristic "fist," the minute elements of style that, like handwriting, were particular to individual operators.[148] Meanwhile, the civilian "voluntary interceptors" became the Radio Security Service.

The materiality of transmission and reception took on strategic dimensions far beyond the value of the information they transmitted. The Royal Navy's embrace of Marconi sets produced a proto-cybernetic system of command, control, communications, and intelligence.[149] Land-based traffic analysis was deployed in the trenches in 1915, establishing the capacity for over-the-horizon detection and mapping of enemy forces. The art of "signals intelligence" was born, generating a new scientific source of intelligence.[150] Governments have been listening ever since.

CONCLUSION

This chapter has traced the emergence of a new media epoch in the nineteenth century and the reconfigurations of the material techniques of interception that followed. Interception and security from interception were paramount concerns in respect of each system. While interception was ultimately a matter of technical and material knowledge and access, the distinction between interception and the legitimate reception or processing of communication was in each case juridically mediated by law, convention, licensing, or internal administrative practice. Interception remained a question of accessing and controlling access to key points of observation and relaying information.

The temporality of communication and the associated reimagining of space engendered a new epistemic order that reshaped communication in the global and domestic economy. New forms of information storage and retrieval emerged, transforming the way that government collected, generated, and processed information. The paper epoch of books, letters, and scrivening was replaced by an era of files, type, and reference numbers as information was encoded in time-bound sequences. World time had accelerated: communication was no longer limited to the speed of a horse traveling over land or the prevailing winds at sea. A new informational dimension had emerged that stretched over the horizon.

But the primary medium of personal privacy, and thus normative concern, remained that of committing thoughts to paper in the form of a letter, not the new electrical media.[151] The state, through legislation, case-law, patents, and financial investments, had quietly reserved its capacity to secretly intercept and administer communication as and when it was judged necessary. The potential power that this represented would not be demonstrated until the next century.

5

PHONES, SPOOKS, AND THE LEGISLATIVE TURN

In the twentieth century, interception was practiced by different agencies. Within the UK, several agencies gathered intelligence through intercepted communications, primarily the police, customs, and the Security Service (known by its historic codename, MI5). This chapter focuses on MI5—first, because it developed the most complex system of domestic interception and, second, because as an organization it occupied a similar constitutional lacuna to the interception power itself. Interception of international communications is dealt with in chapter 6.

The primary focus of this chapter is telephone tapping, the most controversial and most intrusive form of interception. As telephones became the most common mode of private communication, the privacy of calls became a pressing normative problem. The policy of placing official secrecy above legislative clarity, adopted in the aftermath of the 1844 Mazzini scandal, lasted until the latter half of the twentieth century. A set of critical political and polemical discourses had by then arisen, critiquing the authoritarian secrecy of the state and calling for legal recognition of human rights. Following several political and legal controversies, the Hobbesian model of unaccountable prerogative power that had survived anachronistically from the seventeenth century was replaced by a complex set of rules and norms imported from transnational human rights instruments, introducing authorization and oversight protocols to the interception regime, while maintaining its connection to the office of secretary of state. The legal system—iterative, changeable, and highly technical—introduced new techniques to regulate and oversee powers now held up as accountable and transparent despite their secrecy. The interception power was by then exercised over a privatized telecommunications network.

The legalization process that began in the 1980s reflected a deeper transformation in the rationality of government as polices that aimed to maintain the secrecy and authority of an unaccountable Crown, the inheritance of the seventeenth century, gave way to a system of public laws, judicial review, and specialized oversight bodies that aimed to replace arbitrary power with a neoliberal idea of the rule of law. This chapter draws on constitutional theory to contextualize interception within that broader shift.

We begin with the censorship regime of the First World War, when the full potential of interception was brought to bear in the open. From there, a self-sustaining systemic logic of security and intelligence developed.

CENSORSHIP

In 1909, growing paranoia about German espionage led the Committee of Imperial Defence to create a new "Secret Service Bureau" initially staffed by just two officers, Mansfield Cumming and Vernon Kell.[1] They divided the bureau's tasks into foreign intelligence and domestic counterespionage and, respectively, took charge of each. Within months, the bureau had split into two organizations that eventually became the Secret Intelligence Service (MI6) and the Security Service (MI5). Kell became head of MI5, charged with defending the realm, one of the ancient prerogative powers of the Crown.

In September 1911, Home Secretary Winston Churchill signed general warrants for the interception of postal correspondence, allowing Kell's "Counter-Espionage Bureau," then codenamed MO5, to directly intercept the correspondence of suspected German spies without the need to obtain a targeted warrant for each suspect.[2] The aim was to identify and disrupt "postmen," messengers who received letters from German intelligence and forwarded them to German spies.[3] A "carefully compiled, cross-referenced index of the intercepted letters" was created, gathering around twelve hundred discrete entries between September 1911 and August 1914, when the war officially began,[4] mapping their communications through the postal system.[5] On August 3, 1914, the day before the declaration of war, twenty-two German agents were arrested and two hundred new suspects were placed under surveillance.[6]

Censorship was differentiated from interception practically and legally. Practically, all censored correspondence was marked as such. It was not a secret practice, and it served a dual purpose—to actively suppress communication deemed detrimental to the war effort alongside the production of intelligence. It was authorized not by prerogative but under the broad auspices of the Defence of the Realm Act 1914. This short piece of legislation had one substantive clause that allowed the government to issue regulations, enforceable by court-martial, to "prevent persons communicating with the enemy or obtaining information for that purpose or any purpose calculated to jeopardize the success of the operations of any of His Majesty's forces or to assist the enemy," which extended to efforts to "secure the safety of any means of communication, or of railways, docks or harbours." It authorized not only communication surveillance but, among other powers, permitted the mass internment of any civilian deemed to be an "enemy alien" in camps. This short piece of emergency legislation unleashed the full power of the state over the individual.

Censorship was described in a postwar report as a "complicated machine" that was difficult to grasp "without practical experience" and operated over all domains of communication media under the authority of so-called universal warrants.[7] Externally, the undersea telegraphic system that Britain dominated constituted "a single field which offers facilities for the use of circuitous routes apparently remote from the sphere of action."[8] The initial rules for telegraphic censors were as follows: all languages other than English and French were banned, as were diplomatic and private codes, except those used in communication between allied or neutral governments and their diplomats abroad; all commercial codes were banned then gradually reintroduced, provided they were registered and approved and thus transparent to government; and all commercial traffic was automatically delayed by up to forty-eight hours so as to diminish the utility of any secret messages that did make it through the filter.[9]

Censorship provided the War Office with a constant flow of letters and packets suspected of containing correspondence to or from agents of the enemy. Censorship warrants were the first general warrants issued since 1881 and 1882, when all Irish letters were inspected and opened.[10] Instructions were circulated to all postmasters requiring letters or telegrams to be disclosed on demand to any "Competent Military Authority" in possession of a special censorship warrant. The format, terminology, and mode of address in such warrants were the subject of internal discussions between the Post Office, War Office, and Home Office.[11] They enabled MI5, a group of nine officers by August 1914, to target spies for interception as they emerged from the mass of censorship data. When spies were discovered, they were allowed to continue plotting, with the interceptors sometimes manipulating their messages much like Samuel Morland had two centuries earlier.[12]

Filtering work began with the examiners, most of them women, who worked at tables designated according to different kinds of communication—trade tables, private tables, printed matter tables, press tables—opening and examining letters and packages. Apparently, everyone involved experienced an "involuntary and deep-seated disgust" when first opening private correspondence,[13] although they knew the "primary object of examining all mails . . . was to detect secret communications by enemy agents."[14] According to the internal report prepared after the war, anything that seemed potentially suspicious was selected and passed on to assistant censors. All examiners were paid for their work because volunteers could not be trusted, and each examiner was carefully vetted for the work, providing three references, which were checked by the counterespionage department, MI5, against its registry of cross-referenced index cards. Each examiner signed a declaration of confidentiality that confirmed they were aware of the Official Secrets Act and the penalties that would follow should they disclose information about their work. They read on average 110 private letters or eighty-six commercial letters a day. In 1916 and 1918, the busiest years, around 375,517 letters, 117,300 newspaper packets, and 2,407 parcels were examined daily. Material selected for censorship by examiners went to a deputy assistant censor, assistant censor, or censor for a decision on whether to allow it to pass. In some cases, material was copied in the record room by typewriter and photography. Comments were added and a final decision taken. Packets with comments were returned to the examiner; when expedient, the decision was explained to all examiners concerned. Finally, the packet was either closed and sent on or returned to the record room to be passed on to the condemned room.[15]

The censorship system was adaptive, its parameters constantly recalibrated in response to the enemy. It filtered, condensed, and dispersed information through a central registry that was organized by card index systems. The registry directed traffic into centers of distribution, which in turn modified itself through "the gradual formation of other specialized sub-branches."[16] The problem of filtering and observing communication was described as a mechanism versus individualism.[17] On one hand, the work was necessarily "confined within somewhat mechanical limits." On the other hand, "success . . . depended upon the intelligence of the examiners acting within the prescribed limits." Particularly with commercial and trade messages, special knowledge was required to discern disguised enemy messages hidden in business correspondence. Examiners were encouraged to "err upon the side of caution."

The mechanical limits spoken of provided that the examiners should not open more than one letter at a time, should look carefully at the names and addresses of the sender and the ultimate or intermediate recipient, comparing them with the suspect list. The envelopes were required to be opened, whenever possible, at the short end with a letter opener so that the label when affixed covered no portion of the name and address of either writer or addressee or the postage stamps. Where this was inevitable a note was taken of the name or address and the necessary copy made upon the closing label. . . . Envelopes, postage stamps, seals, tissue linings and blank sheets were required to be carefully scrutinized, and, if suspicion arose, the letter was transferred intact to the Chemical section. No remarks or comments were allowed to be written upon any letters, and only necessary explanatory remarks on the enclosed printed slips.[18]

Censorship and interception were differentiated but interlinked within the machinery, as communications targeted by interception warrant were inevitably discovered by the general filtering operations of censorship. Where sorters identified a targeted name of address, they passed the item to MI5, which decided on the best course of action. Intercept targets were circulated on a constantly updated blacklist, which by the end of the war included around 13,500 individuals.[19] Sorters "needed good memories" to keep track of the changing list."[20] Calibration was important: when the head of MI5, Vernon Kell, learned that some naval intelligence was reaching the Germans, "super-censorship" was imposed on all outgoing correspondence and cables, revealing that two Dutch commercial travelers were sending unusual orders for cigars from naval bases. As with other spies detected this way, they were arrested, tried, and executed.[21]

The full schedule of distribution amounted to sixty-seven subjects, each assigned to one of eleven types of information, from enemy activities in British or neutral territory, military information, naval information, commercial information, evasion of censorship, enemy and allied propaganda, indiscreet letters in breach of the Defence of the Realm Act, letters from prisoners of war, letters from Irishmen interned or convicted (including letters indicating involvement in the 1916 Easter Rising), press information, and miscellaneous types.[22]

By 1917, the following steganographic attempts to bypass the censors had been detected:

handkerchiefs embroidered in Morse Code; imitations of Raphael Tuck's postcards;[23] religious books; newspapers sent in batches, the number of newspapers indicating the number of troops; the colour of the ink of the address indicating the arm of the service; phonographic records and printed advertisements. Importation and exportation of phonographic records was prohibited and all advertisements had to have a police visa before publication.[24]

Artificial invisible inks, known to the British as F and P ink, were infused into scarves and socks. All such items were dipped in water when discovered in parcels to release any chemicals stored within. An escalating series of ever-more sophisticated invisible inks and developing reagents unfolded.[25] The microdot is perhaps the best illustration of the technical evolution of postal steganography. A coded message was typed out, photographed, optically reduced, then printed on approximately 0.05 square inches of film. Using a hypodermic needle, the dot was glued onto an ordinary letter, ideally on a full stop, under a stamp, or inside the lip of the envelope.[26] To the naked eye, it was just a dot. Without forewarning, examiners had little chance of noticing one medium carrying another medium parasitically.[27] But even where the censor was evaded, the delay that censorship caused was effective, and by late 1917, a year when 356,000 suspect letters were stopped and 32,000 cases investigated, German espionage in Britain had effectively been defeated.[28]

By the end of the First World War, MI5 was known as the Security Service, with the name MI5 retained to give the false impression that it was a military organization. By then the registry contained over a million index cards on almost nine thousand suspects and notes on over thirty-eight thousand individuals. It was the "central clearing house as regards precautionary information," and its primary concern was increasingly the "collection, collation, and circulation of such material."[29] Its unbridled self-directed mission had led it to target pacifist groups as elements of "enemy influence." As an MI5 officer reported to Kell, "If they are not for the success of our country it is not unreasonable if they are classed as pro-German."[30] Similarly, spy hunts in the munitions industry mutated into a campaign against any action "likely to lead to munitions not being produced in sufficient quantity," with the labor movement classified as the obvious enemy within, associated with the Bolshevik revolution in Russia.[31] The Security Service was largely independent of ministerial control "precisely because governments found it easier to leave them alone than to risk the political odium of involvement with the Secret Service."[32] Without political control, there was little else in the British constitution to constrain them.

LASKI'S CRITIQUE OF THE CROWN

During the technological and economic transformations of the second half of the nineteenth century, British public law was characterized by a vision of the constitution that both liberals and conservatives shared.[33] This ideal image posited the constitution as an "unwritten"—a set of general, abstract rules. The constitution aimed only at limiting the power of the Crown—an increasingly large bureaucracy—to prevent infringements on the liberty and property of private individuals and to thereby constrain government from radical attempts at reordering society.[34]

The classic account is that of A. V. Dicey. Dicey described the constitution as the combination of the doctrine of parliamentary sovereignty, meaning that the legislature was the supreme source of law; the rule of "ordinary" law, meaning that individuals were equal before the law and the state had no exceptional powers or reason of state beyond what law allowed; and stable political conventions about the relationship between the institutions and principles of government.[35] On the one hand, Dicey thus presupposed a natural and harmonious balance was to be found in society and that this liberal balance was reflected in Parliament, where debate leads to reasoned legislation.[36] On the other hand, Dicey effectively hybridized two distinct senses of the "rule of law." First is the ancient sense by which the rule of law referred to the good character and right reason of those who make legal decisions. Second is the modern sense of legal constraints on the powers of the administrative state to interfere with the rights of individuals.[37] Dicey's orthodoxy of English constitutionalism rested on the assumption that liberty and free markets are naturally occurring and should not be interfered with except following reasoned, restrained deliberation. Government's role is to secure and uphold the normative ideals of liberty and freedom. Much later, Foucault observed that the freedom and security of liberal governmentality is nothing natural but had to be actively produced.[38] In chapter 5, we saw this production at work in the ways that new electrical media transformed the economic and spatial geography of the country and the world, deeply enmeshed with governmental practices, investments, prohibitions, and permissions.

In 1919, having witnessed the exceptional capacities demonstrated by the war effort as it mobilized and regulated production at practically every level,[39] the political theorist Harold Laski took a different view of the constitution. Laski focused on the powers of the Crown, which in the English system stood in for the "vast abstraction we call the state." Thanks to the Crown, the British state as such had "no shadow even of existence" in law and could do no wrong because of the legacy of the fact that at one time the king was the final arbiter of justice, where a wrong might at last be put right.[40] Just as there was no court higher than the king, so no subject could bring an action against the Crown, which was never a defendant in its own courts.

In practice, the prerogatives of the Crown were exercised by ministers answerable in principle only to Parliament for their decisions and the departments under them. Ministers had personal legal liability for wrongs done under their authority, but the growth of the administrative state had put these officials in positions where the courts found their acts "impossible to examine."[41] The Crown was free to take on new functions in the administration of life through institutions and agencies that effectively escaped legal categorization.[42]

The key legal question for servants of the Crown, therefore, was whether they had legal justification for their actions when carrying out their duties. If they acted without legal authority, they would personally bear the same legal liability for wrongdoing as any other private citizen,[43] meaning they could be liable for mistakes of the administrative state, bringing down "liability to an unconscious agent who was also the humblest minister of the law."[44] The Dicean model, Laski argued, was inadequate to the powers exercised by modern government, "beclouded by high notions of prerogative," a situation "legally unnecessary and morally inadequate."[45] Britain needed a new "translation of life into the theories of law."[46]

THE SECURITY SERVICE

Laski's critique has no better illustration than the Security Service and its extensive powers to spy on citizens—as the service itself recognized in December 1943, when an internal review marked "most secret" found that since 1920, the "Security Service ... had for at least 20 years no responsible Minister. Its position was anomalous and unconstitutional."[47] After 1945, political responsibility for MI5 briefly rested with the prime minister, then passed to the home secretary, where it remains today. The organization had no footing in statute, yet used the following techniques regularly: "(i) volunteers who spontaneously reported fellow citizens; (ii) monitoring by Special Branch; (iii) infiltration and the use of informers; (iv) watching and following; (v) interrogation and questioning; and (vi) the interception of communications (mail, telegrams, and telephones); as well as (vii) the use of secret microphones hidden in various locations; and (viii) foreign security and intelligence agencies."[48]

MI5 was a largely self-directing organization with enormous administrative and technical independence to pursue its goals, authorized under the vast abstraction of the Crown. It acted by reference to secret directives from 1946 onward and was supposed in theory to act within the law, but it was unclear what practical limits the law imposed.[49] It was by no means the only organization to use interception powers or enjoy unfettered administrative independence, but it best demonstrates the extent of the Crown's blanket power over private telecommunications.

The Maxwell-Fyfe Directive provided MI5 with a kind of secret charter from 1952 until it was brought onto a statutory footing by the Security Service Act 1989.[50] The directive tasked MI5 with the "Defence of the Realm as a whole, from external and internal dangers . . . which may be judged to be subversive of the state." It was for the director-general to judge what counted as "subversive."[51] Ministers relied on the Security Service for information but kept it at arm's length, turning a blind eye to its methods and activities.[52] Their formal authority was filtered through the cabinet secretary and Home Office permanent undersecretary, who kept themselves much better informed than their elected masters about MI5's activities.[53] For politicians, deniability was preferable to accountability.

INTERCEPTION AND CENSORSHIP

Interception was not only carried out by the Security Service. During the early twentieth century, the Post Office was charged with identifying and intercepting postal packets thought to contain "indecent material" and solicitations to enter illegal lotteries from abroad.[54] In 1920, a general warrant was signed for the interception of any letter suspected of containing solicitations to enter lotteries, a memo stating that it would be "troublesome" to seek a specific warrant on each occasion that lottery correspondence was suspected. In 1934, it was decided that the general lotteries warrant should be replaced by individual, specific warrants. Citing as precedent legal advice obtained in 1866,[55] the memorandum of 1934 discusses section 56(2) of the Post Office Act 1908, which holds that no one may open, delay, or detain a postal packet, except "in obedience to an express warrant in writing under the hand of a Secretary of State."[56] This legislative formulation could not justify general warrants. Although it would be costly in terms of time and resources, government legal officers felt this to be the correct reading of the law, confirming that their lawyers did take the law seriously, even in the absence of judicial scrutiny. A bill on illegal lotteries was being considered, but it was decided not to include an interception power for the Post Office to intercept them without a warrant. Such a power would give rise to the most acute controversy and indeed might throw a doubt on the legality of actions taken in the past, and might also have far reaching consequences on the exercise of the prerogative power generally.[57]

The protection of secrecy took precedence over administrative convenience and legal certainty. The same file includes a newspaper clipping of an article about postal interception. The uncertainty of the law in the absence of legislation was a problem subordinate to strategy.

Interception still occurred and expanded its functions: the suppression of foreign-run gambling and lottery syndicates; the suppression of immoral literature and pornography; the censorship of communist propaganda from Soviet Russia; police attempting to locate missing or wanted individuals; investigations into crooked sub-postmasters. Perhaps prompted by the need in 1934 to consult precedent legal advice dating from 1866 in respect to lotteries, the legality of postal interception was reviewed in updated legal advice obtained from a government legal adviser in 1935. First, registry files were reviewed to produce a series of precedent examples.[58] Then the royal prerogative was analyzed in a detailed eighteen-page memorandum in a separate file.[59] It concluded that the prerogative form was ambiguous on interception, but ultimately, given the precedent and the absence of restraint, the interception of letters and packets was lawful.

SECRECY AND PUBLICITY

Mentions of interception by the authorities in the political press were carefully noted and cuttings were kept. Between 1926 and 1932 the Security Service (MI5) frequently requested Home Office warrants to have the General Post Office (GPO) intercept communist publications and pamphlets posted from abroad. Samples of magazines, books, and pamphlets circulated along with interception warrants between the Security Service, Home Office, and GPO. The spies maintained a file dedicated to monitoring breaches of secrecy around interception in left-wing newspapers, which occasionally reported on tip-offs. "The Black Cabinet in the Post Office" was the headline of a clipping from the *Workers Weekly* of December 10, 1926. In December 1931, a registry slip from MI5 accidentally ended up enclosed in an envelope delivered to one interception target and was duly reported in *The Daily Worker*.[60]

But interest in interception was not limited to left-wing journalists. In 1935, the postmaster general's office received a request from a journalist working for the conservative magazine *John Bull* to take part in a feature on the interception of illicit and communist material in the postal system. The Post Office sought permission from the Home Office, which responded by quoting a statement from Home Secretary Sir William Harcourt, made in 1882: "The very essence of the power is that no account can be rendered. To render an account would be to defeat the very object for which the power was granted."

The statement had in effect become a policy precedent and maxim. The letter to the Post Office continued:

Accordingly, while Parliament is aware of the existence and exercise of the power, it has been the invariable practice to decline, in the public interest, to furnish any information, even to Parliament, as to details. . . . If articles are published it is perhaps better on the whole that they should be inaccurate, and capable of denial, if questions should be asked in Parliament.[61]

Members of Parliament (MPs) were potential subversives, after all.

TELEPHONE TAPPING

Telephone tapping was a primarily mechanical process, with techniques that changed in line with the configuration of the network. Early telephones used the microphone to generate an acoustic signal that modulated the current flowing from a battery. The battery electrified the line and was passed along relays to the receiving earpiece, but the resistance of the wire caused noise and signal loss, limiting the length of the possible connections.[62] The invention of the repeater amplifier to periodically amplify the power of a signal allowed for modulated electrical waves to be amplified in both directions. Repeaters were first installed by the GPO in 1916, just as the first Strowger automatic telephone exchange systems were being deployed.

Repeater amplifiers decoupled "the wave that represented the conversation from its physical embodiment in the cable,"[63] an abstraction of information from its material substrate that created the conditions for experiments with feedback and, ultimately, the mathematical abstraction of information theory as a quantitative science. Information became quantified as binary digits, or "bits," distinguished from the semantic meaning and technical medium in question.[64]

The simplest place to tap a line was somewhere between the subscriber's telephone and the distribution side of the local exchange mainframe. That would give the interceptor access only to the target's line. The early work was physically difficult—inspectors from the Post Office's investigation division would physically climb into a junction cupboard and attach wires to the target line, then wait patiently to note what was said. It was not a job for tall individuals.[65] In general, it seems that tapping was too labor-intensive for the intelligence that it produced. Frederick Booth, an MI5 "special censorship" investigator at the Post Office, recalled that during the First World War, the "only method of recording the conversation was by handwriting. The results were not accurate or useful and the written returns showed increasingly the remark 'Conversation in a foreign language—not understood.'"[66]

Local exchange buildings with telephone operators and engineering staff were, in principle, ideal for interception work, but in practice, they were considered insecure "gossip shops." It was much wiser to connect a jumper line to the target line then feed the signal elsewhere. From the 1930s onward, that was possible using "special observation" circuits, which allowed a GPO engineer to listen in on any line for diagnostic purposes. Although this was their primary purpose, they were widely and correctly regarded as tapping circuits. The distinction between interception and engineering was a question of who listened in.[67]

A specialized transcribing unit created during the war for recorded intercepts was absorbed by MI5 afterward. Wax cylinder recording was used until recording systems using magnet tape appeared shortly after. The aptly named Frederick Booth arranged for Dictaphone recorders, buying time for analysis and translation.[68] Police-owned magnetic audiotape recorders were applied at the local exchange by Post Office engineers.[69] In 1957, the Birkett Committee reported that telephone tapping had become a wholly "mechanical operation." But telephones were often used to quickly arrange meetings, so a transcription made much later was not always useful. The painstaking work of waiting and listening was maintained alongside the tape.[70]

Around the late 1950s, the capacity was built into the fabric of the telephone network.[71] By the 1970s, there were too many targets and too much demand for the decentralized approach for telephone tapping to work. By then, operators had been made redundant by fully automated switchboards and exchanges. The new backbone of the national telephone network had a special set of trunk lines reserved for military and governmental use and marked as defense circuits. To tap a line, a specially vetted team of engineers would arrive at a local telephone exchange, send the usual staff away for a break, then install a red jumper cable on the target line in the main exchange frame. The red cable was used for all emergency services—a sign for other engineers not to touch it. Red lines going to the national defense circuits meant that all calls and all numbers dialed would be relayed in parallel to a national tapping center, where tape recorders started up automatically when a call came on the line. It was nicknamed "Tinkerbell" and housed in a drab GPO building that stood on Ebury Bridge Road, in Chelsea, close to military barracks. There, up to a thousand individual lines could be simultaneously intercepted. To save tape and transcription time, a computer controlled the recorder and was programmed to start only if, for instance, a target called one of a list of specific selector numbers.[72]

Telephone tapping became an intelligence priority as encryption standards on telegraphic and wireless communications improved throughout the Cold War.[73] Security Service transcription rooms were located on the upper floors of Leconfield House in London, where a team of Russian-speaking transcribers, all women, produced typed reports. A case officer, on requesting a line tap, would provide the transcription department with a written brief of the material sought from the intercepted audio. They then scanned the conversation for the passages corresponding to the brief, first randomly sampling acetate recording discs at various points, then listening for clues that useful information was being discussed at that part of the recording. They marked the disc with chalk where there was something potentially useful to transcribe, then went back over the recording to make the transcription.[74] Transcription turns voices into text, the medium of state intelligence.

The network did not automatically record connections to and from the subscriber until the advent of digital exchanges. Until then, bills were calculated using analog meters at the local exchange, which counted the time that each line was engaged by outgoing calls in discrete units at rates determined by the dialing code and time of day. The meters were photographed on a quarterly basis in groups of a hundred, with each subscriber's bill determined by magnifying the image and deducting the previous quarter's meter reading from the latest. If customers queried the accuracy of their bill, a meter check printer (MCP) was attached to their line. As each outgoing call was dialed, the MCP printed each dialed digit alongside the time of day and duration of the call. The police and intelligence services also used "metering," applying it to targets without warrants. The printed list of numbers revealed patterns of use that could be collated, compared, and analyzed, providing telephone traffic data and contact chaining, a forerunner of digital metadata analytics now performed automatically.[75]

In Belfast during the conflict in Northern Ireland (1968–1998), a different regime was applied in a tapping center run by the army from the top of the GPO's Churchill House.[76] Dubbed the "hen house," it was the place of work for around thirty local women, recruited by the Royal Ulster Constabulary. Collectively, the station permanently listened "live" to the telephone lines of targeted paramilitaries and politicians (and probably a few lawyers, journalists, and others) for information. The targets, who understood the capacities of the state, knew their telephones were probably being listened to. Small inflections, significant silences, unusual hints—these were the codes used, and knowledge of local accents and vernacular was essential.[77] Then, to be useful, the voice call had to be symbolized and processed, converted to an object from which information is elicited.

TELEPHONE INTERCEPTION WARRANTS

Telephone interception was conducted without warrant until May 1937.[78] Six months later, Labour Party MP Reginald Fletcher raised the matter in Parliament, asking the home secretary when the government's policy on telephone interception warrants was established and what the practice had been beforehand. In preparing a response, the home secretary consulted Sir Vernon Kell, the director of the Security Service. A memo on the file states that warrants were introduced "as an additional safeguard against a too free use of this procedure," but that there was no legal requirement to have one for a telephone tap. Perhaps self-authorization had become excessive.[79] The file notes that "authorization" had always been sought from the Post Office director-general,[80] and a handwritten note in the margin emphasizes that this information should not become public. A draft warrant was sent to Kell for inspection, based on a pro forma telegram warrant, but it was deemed inadequate because it described "detaining" or "opening" phone calls as if they were physical objects. A note suggests that time limits should be included to prevent the Post Office or police from having to indefinitely listen in to calls on the targeted line. A form of words was eventually agreed and confirmed in a secret letter sent to Kell on behalf of Sir Russell Scott, the permanent undersecretary of state (see figure 5.1). In other words, telephone warrants were imposed and designed by unelected and unaccountable Crown servants, not by the legislature or even the home secretary.

The distinction between warranted interception and other modes of listening to calls was, at least in theory, important. During the Second World War, mobile telephone censorship units were deployed under a general warrant, signed in 1940, to listen to targets' calls at their local telephone exchange. The mobile units were to listen in on calls in an area, documenting the public mood and morale, and cutting off any calls in a foreign language or any in which sensitive information was disclosed. However, they were not to carry out investigative work. Only in exceptional cases were they to actively target individual lines for ongoing monitoring under the general censorship warrant.[81] If censors detected there was cause to suspect criminal activity or espionage, they were to inform the police or Security Service, who in turn would obtain an interception warrant for the target. In other words, there was an internal juridical distinction drawn between interception, which targeted an individual, and general censorship, which concerned general monitoring of the population.

Strictly speaking, a telephone interception warrant targeted the telephone line and not the individual concerned.[82] In May 1942, standardized procedural guidance notes were issued regarding letter and telephone checks,[83] bringing all interception warrants together into a carefully prescribed protocol. Preformatted slips carried their own identifying catalog

SECRET   1st May, 1937.

Dear Kell,

Sir Russell Scott asks me to let you know that he agrees to the proposal that telephone conversations should not be tapped and recorded except under specific authority of a Secretary of State's Warrant. Warrants in such cases should be in the following form:—

"To the Postmaster General and all others whom it may concern,

I hereby authorise and require you to record all telephone conversations on the telephone line number .... and to produce the record for my inspection;

And for so doing this shall be your sufficient Warrant.

One of His Majesty's Principal
Secretaries of State."

Colonel
   Sir Vernon Kell, K.B.E., C.B.
                                          Yours sincerely,
                                              J. M. ROSS

5.1 Letter to the head of MI5, Vernon Kell, stating that the permanent undersecretary of state, Sir Russell Scott, agrees that warrants should be obtained prior to tapping and recording phone calls, May 1, 1937. *Source*: The National Archives HO 144/20619.

numbers. Instructions and examples of warrants and warrant cancellation forms were distributed. Preprinted forms ensured standardized feedback so that any of the intelligence analysts receiving data, regardless of their prior knowledge of the file, could immediately see all relevant information in a single location.

Forms take on agency in the actions they prompt and constrain, instructing users in their operating procedures.[84] In the registries of the Security Service, where connections between communications were often more revealing than the communications themselves, a warrant was no longer simply a command but a device that anticipated and prompted feedback: a paper-based proto-cybernetic system of control and observation. The document became an element of the file, wrapped up in protocols and connections that unfolded around it, validating those operations by its symbolic authority; not for the public, who were forbidden to know anything of it, but for the benefit of those who were tasked with the processing of files. For this reason, procedural practices were much less formal than was officially required.

In 1945, when the function of the Security Service was secretly reviewed by Sir Findlater Stewart, he was informed that officers had to submit a formal warrant application to the home secretary for each case, along with a statement of reasons. The home secretary in each case must then "satisfy himself personally" of the warrant's necessity.[85] But the common practice evidenced in the files, now publicly open, was for MI5 to contact the Post Office directly and begin a line tap by working with a single contact in the GPO special investigations unit.[86] This individual was careful about requiring officers to eventually have a warrant, but not necessarily before beginning surveillance.[87] Warrants were frequently backdated to the date of application rather than the date of approval, and interception frequently began "in anticipation" of warrants. The reasons supplied in warrant applications were brief and cursory, with "suspected communist" often regarded as sufficient. Warrants targeted phone lines, regardless of who used them, and were of open-ended duration.[88]

Whereas in the seventeenth century, the secretary of state exercised the personal authority of the sovereign to decide on the necessity of the interception power, by the twentieth century, the permanent staff of the Home Office exercised much of the decision-making power assigned to the secretary. The home secretary, after all, was a political appointee. Appointees came and went. By contrast, the permanent undersecretary was, in practice, frequently the true judge of warrant applications,[89] adept at getting the minister's agreement and heading off refusals by ensuring that warrant requests were adequately formulated from the "point of view of the Defence of the Realm or the security of the state."[90]

Interception was not limited to telephones. A "letter check" request required the Post Office's internal investigators to write down everything on a targeted envelope: its origin, its destination, and details about the stamp. The letter remained unopened and therefore required no warrant. Around 155,000 postal items were selected and opened under warrant in 1961, growing to 221,000 by 1969. Interceptors were stationed securely out of sight in Post Office sorting rooms, selecting items to inspect according to a rolling list of targets, copying the content, and sending on the item for delivery as usual.[91] Wearing rubber gloves, they worked side-by-side at a long table. Each investigator was equipped with a lamp, a photostat machine or pedal-operated camera, and an electric kettle for steaming open envelopes. The work was repetitive and mechanical.[92]

Beyond interception, the Security Service operated a form of remote bugging by directing high-frequency radio beams at a telephonic handset, effectively turning it into a live microphone. A line tap then provided a link to hear conversations that were thought to be confidential. The technique is referred to as Special Facilities (SF) in Security Service files and by Peter Wright,[93] and it was directed under Home Office warrants, although no warrants were ever used when MI5 officers broke into buildings to implant covert listening devices, despite the illegality of such actions.[94] Technoscientific techniques, effectively hacking the operations of telephones, were at least as legally ambiguous as phone tapping and certainly more so if trespass or property damage occurred when installing or activating a listening device. Legal requirements for warrants for such operations were introduced only with the Security Service Act 1989. The earlier use of warrants was more likely intended to limit knowledge of the SF techniques rather than to limit their application.[95]

THE BIRKETT REPORT

In the mid-1950s, the police tapped the phone of a London gangster, Billy Hill. The tap was not mentioned during his trial in 1956, but apparently the details were sent to the prosecution, which accused Hill's counsel, Patrick Marrinan, of obstructing the course of justice in a letter sent to the attorney general after the trial, claiming that the police held evidence of professional misconduct. With the permission of the home secretary, transcripts of intercepted calls were shown to the Bar Council, the senior barristers of Lincoln's Inn where Marrinan practiced, and to Marrinan himself. He was eventually disbarred and left England, but first he became the focus of the second great interception scandal, after his MP raised the matter in Parliament.[96] The interception and disclosure of legally privileged communication between a barrister and his client could not be easily dismissed. Prime Minister Harold Macmillan announced a judicial inquiry led by retired Lord Chief Justice Norman Birkett and two other privy councillors.

The report they produced is forty-three pages long.[97] No mention whatsoever was made of international interception powers, the Government Communications Headquarters (GCHQ), or signals intelligence in general. It deals only with telephone tapping in the context of the UK's domestic legal framework. Ultimately, the report came down in favor of telephone tapping as a necessary technique and found that "the interference with the privacy of the ordinary law-abiding citizen or with his individual liberty is infinitesimal. . . . It has produced no harmful consequences."[98]

However, Birkett failed to pinpoint a legal foundation for the power to intercept telephone calls. There were several arguments put to the privy councillors by government lawyers on this issue, but none convinced them. First, it was suggested that the power represented a prerogative right of the Crown, in line with the view adopted in secret by successive government legal advisers over many years. As Birkett put it, they claimed there was "a prerogative power to intercept, examine, and disclose for certain purposes connected with the safety of the State or the preservation of public order, any messages carried by the Crown; and this Prerogative attached to the new methods of carrying messages that were undertaken by the Crown in the nineteenth century by means of the telegraph and the telephone."[99] But to the committee, it was unconvincing. There was no mention of a prerogative power to intercept communication in any judicial ruling; the textbook writers did not mention it, except Sir William Anson, who in the second volume of *The Law and Custom of the Constitution* (published between 1892 and 1896) had noted that the home secretary had the right and duty to detain and open letters at the Post Office if required—a power already clear from Post Office statutes. Since the common law held that there could be no "new" prerogatives created after the passage of the Bill of Rights in 1689, the existence of a prerogative to intercept telephone calls, or communication in general, was uncertain at best, although it had been assumed within the bureaucracy.[100]

Another argument suggested that interception is not part of the prerogative but nonetheless is recognized as an inherent, ordinary power of the Crown to protect against the misuse of postal facilities, as recognized in successive Post Office statutes. The interception power had simply existed "from the earliest times. . . . How it arose can only be conjectured because historical records are wanting, but that the power existed and was used permits of no doubt whatsoever."[101] This argument, which was based in practice, not principle, was dismissed for the same reason as the prerogative argument. There was no evidence to support it and no doctrine to justify it.

The government also suggested that section 20 of the Telegraph Act 1868, which allowed the postmaster general to make "regulations" on the disclosure or interception of a telegraphic message, extended to telephone tapping. But no regulations had ever been made with respect to telephones, and the committee members were unconvinced by the idea that Parliament could have contemplated that this power should extend to telephone calls, notwithstanding the case of *Attorney-General v. Edison Telephone Co of London Ltd*.[102]

The Birkett report concluded that the "power to intercept letters has been exercised from the earliest times, and has been recognized in successive Acts of Parliament," the power "extends to telegrams," and it "is difficult to resist the view that if there is a lawful power to intercept communications in the form of letters and telegrams, then it is wide enough to cover telephone communications as well."[103] But this seemed to implicitly endorse the very arguments the committee had rejected. The committee added that if "it should be thought that the power to intercept telephone messages was left in an uncertain state that was undesirable, it would be for Parliament to consider what steps ought to be taken to remove all uncertainty if the practice is to continue."[104]

On one hand, legislation would clarify a doctrinal lacuna; on the other hand, maintaining the "uncertain state" of the law might be politically acceptable or even advantageous. The unstated implication was that nothing expressly prohibited unauthorized tapping. The committee found that there was no evidence that private enterprise tapping took place—for "technical reasons," they reported that it was more difficult to do in Britain than in the United States, where it was known as a serious and persistent problem.[105]

The rest of the Birkett report is concerned with confirming that the home secretary authorized warrants for telephone tapping and outlining the circumstances in which it was used. In the absence of doctrinal right, procedural propriety is emphasized. For example, it reported that fourteen different agencies applied for warrants between 1937 and 1956. Seventeen were issued in 1937 and 242 in 1956, indicating growth in utility and capacity.

Most applications came from just three agencies: the police, customs, and the Security Service. Each had its own internal application procedures. The police and customs sought warrants for the detection of crime on grounds set out in a letter from the Home Office sent in 1951. The offense concerned must be "really serious," "normal methods of investigation" must be unlikely to succeed, and there must be "good reason" to think that interception would lead to a conviction. A serious crime was one that could lead to "three years imprisonment" for someone with no prior convictions or one in which a "large number of people were involved."

Customs offenses were concerned with "substantial and continuing fraud which would seriously damage the revenue or the economy of the country."[106] The Security Service did not pursue criminal convictions. Its conditions were that "major subversive or espionage activity that is likely to injure the national interest" had to occur and that the material intercepted be of "direct use" in "compiling the information" necessary for their purposes.[107]

The report emphasized the importance of administrative controls:

> the keeping of full and accurate records is a necessary part of any procedure to ensure that the use to which interception may be put is effectively controlled. The Home Office records of warrants issued for the detection of crime are reasonably full. Each case is separately recorded in a file. These all contain the ground on which the warrant was issued, a copy of the warrant itself and the date of its cancellation.[108]

Warrants for the Security Service were less well kept. Until 1947,

> the Home Office kept a card index of names and addresses showing alphabetically by name and geographically by area all the warrants issued for security purposes. In 1947, at the suggestion of the Security Service, which was disturbed by the existence of these records in the Home Office, all of them were destroyed and no complete records were kept thereafter except for the serial numbers of the warrants issued. . . . The Security Service also destroyed detailed records before 1952 although it kept figures of the numbers of warrants issued. It was not possible to discover the exact number of interceptions in earlier years, but only the number of warrants issued; the discrepancy between these two figures would, however, be very small indeed.[109]

The report recommended standardizing applications across the agencies to implement consistent procedural norms. For instance, individual warrants should be sought for each individual target, rather than continuing the practice of issuing single warrants for batched lists of targets. Reasons for each target should be provided, and records kept of any refused applications. Time limits should be built into every new warrant so that their validity would automatically lapse unless positively renewed by further application, and responsibility for making cancellation and renewal requests to the Home Office should always rest with the agency concerned. Since the inquiry began, the Home Office had changed its protocols to record the grounds of the application, all decisions taken on it, a copy of the issued warrant or a note of its rejection, and the date and reason for its ultimate cancellation.[110] The statistics derived from this internal disciplining of files and forms would in turn be made the subject of regular reviews.[111] This audit work was to be done in secret and certainly without involving judges in the process of reviewing warrant applications, which would remain the provenance of the secretary of state.[112] With procedural adjustments, the system could continue as normal.

One member of the three-man committee, Labour MP Gordon Walker, wrote a "reservation" disagreeing with the majority report to the extent that he recommended banning the use of interception for criminal investigation, to avoid damaging public approval of the police. He felt the Security Service alone should be able to use it, with applications accompanied by affidavit, to protect "high secrets of State" and to ensure "the prevention of the employment of Fascists or Communists in connection with work, the nature of which is vital to the State."[113] This position was mirrored in the resolutions of the Post Office Engineering Union and the Trades Union Congress, but it was not adopted by the Labour Party as a whole.[114]

In fact, when the Birkett report was finally published, after a period of delay when the Security Service unsuccessfully sought to have parts of it redacted, there was no discussion or debate in Parliament about its contents. The home secretary and prime minister announced that the report was instead to be discussed through "the usual channels." Not one opposition MP from the Labour Party challenged or questioned this decision. The usual channels referred to the back channels by which the main parliamentary parties agreed not to draw attention to sensitive matters. The hegemonic silence between Conservative and Labour party members was reflected in the press, with *The Times* announcing that the report "should allay the worst fears" as the powers were "very rarely misused."[115]

For Birkett, good filing techniques, recordkeeping, and reliable administrative control were the criteria of propriety. The internal procedural norms recommended in the report were formally adopted; indeed, a secret report prepared in 1979 by a Working Party of the Home Office (discussed further below) refers frequently to the "Birkett arrangements," which all intercepting agencies concerned confirmed had been complied with since 1957.[116] In the absence of legislative control, constraints on arbitrary power took the form of a well-ordered filing system.

According to Phil Glover, the report was the apogee of judicial deference to the executive.[117] Others go further in calling it a "fudge" and a "whitewash" and its findings on legality "extraordinary."[118] The report's assurances of procedural propriety were essentially unevidenced and contradicted by the finding that in "some cases," the "consultations" for warrants had been orally mediated.[119] Security Service files now open to the National Archives demonstrate that in practice, interception regularly proceeded before receiving the home secretary's approval, and that permanent undersecretaries—senior civil servants—filtered applications to ensure that secretaries of state signed the warrants presented to them. There are suggestions that the Security Service seems to have deliberately narrowed the scope of papers it revealed to the committee.[120] The security of the state, its continued powers of access to communication, its revised procedures of internal self-review in place of public accountability, and the effective suppression of further discussion were prioritized over any sense that individuals had rights worthy of legal protection from arbitrary power.

Unlike the US Constitution, which provides an evolutionary set of grounding norms for contesting and limiting political power, the British constitution, Laski's "deposit of a grim civil war,"[121] provided little by way of resources to legally problematize its administrative power and practice. An underlying hegemonic consensus on the priority of private property, capitalism, and parliamentary representative democracy was consistently held across all key positions in the judiciary, civil service, defense forces, police, and political parties.[122] Thus, the meaning of "subversive" extended to anyone potentially opposed to these fundamental political facts or to the operations of capitalism and state more generally.

Interception was a key technique. The Security Service had no powers of arrest. Its ways of monitoring spies, so-called "subversives," and enemy agents were subtler, and the responses it took remain unknowable. The point of interception was ensuring that targets were closely observable, the minutiae of their private lives and interests investigated and recorded, and any opportunity to influence, blackmail, or interdict them noted and kept open. This reflexive, preemptory power was aware of the contingency of its own operations.

Birkett's report mirrored and extended the long-standing practice by which the judiciary restrained itself from making legal findings about the security and intelligence priorities of government, whether referred to as "security" (as in Birkett's report) or the "defence of the realm."[123] Had Birkett broken with that tradition, it is impossible to imagine his report appearing at all. His report is, to this extent, innovative. In grounding the power in long-standing practice, it seemed to perform the fundamental common law technique of finding in the past a rule that could stabilize the future. The difficulty was doing so with respect to an apparatus that had for so long obscured its own origins and erased its traces as a routine practice.

It was the future that counted, not the past. The priority for the government in all interception scandals is to find a way for things to continue as before. Birkett's findings, as improbable as they were, were politically accepted and effectively legitimated by Parliament's de facto acceptance, signaled by silence.[124] No legal mechanism for complaining, challenging, reviewing, or giving redress in cases of abuse of the power was provided, despite the implications for civil liberties.[125] Birkett's report only outlined the procedures through with which this power was applied, in theory if not in practice.

THE RULE OF LAW

From the 1970s onward, mass media reporting and left-wing political activism drew attention to the threat to civil liberties presented by an unaccountable self-directing security apparatus.[126] In May 1976, journalists Duncan Campbell and Mark Hosenball wrote a report for *Time Out* magazine revealing the existence and operations of GCHQ, calling it "Britain's largest spy network."[127] In November 1976, Hosenball was informed that the home secretary had decided to deport him to the US in the interests of national security, a decision that he was not permitted to appeal except to a secret panel, in a procedure that he unsuccessfully challenged by way of judicial review.[128] In February 1977, Campbell was arrested along with *Time Out* journalist Crispin Aubrey and a former soldier named John Berry, whom they had been interviewing about his work in British signals intelligence in Cyprus. All three were charged with offenses under the Official Secrets Act, with Campbell facing thirty years in prison and his codefendants fourteen.[129]

The "ABC trial" was closely covered in the media. When a television journalist found evidence of possible jury tampering by the Crown, the first trial collapsed. At the retrial, Campbell demonstrated in evidence that his writing was based almost entirely on open sources of information. No

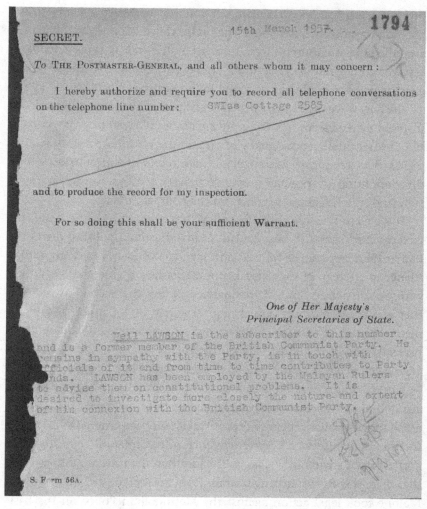

5.2 Warrant for the tapping of the home telephone of Neil Lawson, a barrister with alleged communist sympathies, with reasons typed onto preprinted Form S 56A, March 15, 1957, three months before the Birkett Committee was formed. *Source*: The National Archives KV 2/3593.

official secrets had been violated, but a mosaic had been assembled. The decision to prosecute, which the trial judge called "oppressive," had only amplified the attention his work received. In the end, all three defendants received minor sentences, and an "irreversible change" in the ability to exercise power secretly had occurred in the British political system.[130]

The new wave of critical reporting exemplified by Campbell's work was inspired by American reporting on the domestic espionage programs of the Central Intelligence Agency (CIA) and the National Security Agency (NSA).[131] As a mode of resistance, journalism and historical investigation drew attention to the unaccountable powers of the secret apparatus of state and its immeasurable effects on the political sphere.

There were two key shifts in policy that resulted. On one hand, the government moved to take control of historical and political discourse. Rather than responding to leaks and scandals while maintaining formal silence, a strategy of managed historical narration emerged, beginning with an official account of intelligence during the Second World War that was published only after being "screened by a platoon of government weeders."[132] On the other hand, the government accepted the necessity and utility of legislation, particularly after the case of *Malone v. Metropolitan Police Commissioner* came before the High Court in 1979.[133]

James Malone was an antique dealer in Dorking, Surrey, who was arrested and tried for handling stolen property. In court, his barrister asked to see a police officer's notebook that had been entered as evidence. In the notebook was a cryptic reference to information that obviously derived from a wiretap.[134] The police admitted the interception and said that there was an authorizing warrant from the secretary of state in place. Malone took legal action against the Metropolitan Police on the basis that the interception was unlawful. The solicitor general intervened on behalf of the home secretary. The case was heard by Mr. Megarry, vice-chancellor (VC) and member of the privy council.

Malone sought an interlocutory injunction to prevent further tapping, orders for the delivery of recordings, the destruction of all material held by the police, damages,[135] and a subpoena requiring the Post Office to produce the warrant in court.[136] A Post Office employee attended with a copy that "lay, like some sacred scroll, untouched upon Megarry's bench inside a sealed envelope."[137] The arguments put to the Birkett Committee were rehearsed again, but now before a court. Whereas a committee could describe a situation and offer recommendations, a court must pronounce the law. Crucially, it did so in a manner that ensured the warrant in its envelope remained unopened.

First, Megarry VC ruled in an interim judgment that the legal basis of Malone's case had to be decided before any interlocutory injunction to stop the wiretap could be made. Consequently, the case shifted from the factual issue of interception (and the warrant hidden in its envelope) to the prior question of the interception power in the abstract.[138] Second, he found a place in the common law to accommodate the power.

The court's judgment is remembered for the finding that the Crown is analogous to a private individual, free to do whatever is not prohibited by law. The Crown requires no positive legal permission to act, as long as its actions do not infringe on recognized legal rights. This was decisive because it followed findings that tapping did not violate any such rights. Malone had sought to establish a right to privacy on the telephone on several grounds: private property, personal privacy as protected by the European Convention on Human Rights, and confidentiality.[139] Megarry found none of these applied. The final argument concerned the principle of legality—meaning the absence of a positive basis for interception was enough to render it unlawful. But as Megarry put it, "England is not a country where everything is forbidden except what is expressly permitted ... [telephone tapping] can be lawfully done simply because there is nothing to make it unlawful."[140]

Warrants were thus held to be optional in respect of telephones, mere administrative devices. They carried no legal force either way and could be lawfully ignored or dispensed with. Confidentiality, the judge added in passing, was never to be reliably expected on the telephone. Nevertheless, he emphasized that telephone tapping "is a subject which cries out for legislation."[141] Furthermore, he said that his ruling was "confined to the tapping of the telephone lines of a particular person which is effected by the Post Office on Post Office premises in pursuance of a warrant of the home secretary in a case which the police have just cause."[142] The reticence is understandable. He was effectively pronouncing not only on

Malone's case but on a practice with three hundred years of deliberate ambiguity behind it.

In strategic terms, the judgment was an effective stopgap. It permitted telephone tapping to continue, kept the material facts of the warrant out of the public domain, and foreclosed further legal challenges. It found an unconvincing, troubling, yet nonetheless plausible place in the law for telephone tapping. However, as the judgment recognizes, the UK was a signatory to the European Convention on Human Rights, although at the time the Convention was not yet directly enforceable in the courts.[143] Malone took his case to the European Court of Human Rights in Strasbourg, where in 1984 he won. The court found that any interception of communication in the UK violated the right to private life under Article 8 of the convention, because while states can in principle use secret surveillance powers, Article 8(2) requires that any interference with privacy be "in accordance with law" and only conducted to the extent necessary in a democratic society. As the UK lacked a public legal framework to govern interception this way, telephone tapping could not be in accordance with the law.[144]

To remedy the problem, legislation was required. It would need to be accessible to the public and "foreseeable" in its effects so that the public could have confidence that their rights would not be arbitrarily violated. Foreseeability does not extend to individuals knowing that the authorities are in fact planning to intercept their communications, as that would allow targets to adapt accordingly. It just means that citizens should be able to form reasonable normative expectations in general terms. The legal system is thus required to assess itself as a medium for communicating norms. Human rights law has a publicity function alongside its regulatory function.[145]

Unlike the situation in the 1950s, whereby the prospect of legislation remained subordinated to the strategic imperatives of secrecy, interception practices now had to be aligned with public-facing rules. Political authority was no longer sufficient. Just as absolute sovereignty had been a strategic discursive form deployed as a solution to seventeenth century problems of stability, human rights law took on a similar strategic discursive function in maintaining the security of the security system and the legitimacy of power in the face of contingencies, leakages, and political dissent.

THE LEGISLATIVE TURN

The *Malone* case meant that legislation was, at last, inevitable. The government published two white papers in 1981, seeking to normalize the procedural controls that operated internally and appointing a judge as an official overseer of the use of interception powers.[146] As early as 1979, a secret working party began convening within the Home Office to design the legislation that became the Interception of Communications Act 1985 (IOCA).[147] The legislation prohibited interception of communication without a warrant. Section 2 permitted the secretary of state to issue warrants requiring their addressees to intercept "communications" sent by post or "public telecommunications" systems and "to disclose the intercepted material to such persons and in such manner as are described in the warrant."[148]

Interception had to be justified on one of three broad grounds specified at section 2(2), derived from Article 8 of the European Convention on Human Rights: the interests of national security, the prevention or detection of serious crime, or the safeguarding of the economic interests of the UK. None of these terms were defined, but they overlap with the three key areas that Birkett identified: police work, security work, and customs work. The economic well-being provision applies only to communications "relating to the acts or intentions of persons outside the British Islands," which would include customs inspections and foreign economic espionage but not domestic economic espionage.

Under section 3, warrants targeting a person or "set of premises" within the British Islands had to provide a description of the target. Warrants targeting "external" communications required only a description of the communications sought. In other words, external communications could be collected in bulk and trawled electronically, as was already established practice. Where the purpose concerned "preventing or detecting acts of terrorism," the trawling method could be deployed internally, a provision doubt applied to maintain bulk surveillance of communications within Northern Ireland.

IOCA created an oversight mechanism, a commissioner tasked with inspecting the agencies using interception powers and reporting annually to the prime minister. It also created a specialized judicial panel, the Interception of Communications Tribunal (ICT), to secretly review complaints against the agencies. In the 1997 consultation document announcing the reforms introduced by the Regulation of Investigatory Powers Act 2000 (RIPA), the commissioner reported that between its establishment in 1986 and the end of 1997, the ICT had considered 568 complaints. In only eight of those cases was interception in fact carried out by a government agency. In each of those eight cases, it was authorized by a valid warrant. As such, no complaints had ever been upheld. The system worked precisely as planned.[149]

Under section 9 of IOCA, "no evidence shall be adduced and no question in cross-examination shall be asked" in court if they risk disclosing intercept material or the fact that an interception warrant existed. GCHQ intercepts were used in evidence against East German spies during *in camera* trials in the 1980s, but never in open court.[150] This would prevent any further errors like the one that led to *Malone*. Public law ensured the secrecy of administrative documents. That prohibition, in a different, updated form, remains in effect today.

IOCA was received by critics as a "cynical gesture towards civil rights."[151] But the realization of the utopia of human rights was never the intention of the law. It was a strategic response to a changing communications environment, a way of implementing reliable warrant procedures to maintain access to communication systems that were recently privatized, while signaling to a hypothecated public an outline of a system based on normative proportionality, oversight, and foreseeability. The interception apparatus has ever since included a set of legislative prescriptions and requirements that define and structure its internal operations, while ensuring that further legal challenges, or leaks of information, are contained within its legislative framework.

It is significant that Britain imported the right to privacy from the European Convention on Human Rights. In the 1970s, global resistance to authoritarian and totalitarian regimes increasingly took the form of the discourse of international human rights. Human rights inspired new forms of political activism, articulated diverse aspirations, and led to the rise of new legal instruments aimed at constraining the sovereign powers of states.[152]

Yet, at the same time, a renewed discourse of the rule of law was asserting itself in governmental rationality. The nineteenth-century liberal rationale of constitutional law, exemplified by Dicey, was revived as neoliberalism, with an emphasis on free markets supported by a strong yet constrained state.[153] The government of Margaret Thatcher, which took power in Britain in 1979, the year of the *Malone* case, is synonymous with the beginning of the neoliberal transformation that brought ever-more facets of social and private life into the market.[154] In 1979, the government began the process of privatizing the UK's telecommunications services. British Telecom was created in 1981 and sold off in 1984.[155]

In this respect, the legislative turn had a regulatory function that human rights discourse coincided with and legitimized. Although it was presented as a comprehensive law for communications surveillance, IOCA must be read alongside the Telecommunications Act 1984, which regulated the newly privatized market. Section 94 of the Telecommunications Act granted the secretary of state a broadly defined power to give secret directions to licensed operators in the name of national security, requiring them to "do, or not to do, a particular thing specified in the direction." This broad power had no oversight and no explicit purpose. While the immediate aim was no doubt to ensure that the capacity to intercept communications was maintained, in 2015 it was revealed to be the mechanism by which the Security Service and the GCHQ had obtained bulk digital communications records with no oversight and no express legislative authority. In short, legislation served to ensure that privatized media "remained covered."[156]

In the neoliberal spirit, it is helpful to think about the transformation of interception power using Friedrich Hayek's distinction between law as *nomos* and law as legislation (*thesis*). The concept of *nomos*, for Hayek, refers to law as general rules of just conduct that organically emerge through a "spontaneous order" that arises when people are free to go about their business without interference.[157] The common law's traditional defense of a sphere of private interests, which so influenced Megarry's ruling in *Malone*, reflects this ideal: the state was akin to a private individual, just as private individuals were free to act without permission from the state.

By contrast, Hayek argued, legislation is nothing spontaneous; it is a mode of intentional organizational design by which government agencies and officials are told what to do in specific situations. For this reason, Hayek believed legislation risks supplanting the "spontaneous order" of *nomos* and could even serve as a means of implementing socialist and totalitarian ideologies.[158] While government required organizations with legislative "compulsory powers" to provide security for market society, Hayek was critical of state provision of other services, including the postal monopoly, which only existed through the "government's desire to control communication between citizens."[159] Hence, the legislative turn to regulate interception represents a dovetailing of the turn to human rights and the rise of neoliberal economic rationality. Where human rights require that governmental powers to interfere with private life be limited, accountable, and proportionate to legitimate purposes, neoliberalism requires that government not be permitted to interfere with the spontaneous order of the market in the name of the people.[160] Both require that sovereign power be constrained and that individuals be enabled to anticipate government actions. The point is not to suggest that the rise of human rights is a mere symptom of neoliberalism, but to stress that a particular vision of capitalism arose congruently alongside a distinct, yet compatible, vision of the relationship between state and subject, giving rise to new techniques for governing the social order.[161]

CONCLUSION

The immediacy of the telephone and its intimate connection to the voice personalized communication in a way that no other medium had done before. It produced virtual intimacy that paradoxically highlighted the impossibility of unmediated understanding. The noise on the line represents the ever-present possibility of disruption, interruption, or interception.[162] How was the parasite to be contained? Laski's critique of English constitutional thought was demonstrated by the lack of any control over the activities of the Security Service, police, or the interception power until the 1980s. The Birkett report's contribution was to improve administrative procedures and file hygiene.

The domestic interception warrant regime first introduced in 1985 promised that targeted interception could only occur to ensure national security or the prevention and detection of serious crime, and only in cases where the interference is proportionate when weighed against the target's human rights. But this remained a decision for the secretary of state, filtered by the permanent bureaucracy that applied its own governmentality to the question. By then, MI5's registry was digitized, with a mainframe computer and network of around two hundred terminals supplementing the extensive paper records on subversives, spies, trade unionists, and activists of all kinds.[163] File management, a rudimentary foreshadowing of data protection principles, was now indexed by legislation to the dignity of the individual.

The complex nexus between human rights and neoliberal discourse raises a larger debate,[164] but it provides useful context for understanding the turn to legislation. A confluence of human rights and liberal rule of law discourse set the stage for the interception apparatus to shift its juridical basis and normative self-description. The fundamental capacity to intercept and control communications in the name of reason of state was not extinguished, but the once-secret power deliberately held outside the law under the blanket of organized silence was folded into a complex web of legislation, guidance, audit regimes, oversight mechanisms, secret tribunals, and legislative reporting that now described itself, in carefully chosen and limited terms, in order to engender foresight amongst an imaginary public.

6
COMPUTATIONAL POWER AND THE RADIO EPOCH

This chapter traces the development of global radio interception and its role in the development of electronic computing in the twentieth century. If the First World War revealed the potential use of radio for military power, the Second World War confirmed it. Meanwhile, improvements in wireless and cable media made it possible to send international and imperial messages at ever-higher frequencies, but those same electromechanical developments made it possible to design and build unbreakable encryption systems. The era of human computing came to an end before being superseded by the advent of digital computing at Bletchley Park, where Alan Turing helped give form to his universal discrete machine, the medium that can imitate any other.[1] From that point on, Britain began integrating its interception apparatus with the US, setting the stage for a global interception apparatus that by the close of the century was absorbing, processing, and analyzing electronic communications at an unprecedented scale, producing the global interception network that today overlays the communication networks of the western hemisphere.

All telecommunication systems have spatial dimensions and all reconfigure the territory they connect. If, as Harold Innis showed, a postal system is a prerequisite for the distribution of power over space, then telecommunication reconfigures territoriality itself.[2] Territory is nothing given or natural, but the mutable and contingent precipitate of political technologies that territorialize the world, rendering it visible and governable in its "economic, strategic, legal and technical" dimensions.[3] We begin by returning to the mass interception of communications during the First World War, when blanket censorship was applied to domestic and international communication alike. This enable new techniques of intelligence-gathering to emerge, precipitating the formation of modern intelligence agencies.

WIRELESS INTERCEPTION

Just as the telephone network became the defining technology of the domestic order of the state and its relationship to private subjects, so cable and wireless communications transformed the relationship between the imperial core and its colonized outposts. Wireless transmissions propagate through space, decoupling communication from physical terrain. The criteria for successful transmission and reception of signals are contingent on other physical factors such as the mode of transmission, available electrical energy, interference from the terrain or other transmitters, and contingent interactions with the earth's ionosphere and other sources of noise that can interrupt the successful reception of a message. Otherwise, and unlike physical transmission media, radio waves are indifferent to the locations and identities of their receivers.

Moreover, senders and receivers were mobilized once valves and batteries were sufficiently miniaturized. The ability to deterritorialize transmission as well as reception made communication possible at any point on the earth's surface, and eventually in outer space. That is precisely why radio was initially pioneered by the Royal Navy.[4] Radio transformed the operations of armies and navies between the world wars, turning the world into a universal battlefield and making wireless interception into a permanent necessity.

According to John Ferris, the authorized historian of the Government Communications Headquarters (GCHQ), the outbreak of the First World War marked the first pillar of a new age of British intelligence that lasted until 1996. The other pillars are mechanized cryptanalysis in 1940, computerized cryptanalysis in 1955, satellite interception in 1970, and the turn to the internet in 1996.[5] Radio and computer processing produced a cybernetic intelligence system that not only altered the juridical distinction between the "inside" and "outside" of the territorial state but incorporated the geopolitical boundaries of the waning British Empire into new circuits of transnational power. With postal and telegraphic communication, the distinction between internal and external communications is manifestly obvious, as physical objects are literally carried in bags or linked in relays that physically cross a border. Radio, by contrast, dissolves not only the lines of the network but also the locations of sender and receiver. Whereas a letter or telegram carry their addressee with them, radio waves must be received and resolved into language, whether textual or geometrical, before they can be indexed to an addressee. This is why radio refers to broadcasting: mass media signals addressed to no one and everyone. The inability to technically differentiate between reception and interception prompted the escalation of another technology, cryptography, as we shall see. Yet it also prompted juridical reconfiguration of the relationship between space and communication.

This chapter primarily focuses on communications intelligence, that is, intelligence gleaned from reading the content of messages, as that is where the juridical status of wireless interception arose as a problem. But only the law retained this anthropocentric concern. Wireless media and the escalations they provoked between rival intelligence agencies and militaries were more concerned with the materiality and spatiality of signals than with their content—traffic, rather than messages, became the key focus. In this sense, signals intelligence was conceived of and developed as a form of interception largely indifferent to individual communicants, their right to privacy, or their personal intentions. Mass electronic interception is strategic in scope.

TOTAL INTERCEPTION

We begin with war and censorship. As demonstrated in chapter 4, international cable censorship was first deployed by Britain in its colonial war against the Boers. Its wartime manifestation in the First World War was an instance of what Aimé Césaire identified as the "boomerang effect" of colonial powers coming home.[6] A cable ship conducted Britain's first offensive action on the night of August 5, 1914, cutting submarine cables connecting Germany to transatlantic cables. Russia cut German cables to the east. Enemy telegraphic communication was channeled toward the censors so as "to examine and dispose of, in any reasonable way, all communications so far as the public safety demands."[7] As the war began, the government issued warrants to international cable companies under the authority of either the company's landing license or section 52 of the Telegraph Act 1863, which gave "control over the transmission of messages by the company's telegraphs . . . either wholly or partly, and in such manner as he directs."[8] With Home Office Warrants (abbreviated to HOWs) covering the internal communication relays owned by the General Post Office (GPO) and section 52 warrants and licensing arrangements covering external links, all communication traveling through formal channels was filtered, while the police used radio direction-finding to seek out illicit radio transmitters.[9]

By 1915, British control over cable communication meant Germany was wholly dependent on long-wave radio transmission for long-range international communication. Knowing the risks of radio interception, the German government used the ostensibly neutral Swedish embassy to smuggle encrypted messages by cable to its embassies in the Americas. Neutral diplomatic traffic sent by cable was not checked by British censors as it was relayed through British cable stations. But when British intelligence discovered that the Netherlands, also formally neutral, was secretly providing Germany with imported materials to relieve the blockade, the censors started filtering neutral cable traffic.[10] As an unexpected consequence, known German codes were spotted among Swedish diplomatic traffic, and a new source of intelligence emerged.

Shortly thereafter, on January 16, 1917, the "Zimmerman telegram" was intercepted. Addressed to the Mexican government, it promised that if the Mexicans were to attack the United States in response to a US declaration of war against Germany, Mexico would be rewarded with Texas, Arizona, and New Mexico. The telegram is credited with influencing President Woodrow Wilson's decision to declare war on Germany, providing a propaganda device that united the American press and public opinion behind the war.[11] It was uncovered and deciphered by the codebreakers of "Room 40," under the command of the Admiralty, and was decoded with the help of a mechanical device called the "Pianola," which used punch-card computation to reduce the time taken to attack two-part handmade encryption algorithms. The Pianola could test nine possible solutions per hour and is among the first use of machines to break cryptography.[12] The use of machinery to outpace human computation was a key theme in what followed.

COMMUNICATIONS INTELLIGENCE

Beyond the Zimmerman telegram, intelligence derived from cable censorship and wireless interception was most effective in naval warfare and in relation to the economic blockade of Germany. While blockades were traditionally enacted by naval forces acting on enemy ports, the War Trade Intelligence Department (WTID) operated at a remove, utilizing information and law as its tools.[13] Careful analysis of all commercial correspondence, mostly transmitted in plaintext thanks to censorship, allowed action to be taken against individual firms at the Probate, Divorce, and Admiralty branch of the High Court, which granted enforcement orders to the Ministry of Blockade based on WTID intelligence.[14] This included the embargoing of ships and the seizure of shipments bound for Germany. The intelligence emerged not from singular intercepts but from an accumulated card index registry of over a million entries, categorized alphabetically, which contained cross-referenced data such as names, firms, commodities, payments, and ships derived from over a billion individually censored messages and intercepts.[15]

The success of this entirely second-order form of observation depended on the internal reconstruction of the international commercial environment. It marked the differentiation and formalization of what later became known as communications intelligence, or COMINT.[16] Alongside it, the development of intelligence derived from monitoring and collecting enemy radio signals—recording both the content of the message and the spatial dimensions of the transmission—marked the beginning of SIGINT, or signals intelligence.[17] After the war, a permanent intelligence service was created combining military SIGINT with diplomatic COMINT. It was known as the Government Code and Cipher School (GC&CS).[18] Although economic surveillance ended as censorship was lifted, GC&CS was tasked with maintaining a permanent policy of intercepting and deciphering foreign diplomatic communication gathered from international radio telegraphy, cable companies, and intercepted military signals.

The terminology is specialized and complex. Signals intelligence is broader than COMINT. It too was driven by radio and includes all dimensions of wireless media, such as the enemy's radar and weapons systems that use radio technology.[19] Electronic intelligence, or ELINT, is differentiated from COMINT in that it concerns the electrical properties of signals and equipment rather than the messages or data carried. From the beginning, "traffic analysis" has involved measuring the position, movements, quantities, and other dimensions of signals and related technologies to remotely map physical movements, anticipate plans, and take technical countermeasures.[20] In many cases, COMINT and ELINT are combined: the externalities of the signal can be suggestive of the likely content, simplifying codebreaking.[21]

As explained in chapter 4, the directional devices and techniques for analyzing wireless signals generated a new order of knowledge about the surface of the earth and thus a new ontological relationship toward the enemy, who in turn was mobilized in the air, at sea, and on land in entirely new ways. Command and control radio signals that had no communicative content were productively intercepted. German night-bombing during the Second World War, for instance, was conducted by beam radio navigation, enabling relative accuracy without any visual cues. The *Knickebein-Verfahren* system employed one narrow shortwave beam to guide pilots to their target, where an intersecting narrow beam triggered the release of bombs.[22] During the course of the war, radio-based countermeasures rapidly evolved. Both the "passive" reception and directional pinpointing of radio emissions from enemy aircraft, submarines, and ground stations, as well as the "active" use of radar to sweep the horizon, became increasingly important, as did frequency jamming and other countermeasures.[23] Wireless media turned the electromagnetic domain into its own scene of strategic and tactical escalations. Transmissions no longer had to carry meaning to be informative. Individual messages revealed tactical commands, but techniques of traffic analysis revealed entire networks of strategic operations.

The story of external communications interception in the twentieth century is inseparable from the integration of communications with science and technology. Interception prompted an escalation in statistical methods, electrical engineering, encryption, and programmable computers. Modern signals intelligence subsumes communications intelligence just as digital code subsumes human language. Intersubjective meaning—COMINT—is just one element of the apparatus known as SIGINT.

COMINT AND WARRANTS

Following the war of 1914–1918, it was necessary to pass legislation to make cable interception permanent. In 1920, tensions with the Soviet government in the newly formed Union of Soviet Socialist Republics (USSR) led to a general postal interception warrant being issued over correspondence between British and Russian prisoners of war. In March 1920, with tensions high over Soviet "subversion" in Britain,[24] an experimental warrant was signed for three months requiring that all "non-official telegrams" should be "sent for examination." In June, a query on the file asked after the authority by which telegrams were being sent to GC&CS, and a general warrant was issued for all telegrams to or from those parts of Russia under Soviet control.[25] Now, the warrants were authorized by the foreign secretary, and copies were to be sent to their officials (see figure 6.1).

While there was no problem making such warrants for intercepting messages sent via the Post Office cable between Peterhead and Alexandrovsk, the privately owned Marconi wireless telegraph service was a different matter. To exercise control over private international companies, an updated Official Secrets bill was introduced to Parliament. It contained at section 4 the first explicit interception power in UK legislation.[26] The Official Secrets Act 1920 came into force on December 23 that year. A week earlier, the president of Western Union, Newcomb Carlton, openly informed a US Senate subcommittee of ongoing cable censorship in Britain. Carlton said he had been told that the content of messages was not deciphered and that the government simply wanted "to keep general track of who was cabling" to gain "an inkling of pending disorders" connected with "Irish unrest" and "Bolshevik propaganda."[27] Yet the potential for economic espionage against the United States and its commercial interests was obvious.

Section 4 of the Official Secrets Act conferred on secretaries of state a power to require the production of the originals and transcripts of any or

To the Postmaster General
and all others whom it may concern.

I hereby authorise and require you to detain open and produce to the Secretary of State for Foreign Affairs or his officers or agents copies of any telegrams which have been received or transmitted from or to those parts of Russia which are under the control of the Soviet Government or from or to any officers or agents of that Government.

And for so doing this shall be your sufficient warrant.

(Sd) E. Shortt

One of His Majesty's Principal
Secretaries of State.

HOME OFFICE,
WHITEHALL,
16 June, 1920.

6.1 General warrant for the interception of telegrams to or from "those parts of Russia which are under the control of the Soviet Government" or its officers. The foreign secretary is to receive the copies. June 16, 1920. *Source:* The National Archives HO 144/1684/400430.

all telegrams, or any class or description of telegrams, sent or received by cable or wireless telegraphy to or from "any place out of the United Kingdom."[28] In short, the state was to be granted the same unlimited access to international traffic that it already enjoyed over domestic Post Office traffic, and they were to be penalized if they disclosed the fact. From then on, one general cable interception warrant was in force and renewed each year. A copy of the warrant was supplied to all international telegraphy companies requiring them to supply the government with "drop copies" of their traffic every day. The warrants seem to have allowed the government to delay the return of messages for up to ten days, although in practice, they tried to sift out diplomatic traffic along with messages concerning "occasional suspicious characters in whom our security authorities were interested."[29]

Such characters were also the subjects of targeted interception warrants, as were used against labor leaders during the General Strike of 1926.[30] There were occasional political questions asked about this entirely secret regime. In 1955, Foreign Office lawyers queried the validity of the practice, as the function of the Official Secrets Act was counterespionage rather than the collection of foreign intelligence, and in 1969, the practice was altered so that the warrants were updated on a six-month basis.[31] Otherwise, these singular, general, and renewable warrants formed a strong coupling between the legal system and private telegraphy companies, allowing interception of world telegraphy, an international network with Britain occupying the maximal vantage point.

The Official Secrets Act did not only concern telegrams. Section 5 addressed private postal systems, requiring them to register their business with the police and to keep and make available for police inspection records of their customers and the letters and packets they received or sent. The communication records of postal transactions collected during the censorship regime continued,[32] now through the medium of registries, those "universal exchangers" of data.[33] Private communication networks were thereby integrated into the interception apparatus.

GC&CS had several functions: (1) organizing, developing, and coordinating the wireless interception and analysis of foreign communications received at listening stations across the Empire;[34] (2) receiving and processing radio and cable intercepts of international diplomatic correspondence passing between foreign countries; (3) processing and examining radio signals picked up from foreign armies and navies; (4) helping to develop and coordinate technical methods for detecting radio broadcasts from clandestine agents broadcasting from within the UK; (5) analyzing intercepted commercial cable traffic. Warranted copies of telegrams were delivered daily to naval intelligence for vetting.[35] Finally, GC&CS was responsible for communications security, supplying codes and protocols for British government and military services.[36] So-called cable vetting was a key source of raw information. According to Alastair Denniston, deputy head of GC&CS:

> Throughout the twenty years (1919–39) it was our aim to make this procedure work smoothly with the companies (British and foreign). . . . To carry out the work of sorting and copying we took over a comparatively small body of GPO lower grade staff that were accustomed to this work. Our aim was to inconvenience the companies as little as possible, and throughout we tried to let them have their traffic back within twenty-four hours. . . . Between us and the companies there has never been any question as to why we wanted the traffic and what we did with it. The warrant clearly said scrutiny, and the traffic arrived back apparently untouched within a few hours. I have no doubt that the managers and senior officials must have guessed the true answer, but I have never heard of any indiscretions through all the years with so many people involved. In short, barring the delay, we always had as good service of cables when we dealt direct with the companies as in the periods of censorship.[37]

The secrecy of the permanent cable-vetting arrangements lasted until February 1967, when the *Daily Express* published a story under the headline "Cable Vetting Sensation," reporting on the daily delivery of telegrams under section 4 of the Official Secrets Act 1920. The political response in government focused less on bulk interception than on the fact that the story violated the D-Notice system, by which the British press voluntarily refrains from publishing stories where the government indicates it would be contrary to the public interest. Consequently, an inquiry was formed to inquire not into the power itself but the failure to effectively suppress the story.[38]

SHORTWAVE

While cable vetting permitted bulk interception of telegraphic traffic flowing in and out of Britain, it relied on the same control over sorting operations as postal interception. However, the spatiality of interception was more profoundly transformed entirely by the affordances of wireless media. By the close of the First World War, Britain had around one hundred radio interception stations searching the wavelengths using customized radio receivers and paper recording apparatus.[39] Under cover of policing domestic licensees, as authorized by section 5 of the Wireless Telegraphy Act 1904, the interception network grew. A GPO memorandum from February 29, 1929, concerning a new "interception hut" at Sandridge, near St. Albans, records that it was needed "for the purposes of ensuring that amateurs do not wander outside their allotted bands, and of detecting illicit transmitting stations."[40]

Once high-frequency short-wavelength radio technology was developed in the 1920s, transmissions could be sent and received from locations previously far out of range. Shortwave radio involves focused beam antennae that generate radio waves less than one hundred meters long. Signals in this range are reflected and refracted by electrically charged gases in the band of the atmosphere known as the ionosphere. By "skipping" signals between the surface of the planet and the ionosphere, shortwave signals could bridge over the horizon locations on opposite sides of the planet. With shortwave, messages cost about 5 percent of the price of longwave transmissions, needed only 2 percent of the electrical energy, and could be multiplexed to carry three times as much information, allowing radiotelephony to become an expensive but practical service.

Undersea cable networks, by contrast, did not have the bandwidth required to transmit voice information until coaxial submarine cables replaced Victorian-era multicore cables after 1945. The commercial undersea cable companies therefore faced bankruptcy. They were too slow, too expensive, and unable to match the prices offered by shortwave systems. The financial threat to the undersea cable network was quickly identified as a threat to Britain's imperial communication security, so in 1927, the Subcommittee on Competition between "Beam" Wireless and Cable Services created a communications company to acquire all British cable assets. No more than 25 percent of shares would ever be owned by foreign interests, and an Imperial Communications Advisory Committee would supervise the whole operation. In 1929, the government founded Cable and Wireless.[41] During the Second World War, Cable and Wireless (C&W)

integrated with British intelligence agents of the Secret Intelligence Service (MI6) and the British Communications Service. C&W brought the entire telecommunication network of the British Empire together in a single cybernetic feedback loop that has persisted beyond the life of the company itself.[42] The company was an extension of the listening apparatus of the empire.[43]

Alongside cable vetting, radio interception allowed the collation and analysis of sources of external communications at GC&CS on a grand scale. This relied on the "infinite pains" taken to carefully record, index, and process intercepted information. Transcriptions and comparisons were made by hand using pencil, paper, and index cards. The underlying aim was to break codes in order to read messages, a task which demanded as much raw information as possible. The more a targeted codebook was used in intercepted foreign messages, the more information was available to identify patterns, test possible permutations, and thereby unlock the code.[44] Contextual knowledge was helpful for making educated guesses about the content of the plaintext beneath the code, so intelligence on persons of note, newsworthy events, and political developments was collected and compiled in relation to all target countries, in order to provide possible cribs for decryption, while traffic information gave useful context to wireless transmissions.

Ironically, despite knowing the vulnerability of codebook methods of encryption, the security of Britain's undersea cable network made GC&CS overestimate the security of British code protocols. The assumption was that important traffic would be sent by All-Red cables, so coded messages would be protected from interception, and it was further assumed that the impact of interception on the First World War meant future wars would be characterized by radio silence. Codebooks therefore remained in use long after enemies had compromised them, despite GC&CS having broken enemy codes of a similar standard. Britain also failed to integrate electromechanical encryption machines into its government and military apparatus until after the Second World War began. By then, the Germans (and others) were reading British transmissions with ease, while the electromechanical Enigma machine used to coordinate the highly mobile German forces as they conquered much of Europe left GC&CS in the dark.[45]

MECHANICAL TRANSMISSION

Mechanical encryption machines like Enigma became possible only once teletype systems could convert alphabetic symbols into discrete binary groups and automatically transmit them. For around the first seventy years of telegraphy, practically every telegraphic messaging system required an element of human processing. To send and relay encoded messages, someone had to be "in the cage" or perhaps operating a relay station in the middle of the ocean.[46] Error-free communication required human coordination until the development of the first teletype machines.

Whereas Morse code deployed a two-bit code comprised of two elements defined by time intervals—dots and dashes—alternative code systems were available from the early days of telegraphy, enabling more data to be transferred. The Baudot code, for instance, was designed to allow multiplexing of messages.[47] In this system, alphabetic signs, punctuation marks, and control signals are all assigned a five-bit symbolic combination of binary switching operations. The system states are designated "on" or "off," as in Morse code, but alternators were widely available that maintained a steady voltage while switching the polarity of the current. It is not the two states themselves that are significant but the patterned differences between them.[48] Each reversal of polarity was an instruction to the system.

Electromechanical switching decoupled telegraphy from the processing time of human consciousness because messages no longer had to pass through the processing medium of the telegrapher. Once the synchronization problem was solved by incorporating automated "stop/start" instructions from one machine to another, messages could be mechanically queued and printed serially, regardless of the rate of input. The human was removed from the telegraphic apparatus as teletype messages passed from machine to machine in coded transmissions, the continuous signals resolved into discrete alphabetic signs and back again—in short, global text messaging was invented.

Telegraphic coding became an object for statistical mathematicians, defining and refining codes for compressing information. The patterning of alphabetic text in human language—the statistical prevalence of letters, the probability that one letter would follow another, and so on—meant that information was differentiated from its semantic meaning. Communication, coding, and therefore encryption became a theoretical question of statistical probabilities.

Interception practices followed. In 1939, new Y stations were created at Brora, Cupar, and St. Albans in anticipation of war.[49] Seven officers were required for each station, working in shifts to intercept communications. A further five officers would carry out "scrutiny work" that

consists of scanning "dead" telegrams and extracting certain of these in accordance with a prescribed list. A retentive memory is necessary to the performance of this duty which, owing to the large number of forms falling to be examined, has to be discharged at a fair speed. This work must, after some time, tend to become monotonous in character but it is of a purely routine nature and is not considered to call for any exceptional knowledge or skill ... any telegrams sent to or by Foreign Governments ... are easily distinguishable from other traffic by prefix and/or address. Accumulations of slip are examined very speedily as soon as opportunities offer, a very great percentage of the slip being of course discarded.[50]

Records of intercepted transmissions list signals picked up from around the world.[51] The interceptors had targets, specific frequencies to tune to on schedule, but they also had periods of "General Search,"[52] scanning all frequencies, noting time, language, signal types, and the likely location and topic of intercepted transmissions. Encrypted messages were passed to GC&CS, while plaintext messages were analyzed on site. There were Y stations overseas in Malta, India, Hong Kong, and the Middle East and on ships of the Royal Navy.[53] The work was difficult. There were technical difficulties in tuning in, monitoring, and relaying encrypted messages for processing. Aural processing of signals using headphones was required where the intercepted radio signal was too weak for the teleprinting apparatus to differentiate signal from noise, with such signals noted by hand and forwarded to Bletchley codebreakers by teleprinter.[54] The codebreakers in turn disliked handwritten intercepts compared to automated messages due to the risk of transcription errors that made the puzzle impossible to solve.[55]

Encryption was a simple inflection on the teletype principle. In 1917, an AT&T engineer realized that the transmitted letter codes could easily be combined with a second synchronized source containing random key characters similarly encoded on punch tape. With each stroke of the keyboard, the transmitting machine would read a random symbol from the tape, combining it with the plaintext input to generate an encoded output value. In other words, a random string of parallel text served as the encryption key. Provided a copy of the same key was correctly synchronized in the receiving machine, it would be automatically subtracted from each symbol received to print the original plaintext.[56] This way, cryptography could be automated.

The Telekryption machine that AT&T initially manufactured on this principle used duplicate key tape for sender and receiver. This made it an electromechanical One-Time Pad (OTP), the only theoretically unbreakable method of cryptography.[57] An OTP is a completely random, non-repeated key to be used only once. Unlike a reusable codebook or encryption algorithm, an OTP is effectively unbreakable because it contains no patterns. Each transformation is random and never repeated, so there is no information for the interceptor to use to attack the code. It is effectively indistinguishable from random noise. The practical drawback is that key copies must be held by all parties and perfectly synchronized, so they are best applied to fixed two-way channels.[58]

Electromechanical code-wheel systems followed. From 1927 on, Soviet diplomatic communication became almost impossible to read.[59] Other models were Hebern's Electric Code Machine in the US, the Swedish Hagelin M-209, the British Typex, and the famous *Geheimschrijfmachine*, known as Enigma.[60] In each of these devices, a set of combinatory rotors performed complex transformations that perfectly encoded and decoded messages. The key was determined by the starting position of the rotor wheels, rearranged daily on every machine. Rather than a codebook, there was a key book. It was effectively impossible to break the daily encryption code using hand and paper methods. Every combination was one among several billion possibilities.

MECHANICAL CRYPTANALYSIS

GC&CS initially believed Enigma messages were unbreakable. In fact, because every Enigma setting produced a linear set of transformations, and because Enigma was a machine, its mechanical transformation operations could be inverted like any other discrete mathematical algorithm.

With enough intercepted messages to use as raw data, codebreakers could begin to guess the correct encryption key for the day. The weakness was that the encrypted text always connected back to alphabetic language. Languages limit the probability of one letter following another, thanks to the structure of grammar and spelling or the inherent connections between certain words or letters in each language. The more that simple repetitive messages are broadcast, the weaker the code becomes.[61] Hence the key changed on a daily basis.

To make progress, vast numbers of intercepted transmissions were required, augmented by traffic analysis of the time, location, length of message, signature "fists" of known enemy operators, and repeated phrases, which all provided potentially useful clues, known as "cribs." Second-order analysis of such data, or "cribtology," was essential to narrowing the range of guesses in brute-force attacks on the code.[62] Everything thus had to be categorized and recorded, even trivial enemy communications, as they provided clues for possible solutions.[63]

Enigma was thus defeated by the Ultra program, involving large banks of bombes, which were the "most complicated electro-mechanical devices yet built."[64] The machines cycled through possible key settings to match intercepted code phrases to likely plaintext words. Once the machine found a pattern that matched a coded message to the assumed plaintext, it stopped working, and its final configuration was the solution. Once the production of bombes reached a critical level in 1942, the German Enigma machine was effectively defeated. During the war, the use of its intelligence was masked by "cover," such as sending up a "lucky" reconnaissance flight to spot a long-expected maneuver.[65] Ultra's success against Enigma remained a secret for decades afterward.

German high command messages were encrypted with the Siemens T-52 *Geheimschreiber* (Cryptwriter) and Lorenz SZ40/42, more complex machines than Enigma. They were defeated by the first programmable computer, Colossus, which had fifteen hundred vacuum tubes arranged to operate as a matrix of two-state binary switches. Crucially, Colossus Mark II had the capacity to automatically switch programs, making "conditional jumps" that determined the most probable next guess based on previous guesses. Previously, the job of cryptanalysts using bombes had been to input the most likely possible solution for analysis, but Colossus decided this for itself, sorting, and discriminating between different possible programs.

Although Alan Turing's role in the invention of the computer is sometimes overstated, the logic underlying Colossus materialized an idea that Turing first conceived of as a thought experiment in 1936 as an effective method for solving the *Entscheidungsproblem* in mathematics: the Universal Discrete Machine, or "Turing Machine." The *Entscheidungsproblem* concerns whether there is a method for determining which mathematical statements can be proven within a given formal system, and which cannot. If such a method existed, it would be possible to use it to assess whether *any* given mathematical assertion is true or not. Turing posited a hypothetical machine that could compute everything humanly computable, simulating any algorithmic process by changing its "program," thus processing all computable numbers and functions. Through this, Turing showed that the enumeration of all computable functions produces the condition for another function that by itself is incomputable. By the same logic, it is impossible to program a Turing Machine that could determine whether another Turing Machine would stop running (halt) on any given input. Hence he showed that incomputable numbers must exist, and thus there are limits to what can be computed.[66]

The Colossi developed at Bletchley Park actualized the idea of a specialized programmable machine that could be programmed to simulate another. Friedrich Kittler sums it up: "Only automata like COLOSSUS could read what automata like ENIGMA wrote."[67] For Kittler, the realization of a machine that could compute any computable function was a revolutionary moment in media history. Thereafter, digital media come to simulate all media, to unify their forms, and to transform the parameters of human self-understanding. After Turing, "an automated discourse analysis has taken command."[68]

THE UKUSA ALLIANCE

After the war, material power and capital shifted across the Atlantic. As encryption systems developed in complexity, targeting diplomatic and commercial cable traffic became increasingly important to Western intelligence services.[69] Each Soviet communications encryption key was a "one-time," never repeated key, a constantly modulating stream of information masked by noise. This made it impossible to identify individual messages within the signals and to differentiate meaningful signals from "dummy" data. Traffic data was similarly masked, offering no way to determine the start, end, duration, or format of intercepted radio signals.[70] The Cold War protagonists achieved communication secrecy over their high-level political communication. As a result, the British SIGINT installation, now called GCHQ, relied on radio interception for traffic analysis, listening for clear-channel radio communications and devoting ever-greater focus on scanning commercial radiotelegraphic transmissions sent by International Licensed Carriers (ILCs).[71]

The bipolarity of the Cold War made it increasingly important to integrate operations with the dominant hemispherical superpower. The Western signals intelligence agencies created a transnational network organized around a secret international agreement that governed an exchange of capital and computational power for territory and technique. In his authorized history of GCHQ, Ferris argues that the wartime Allied powers' willingness to share cryptological data, technology, and technique was a key advantage, especially given that the Axis powers refused to share theirs. After all, the more instances one has of a code, along with data about the traffic bearing it and the techniques for revealing the encrypted language, the greater the chance one has of breaking it.[72] Cooperation is a force-multiplier in an informational war.

In 1943, the BRUSA Agreement acknowledged the emergent practice of sharing SIGINT between British and American agencies, and in 1946, the British–US Communication Intelligence Agreement (now known as UKUSA) formalized the relationship. A month beforehand, Canada, Australia, and New Zealand had agreed to integrate elements of their signals intelligence with GCHQ and gave the British permission to negotiate on their behalf.[73] UKUSA is a formal agreement but not a legal treaty.[74] It was negotiated and concluded in secrecy, with government approval but without public knowledge. It is more accurately a series of agreed internal regulations, all formally provisional and without force of law.[75] The original agreement mandated the sharing of techniques, intelligence reports, and intercepted material unless explicitly excluded by agreement, with a shared classificatory scheme for different levels of secrets. Secrecy was paramount. Both sides promised "complete and absolute silence" about not only the agreement but signals intelligence methods generally, in perpetuity.[76]

In practice, the two prime partners, GCHQ and the US National Security Agency (NSA, created in 1952),[77] frequently function as a unitary signals intelligence apparatus for their respective governments. Further, the interests of the alliance have had a major impact on intelligence policy and government investment decisions.[78] Although the British Ultra program was far ahead of US cryptology in 1945, within a few years American resources tilted the balance, particularly in terms of money and brute force computation. Much of what Britain offered to the alliance from 1960 onward involved the territoriality of the collapsing British Empire.[79] Decolonization was underway, but Britain "retained ample areas for antenna farms,"[80] and newly independent states unknowingly agreed to allow British communications relay facilities to remain in place.[81] Hong Kong, two "sovereign base areas" in Cyprus,[82] and the island of Diego Garcia in the Chagos Archipelago were valuable sites for major wireless interception installations. Diego Garcia remains a British oversees territory, subject to ongoing colonial occupation in the name of military and sigint priorities.[83]

The new geostrategic order of the world was reflected in the postwar reorganization of the cable industry as coaxial lines were developed and laid undersea. International connections were organized by consortia of companies connected to national authorities. As Nicole Starosielski puts it, the "terrain to be secured was no longer the country's territory, but the circuits of the cables: each nationally affiliated company would own a percentage of the cable or a specific number of circuits."[84] Western strategic interests determined the composition and shape of cable networks. In anticipation of nuclear war, cable stations were hardened, with critical connection systems and living quarters encased in reinforced concrete and stocked with long-term food supplies, and redundancy was included in the network.[85] Under the ideological rhetoric of interconnection and the material integration of electronic circuits, a new generation of critical infrastructure took shape.[86]

COMPUTING COMMUNICATIONS

As the volume of international communications intercepted globally grew exponentially, the movement of money, commodities, and third-party diplomatic communication grew in importance as an intelligence resource. The Soviet Union exercised tight political control over its economy and economic data and encrypted its most sensitive internal communications. Soviet communications channels ran permanent transmissions so that there was no external way of distinguishing where a message ended and randomness began. As the information theorist Claude Shannon demonstrated, true secrecy is indistinguishable from random noise.[87] Once a code is repeated, it is weakened. The solution is to mask codes by masking messages themselves in a constant stream of apparent randomness.

The Soviet Union exercised tight control over the economy, making it difficult for Western intelligence agencies to accurately determine the state of technological and economic development. Hence vast quantities of telegraphic text messages were collected and analyzed in bulk to produce second-order economic and technological intelligence assessments about Soviet plans, economic development, and technological capabilities. As in the First World War, useful information could be derived from tracking market transactions. In particular, raw commodities like iron, steel, and gas offered objective yet oblique indications of political plans.[88]

In the Cold War, the interception of radio (a juridical distinction, as there is no material difference between interception and reception) was partially automated but still depended on banks of disciplined radio operators, many drawn from the ranks of the military. They were low paid and subjected to extremely difficult work, leading to industrial disputes.[89] Yet the cognitive revolution instituted by Alan Turing and the Bletchley cryptanalysts continued, as the volume of communications that needed to be analyzed and the sophistication of the encryption systems meant that the purest forms of state intelligence became a function of computational power and bulk volumes of interception.

To maximize the take, all signals were of potential interest. Commercial telegraphy signals sent by international licensed carriers were assigned bandwidths on the airwaves and were therefore easily collected and collated alongside data directly received from commercial communication companies.[90] The Wireless Telegraphy Act 1949 maintained the earlier legislative prohibition on using "any wireless telegraphy apparatus with intent to obtain information as to the contents, sender or addressee of any message (whether sent by means of wireless telegraphy or not) which neither the person using the apparatus nor any person on whose behalf he is acting is authorized by the postmaster general to receive."[91] This remained the basic legal position until 2006.[92] The Crown, by its own authority, could "intercept" any message; everyone else required a license that effectively determined what they could lawfully receive. The airwaves were appropriated and divided according to law.

Wireless interception stations targeted different international carriers, depending on their geographic location and the channels they sought to intercept. Cables were intercepted near shore landing sites, licensed by the Post Office in Britain,[93] while radio receiving stations were located according to where shortwave channels were known to "bounce" down from the ionosphere. At twelve radio sites in the UK, intercepted transmissions were automatically filtered and forwarded to headquarters at Cheltenham, when the ILC Control Party used a large wall chart to coordinate the stations.[94] At 8–9 Palmer Street, London, a GCHQ station collected all foreign embassy radio messages in encrypted teletype format and sent them to Cheltenham for analysis.[95]

Intercepted transmissions were combined with those delivered from international telegraphic services, which by the 1960s were computer-controlled, capable of storing and processing around two thousand telegraphic characters at once.[96] The exchanges generated copies of all processed messages on magnetic tape and stored them for at least thirty days in case of queries, delays, edits, or diagnostic reviews.[97] The requirements to enable mass automated processing of daily cable traffic meant it was also readily available for processing by intelligence agencies using computers.[98]

The NSA ran a similar cable collection program, which was co-opted to monitor domestic political activists under the codename Operation Shamrock. Instituted after the Second World War with the cooperation of the international cable companies Western Union, RCA, and ITT, only a small number of NSA officers were aware of it until the 1970s. Tapes of data were couriered to the NSA each day for processing.[99] By the 1960s, the agency processed around 150,000 selected cable messages a month using computers, the rest having been destroyed in the "burn bag." In four hours, the IBM-built Harvest computer could scan about seven million teletype messages, searching for instances or combinations of around seven thousand preprogrammed keywords known as "selectors." Data produced through cable analysis helped produce Minaret, a blacklist of domestic political activists collaboratively compiled by the Federal Bureau of Investigation (FBI), Central Intelligence Agency (CIA), and NSA.[100]

Reducing the complexity of world interception, in short, depended on computation. As a 1956 paper in the *NSA Technical Journal* pointed out, a "computer" at one time referred to a person; someone employed to do arithmetic. Now it was an electronic arithmetical machine. Any sequence of discrete sequential mathematical operations can be computationally performed.[101] The cryptologist working on intercepted material "no longer had a piece of paper delivered to him which contained some meaning but had to plumb the depths of the atmosphere to extract his raw material . . . extracting information from the atmosphere around us by the use of all possible scientific means available."[102]

COMPUTER POWER

Between 1963 and 1973, NSA pulled ahead of its UKUSA partners in technological capability, growing its computing power by 50 percent and lowering its associated costs by 25 percent per annum.[103] Superior computing power became part of the arms race. The first large-scale stored-program computer ever built was the UNIVAC 1101, developed with secret assistance from NSA scientists. In the 1950s, a secret NSA project codenamed Lightning attempted to build a supercomputer. According to a report from 1959:

So long as it is possible to have computing facilities in excess of what others may consider feasible, it behooves us to have them. Eventually we foresee that natural limitations on speed and size will be encountered, and then the inevitable advances of our opponents will corner us, so that the duel will become one of pure wits. But while we can, we must maintain our superior weapons.[104]

That year, the first digital "word spotter" was developed.[105] The prototype could process fifty thousand teletype words per minute up to a maximum of twelve characters. Input data came from different media storing teletype messages, initially magnetic tape or paper punch cards and later a perforated tape reader. In 1962, the NSA acquired Harvest from IBM, which at the time was "the most sophisticated computer ever built . . . certainly the most advanced in the crypt community."[106]

Two Harvests were built, one for the NSA and one for the Atomic Energy Commission. The NSA's version included logical input-processing units specially designed for cryptanalytic operations. A magnetic tape handling system called Tractor selected from 160 stored cartridges, transferring data at over a million characters per second. It was the fastest processing machine in the world for at least a decade, progressively increasing its capacity through efficiencies in programming. Harvest ran its own code language, Alpha, designed to operate on large masses of data.[107] The NSA ensured it remained ahead of commercial computing systems, while its secret research and investment program helped advance the American computing industry.[108]

The UK had no comparable computing industry, but in addition to imperial territory, it had a different form of analytic expertise and approach that differentiated it from NSA.[109] Nevertheless, its relevance depended on computerization. In 1962, a report by Professor Stuart Hampshire, an Oxford philosopher and wartime interceptor, on the cost and value of GCHQ funding emphasized the need to maintain an independent SIGINT capacity with significant investment in computer technology. If the US pulled too far ahead, Britain's "residual ability to influence the policy of the Western alliance . . . will steadily diminish toward zero."[110] Signals and communication intelligence was a field of constant escalation, with a "built-in tendency, arising from the nature of the material itself, for an ever-increasing effort to be required in order to maintain an equal flow of useful intelligence."[111] Computing power had increased a millionfold over the previous decade. The Americans were investing heavily in NSA; if GCHQ was to maintain its importance and Britain, by extension, to maintain the "special relationship," it would have to keep pace as far as possible.[112]

GCHQ's first advanced computer was a UNIVAC 1103A, received in 1958 and paid for by the US government's Mutual Weapons Development Program for subsidizing allies. GCHQ continually purchased computers in the 1960s, primarily from IBM, which were superior to British products and compatible with NSA equipment.[113] Between 1970 and 1977, GCHQ doubled its supercomputing capacity, with two main systems working in parallel, Pole Star for handling cryptanalysis and Twin Star for ILC communications traffic, speech research, and other tasks, using GCHQ designed software.[114] The era of bulk data analysis had begun.

DISTRIBUTION NETWORKS

From 1975 on, the organization and flow of data within GCHQ became a growing topic of internal analysis as the organization adapted its internal complexity to meet the growing complexity of its environment. The age of the index card as the basis of intelligence analysis was decisively over. Computer networks enabled the "automatic distribution of content to consumers,"[115] while analysts interacted with the supercomputers with user interface software.[116]

NSA had the world's largest collection of networked computers by the mid-1960s. Radio interception stations equipped with automated collection systems scanned transmissions for selector keywords, triggering automatic forwarding of data when identified.[117] The average field officer "become a communications tape handler rather than a SIGINT analyst."[118] Programs were written to make computers "conveniently accessible to users, who don't really know much about what goes on down in the basement."[119] Ideally, users would interact only with a software interface. Such interfaces "led to an incisive division between people and lawgivers, or, in computer terms, between *users* and *programmers*."[120] The machine took on the sovereign position of the sorter of data, the architecture of the processing chip replacing the corridors and filing cabinets of the bureaucratic registries in determining the rate and capacity of interception power to generate new information.[121]

According to a senior cryptanalyst, by the 1970s, NSA was "beginning to be a factory," and "one of the biggest developments was when the target countries began to use Teletype equipment and began to send their data electrically."[122] Teletype data links around the world allowed interception and analysis to be digitally integrated. All NSA systems were to be electronically connected by 1980, with users granted access to different computational processors according to their position and role. At every NSA intercept station, a computer "produces an electrically forwardable signal which is sent to NSA and processed by computers. The feedback goes via reverse route such that in effect we are no longer a nice working team; we're a factory."[123]

In 1983, the Department of Defense created MILNET, a network based on the principles of the internet but differentiated from it. The internet was foreshadowed by the networking of NSA, GCHQ, and allied intercept sites. The US Defense Advanced Research Projects Agency (DARPA) established the first operational packet-switching computer network, ARPANET, in 1969, enabling networks using different software languages to exchange data.[124] One of its first instantiations was Platform, a global packet-switched network. Intercepted data from multiple sources could be accessed worldwide. NSA's traffic was encrypted using a system codenamed "Blacker," as one's intercepted data could potentially be intercepted by others.[125] The universality of packet switching gave the Platform the inherent capacity to expand.[126] Rather than switching relays to form a connection between two end points, as in a telephone network, TCP/IP (the internet communications protocols) switches packets into available channels based on their present capacity.[127]

SIGINT circuits populated the datalinks of the early internet before other forms of traffic. Any type of network on the internet, from military circuits to cloud services, should be viewed as "a logical overlay, rather than a physical thing; it is a process, not a static moment."[128] The internal networking of the US military SIGINT apparatus prefigured and anticipated the internet to come.

SATELLITE INTERCEPTION

Until the late 1960s, the distinction between internal and external communications was defined by their transmission medium. Internal communications transited hardware in the territory of the UK, while external communications transited ILCs and submarine cables. This changed with the commercial communication satellites, which relayed multichannel telephony and color television channels on dedicated radio frequencies.[129] By 1970, the second generation of INTELSAT satellites was in place, providing global satellite telecommunications.[130] By 1983, there were around thirty thousand satellite communication channels in operation carrying telephone, telegraph, data streams, and television.[131] Signals transmitted to earth from communication satellites rarely fall entirely within the jurisdiction of a single state. Instead, they illuminate large areas of the surface of the globe. Hence, the international consortia that operate satellite systems devised frequency plans that assigned different baseband transmission frequencies to every governmental or commercial client using their satellites.[132]

The UK's first fixed-point earth station for sending and receiving satellite transmissions was built by the GPO in the early 1960s at Goonhilly Downs in Cornwall. In 1967, GCHQ installed a duplicate receiver station sixty miles along the coast at Bude, collecting all traffic in range. At the site, codenamed Carboy, computers outnumbered humans twenty-two to eight. The system was a "real-time, computer-controlled, receiving, dechannelling, recording, demultiplexing, message processing system, with facilities for data forwarding."[133] Similar "shadow stations" were built in Cyprus and Hong Kong. The data received at each station was correlated, allowing the UKUSA agencies global coverage.[134] The system provided a constant feed of data on the world's financial and diplomatic traffic.[135]

In the 1970s, interception hardware was deployed in outer space. High-frequency radio transmitters, designated as VHF, UHF, and microwaves, transmit narrow beams at frequencies that are capable of much higher rates of data transfer than shortwave signals, and they attract less interference. Microwave beams seemed to solve Marconi's original problem of directing radio waves to avoid their interception. But the NSA discovered that the beams continued beyond their intended receivers and out into space, where they can be collected by a network of high orbit surveillance satellites and retransmitted to ground stations for analysis,[136] such as the NSA installation at Menwith Hill in Yorkshire.[137]

Similarly, high-frequency microwave transmissions can be intercepted by ground stations positioned anywhere in the line of sight of a transmitter dish. With a network of receivers located in Belfast and Derry in Northern Ireland, Anglesey in Wales, and Macclesfield in England, GCHQ collected all voice and data traffic passing over microwave communications circuits in the Republic of Ireland during the conflict in Northern Ireland.[138]

The flood of satellite, microwave, cable, and shortwave data intercepts exceeded all previous sources by several orders of magnitude, prompting the development of digital filtering systems. By the 1970s, an automated selector program used for the purpose of sifting through satellite and intercepted ILC traffic was in use, codenamed Dictionary.[139] Traffic was scanned for key selector terms to automatically select and send for analysis. Thousands of collection tasks were included in Dictionary, yet given the improbability of a match, the function was as much about erasing unwanted data as finding potentially helpful intelligence.[140] Dictionary was used to filter intercepts at international cable switching centers in London, such as Mondial House, a ziggurat building on the Thames through which many international undersea cables carried voice and data overseas.[141] At the same time, it operated throughout the UKUSA network, where NSA computer hardware operated on Canadian, Australian, and New Zealand territory. Discourse analysis was, from then on, a function of search algorithms.[142]

Satellite communications carried a mixture of internal and external communications. The totality of satellite transmissions sent and received on the UK's baseband frequency included communications with both ends located within the UK, as well as communications that transit international boundaries.[143] Consequently, concern grew within GCHQ about the legality of intercepting and processing transmissions on UK baseband frequencies without specific authority. Secret legal advice was obtained stating it was legal.[144]

Technically, there was no way to collect data in bulk quantities from international links without gathering up some domestic messages along the way. The advice may have included a reference to section 11 of the Post Office Act 1969, which also abolished the office of postmaster general and put the Post Office onto a new statutory footing. Section 11 granted a power of "general ministerial control and supervision," allowing a minister to give "directions of a general character . . . in the national interest."[145] If "there is a defect in the general plans or arrangements of the Post Office for exercising any of its powers, he may, after consultation with it, give it directions of a general character for remedying the defect."[146] Section 11(3) of the Post Office Act 1969 stated that if it is necessary, in "the interests of national security or relations with the government of a country or territory outside the British Islands," or to attain ... any other object" in the interests of an international organization or international agreement, the minister

may, after consultation with the Post Office, give to it directions requiring it (according to the circumstances of the case) to secure that a particular thing that it or a subsidiary of it is doing is no longer done or that a particular thing that it has power to do, but is not being done either by it or by a subsidiary of its, is so done.

Section 11(6) allowed the minister to impose secrecy on the Post Office where "he is of opinion that it is against the interests of national security to do so." This extremely broad and obscurely framed power superseded all previous provisions. The international agreement provision could extend to the UKUSA agreement, so attaining "any object" or doing or stopping "any thing" essentially ensured sovereign control over the capacities of the Post Office with no oversight or review.

LEGALIZATION

By the 1980s and 1990s, the existence of a global communications interception network was public knowledge, at least in outline. In the US Senate, the Church Committee hearings of the 1970s exposed the unlawful use of computerized data and communications by NSA to spy on Americans engaged in political protest and reform movements under Operation Shamrock. Coming shortly after Watergate, it added to a radical political distrust in government secrecy and a growing awareness of the potential that electronic communications offered to surveillance agencies. In 1978, the US Congress passed the Foreign Intelligence Surveillance Act, which prohibited the unwarranted targeting of communications pertaining to "US persons," meaning anyone in the United States who is not an agent of a foreign power or any US citizen in the world. Soon after, a lawyer named James Bamford, using open-source information and a few Freedom of Information requests, published a book, *The Puzzle Palace*, which detailed the origins and operations of the NSA.[147]

In Britain, by contrast, the government denied the existence of GCHQ until the late 1970s, a position that became untenable. First, Duncan Campbell and Mark Hosenball's *Time Out* story, "The Eavesdroppers," was published in 1976; it was followed by the attempted prosecution of Campbell, journalist Crispin Aubrey, and John Berry, a former soldier, in 1977 under the Official Secrets Act.[148] In 1982, Geoffrey Prime, a former GCHQ officer, was prosecuted for sexually assaulting young girls and for extensive espionage for the Soviet KGB.[149] In 1984, Margaret Thatcher's decision to ban civil service unions at GCHQ led to a landmark judicial review case that redefined the common law's approach to assessing prerogative powers and national security.[150]

The same year, legislation for a privatized communications market was created in anticipation of the privatization of British Telecom. Buried in the Telecommunications Act 1984 at section 94 was the power to make national security orders, giving undefined and unlimited authority to the secretary of state over the secret capacities required from licensed communication operators within the UK. Little commented on until Edward Snowden's disclosures, the legislation mirrored the provisions of the Post Office Act 1969, integrating communications data into the increasingly automated scanning and search operations of the intelligence agencies' registers.

In 1984, the *Malone* case went before the European Court of Human Rights (discussed in the chapter 5), which found that Britain's interception apparatus was "not in accordance with the law." The resulting legislation, the Interception of Communications Act 1985, introduced two types of warrant. One was for internal communications. Internal interception warrants required that detail be provided of the persons or addresses to be investigated and the reasons for their investigation. The other kind of warrant concerned external communications, which included global communication media. Communication could be intercepted in bulk and analyzed using selectors that related to broad themes contained in a certificate appended to the warrant. The exception to the targeted warrant regime in the Interception of Communications Act 1985 (IOCA) concerned any internal communication related to terrorism, which could be collected in bulk and scanned for selectors as if they were external communications. This brought a war power home, deploying it in the internal networks of the UK, almost certainly with the Northern Ireland conflict in mind.

No warrants from this period are in the public domain—indeed, it is doubtful whether they are easily locatable in GCHQ's archives, as they were certainly less important than the mountains of reports that they facilitated. The legal framework operated secretly, and its statutory auditors and oversight tribunal reported in secrecy. From the perspective of the global interception apparatus, the internal warrant regime created by IOCA is not so much a positive power as a kind of carve-out. Only internal communications are immune to the bulk collection and trawling process. By requiring internal interception powers to be indexable to targeted persons or premises and accompanied by specific normative justifications for those targets, the interior was preserved as a space of freedom and privacy, at least so far as one was deemed to be within the acceptable limits of non-subversive norms.

In 1994, the Intelligence Services Act put GCHQ and MI6 on a legislative footing. With the Cold War over, the radio interception apparatus was downsized. GCHQ secretly began considering the internet as a source of communications intelligence in 1996.[151] By the 1980s, computer architecture was already composed of protocols, rules, hierarchies, gateways, and permissions that ensured the smooth reproduction of networks. Access was contingent not on the text of the law, or the processing of signals, but on the permissions of code.[152] The Interception of Communications Act, which deliberately made no mention of communications data used to differentiated internal and external communications intercepted in bulk from satellites, was overhauled for the internet age by the Regulation of Investigatory Powers Act 2000 (RIPA). RIPA included complex provisions for the collection, handling, and storage of related communications data, or metadata, collected or acquired alongside the content of communications intercepted.

ECHELON

The worldwide codename for the UKUSA surveillance network as it existed at the end of the century was Echelon.[153] It generated a vast amount of data, as the William Studeman, then NSA director, explained in 1992. The "intelligence collection system alone can generate a million inputs per half hour; filters throw away all but 6,500 inputs; only 1,000 inputs meet forwarding criteria; 10 inputs are normally selected by analysts and only one report is produced. These are routine statistics for several intelligence collection and analysis systems which collect technical intelligence."[154] Intelligence was created from the computerized systems that organize, multiplex, transmit, and decode communication in their ordinary course of transmission, with worldwide coverage.[155]

In 1998, Richard Lamont began studying a tower at Capenhurst in Cheshire that had been sold off by the Ministry of Defence. He deduced that it had been used to sweep up Irish telecoms signals in bulk as they were carried by microwave transmissions.[156] Liberty, the civil liberties campaign group, picked up the story and challenged the legality of the bulk interception regime in the UK. At first, the claim was rejected by the newly created Investigatory Powers Tribunal, then it was considered by the European Court of Human Rights. In 2008, the court held that the bulk interception regime that had operated under IOCA had been insufficient to meet the required standards of the European Convention on Human Rights. Once again, the UK's interception regime fell short of being "in accordance with the law." The reason was that the provisions concerning external communications were inadequate to constrain the risks of an abuse of the power and did not allow the public to understand the terms under which any intercepted data or communications would be examined, shared, stored, and destroyed.[157] By that point, however, the law had been changed. RIPA had been in place for eight years, and the microwave radio transmissions intercepted at Capenhurst had become redundant. The law moves more slowly than technology—a pattern that would repeat with the Snowden revelations.

CONCLUSION

This chapter has shown that while the legal definition and practice of interception powers has long turned on internal/external distinctions, the development of a permanent signals and communications intelligence apparatus transformed the meaning of that distinction. The territoriality of communication came to be defined via the addressing data that determined which channel it followed. The distinction between domestic and international traffic, in other words, was determined by the standards and protocols of international cable, wireless, and satellite communication links.

This in turn reveals a co-constitutive relationship between technical media and legal space. As early as 1920, legislation was used to define external communications and to appropriate them for intelligence purposes. For Britain, as a sea-based empire with colonial assets around the world, the freedom to intercept transmissions and messages generated a worldwide listening network that in turn produced the most sophisticated communications intelligence project yet attempted. British territorial reach served as a geostrategic asset in a post-war alliance with the United States, the new hemispherical superpower after 1945. American computational power joined with British imperial space, particularly the settler colonies of Australia, New Zealand, and Canada. The new cybernetic sovereign was increasingly distributed, hybridized, and disguised across new agencies, institutions, registries, and listening stations, unified with the aid of simple yet obscure legal protocols.

7

ENVIRONMENTAL INTERCEPTION

This chapter examines internet interception as described in material drawn from the "Snowden archive," the documents published in various media outlets after whistleblower Edward Snowden disclosed classified National Security Agency (NSA) files to journalists in 2013. It begins with a look at the media-technical epistemology behind Snowden's justification for revealing technical details of the UKUSA interception network, which led to charges against him under the Espionage Act in the United States and his flight to Russia. It reviews three categories of technique among the different programs and operations that were disclosed, corresponding to transmission, storage, and processing. Respectively, these operations are manifested in the interception and bulk collection of data in transit, the acquisition of bulk data at rest, and the covert exploitation and exfiltration of data by hacking or altering vulnerable computer software.

It then examines how the legal and political system in the UK metabolized these revelations, arguing that the effect was to end the era of legal obfuscation and replace it with a reflexive, adaptive legal regime. Compared to the previous media epochs of interception, there has been an inversion of norm and apparatus. Whereas before, the norm was openly stated while the apparatus was hidden, today, the apparatus is openly known but the norm is hidden—or rather, the norm is what is constantly being *discovered* in the endless processes of data mining, leading to a form of power that resembles a system closely attuned to its environment. The legislation introduced after Snowden's disclosures reflects this structural shift. The law integrates and normalizes digitally-mediated forms of *environmental* power, carving out protected categories that are subject to protection from otherwise ubiquitous surveillance.

THE SNOWDEN EVENT

Following the collapse of the Soviet Union, the UK's Government Communications Headquarters (GCHQ) dismantled much of its worldwide radio interception network. It began surveillance operations on the internet as early as 1996, and by 2013, it had a high degree of interception power and specialization in internet-based communications intelligence. As part of the postwar "Five-Eyes" alliance with the US, Canada, Australia, and New Zealand, it continued to exchange technological capacity and intelligence reports with allies. The alliance formed a kind of shadow of the internet, exploring, observing, and experimenting while responding to governmental demands for intelligence on the new strategic priorities of the so-called "global war on terror."

In his autobiography, Edward Snowden emphasizes the contingencies that allowed him a glimpse of the NSA and its global alliance as a totality. Few employees had the same kind of opportunity to review the entire Five-Eyes apparatus.[1] As a systems engineer, his work primarily concerned developing the potential of digital media, rather than the day-to-day intelligence operations they were used for. Along the way, he created a program called Heartbeat, a document aggregator that automatically pulled copies of materials from different intelligence agencies in the US global network and made them readable on one platform, with permissions indexed to each user profile's level of security clearance.[2] In short, he had access to files and documents that were otherwise classified above his grade.

Snowden first became concerned about the NSA's activities after accidentally gaining access to a highly classified report on Stellar Wind, the codename for the bulk collection and mining of international and domestic communications data initiated after September 11, 2001, under the

President's Surveillance Program (PSP).[3] The program began under authority of a top-secret presidential authorization that asserted an "extraordinary emergency" existed, necessitating electronic surveillance within the US for counterterrorism purposes without a court order, contrary to the law. The order was renewed at thirty- to sixty-day intervals, allowing NSA to intercept, collect, and analyze the content of all international telephone and internet communications involving "US persons" and, crucially, all metadata associated with domestic electronic communications and phone calls. Reports generated on suspected terrorists were sent to the Federal Bureau of Investigation (FBI) by secret "tippers" and were not to be disclosed or used as evidence in prosecutions. Less than 2 percent of the leads sent to the FBI made significant contributions to counterterrorism operations. Most were deemed irrelevant.[4]

Since the US Senate's Church Committee hearings into Operation Shamrock in the 1970s and the subsequent Foreign Intelligence Surveillance Act of 1978 (FISA), the NSA had been legally forbidden from engaging in domestic espionage against US persons on US soil. Their bulk interception powers were supposed to be limited to the electronic surveillance of foreign communications. To intercept communications between US persons and foreigners, warrants could be issued by a special closed Foreign Intelligence Surveillance Court (FISC), which reviewed applications and imposed oversight requirements. By secretly bypassing these legislative safeguards, the administration of President George W. Bush, acting on legal advice from John Yoo, a deputy assistant attorney general at the Department of Justice, unilaterally bypassed FISA.[5] The declaration of emergency powers secretly imposed warlike surveillance powers within the US with the aim of creating a preemptive detection system that would reveal terrorist plots before they crystalized.

In 2004, lawyers within the Department of Justice discovered the program and overturned Yoo's advice. The program was quietly moved onto controversial legal footings before the FISC. The domestic metadata collection program continued under the auspices of section 215 of the post-9/11 USA PATRIOT Act, reducing the number of search-term selectors the NSA used and subjecting the program to secret judicial oversight.[6] The interception of "foreign" communications mediated by US companies was moved onto FISA warrants. Strictly speaking, anyone overseas using a US-based email service was communicating with a US company and therefore a warrant based on "probable cause" was required to access their emails, even if the content of those emails had nothing to do with US persons the warrant provisions were designed to protect. The *New York Times* reported on the secret surveillance program in December 2005, leading to the eventual closure of the program.

The question of accessing foreign communications hosted by US servers remained, however. Congress passed the FISA Amendments Act in 2008, creating section 702. This controversial power allows warrantless interception and collection of communications pertaining to non-US persons located outside the US, provided they are expected to have or to communicate "foreign intelligence information." Procedures to minimize the incidental collection of information from US persons must be included under a renewable certificate that is valid for up to a year.[7] The effect is that the government can send requests for data to the world's largest internet platforms seeking data pertaining to overseas targets in the form of selectors, effectively a string of characters that identifies an individual or organization, like a phone number, email address, social media profile, and so on. The platforms are obliged to return all relevant data and communications records to the government for processing. In practice, the program inevitably sweeps up communications of US persons, which must be "minimized." However, the domestic security agency, the FBI, regularly searches communications for counterterrorism purposes, including those of US persons. In 2013, the NSA called it "the most significant tool in the NSA collection arsenal."[8] It remains a controversial power with an uncertain future.[9]

In 2009, President Barack Obama's administration sought to head off further investigation by releasing a redacted internal investigation titled *Unclassified Report on the President's Surveillance Program*.[10] While Snowden was engaged as a systems engineer on NSA servers—ironically, he was supposed to be removing "exceptionally controlled information" from the NSA's internal network—he discovered a document demonstrating that the public report was effectively a fabrication. The key point was that the NSA and a handful of government lawyers had decided that FISA was legislation from the radio epoch, outmoded on the internet. It had unilaterally redefined the meaning of technical terms like "acquiring" and "obtaining" data as if they only applied at the point when data that was already intercepted or acquired by NSA was "searched for and retrieved" by analysts.[11] The physical interception, collection, acquisition, and storage of data by automated systems was effectively regarded as outside the law, the background condition against which the law operated. Stellar Wind entailed the production of a permanent secret record of all digital communications, available in perpetuity.[12] This was not the only internal legal interpretation that Snowden revealed. Section 215 of the 2001 USA PATRIOT Act, which authorized the collection of "business records" of terrorist suspects, was similarly interpreted as grounds for indiscriminate domestic metadata collection.[13]

For Snowden, the distinction secretly introduced between the ontological fact of data collection and the epistemic act of examining it was incompatible with the US Constitution. Not only was it created without democratic oversight, its authors had repeatedly lied about it to Congress. He began gathering evidence. The protocols that allowed the internet to produce, as Snowden put it, a "pleasant and successful anarchy" of anonymity, decoupled from official identities and the real economy, also produced unprecedented scope for automated surveillance.[14] As Alexander Galloway observed, the same protocols that defined the open texture of the internet—whereby different computer networks running different programs could exchange data through a common internetworking protocol, look up repositories of stored data using a standardized addressing protocol, and create a network of hyperlinked connections—also enabled the control and observation of that network. Code enables computers to simulate other media, while operating below the threshold of perception. Computational media are flexible, open, and liberating, and at the same time enabling mechanisms for vast power and concentrated control. Code became the terrain of contemporary questions of freedom, subversion, and resistance.[15]

By disclosing technical documents, Snowden hoped to engender the "technical literacy" necessary for the public to understand the scope of what the law authorized.[16] No one had voted to build a "permanent record of everyone's life," but too few people understood what that meant in practice.[17] As Snowden viewed it, the law is a rule-based system, and a systems engineer's job is to find out where the rules were going wrong:

Imagine a system. It doesn't matter what system: it can be a computer system, an ecosystem, a legal system, or even a system of government.... Because systems work according to instructions, or rules, such an analysis is ultimately a search for which rules failed, how, and why—an attempt to identify the specific points where the intention of a rule was not adequately expressed by its formulation or application.[18]

The isomorphism between law and code often remarked on by legal theorists was tested as a systems engineer sought to reformat the law.[19] In 2013, he resolved to become a whistleblower,[20] contacted the journalist Glenn Greenwald and the filmmaker Laura Poitras, met them in Hong Kong, and handed over files extracted from the NSA's servers.

SNOWDEN AND GCHQ

Broadly observed, Snowden disclosed three types of interception programs operated by GCHQ in partnership with the NSA and UKUSA allies. The first is interception of data in bulk as it transits high-speed fiber-optic cables and other datalinks; the second is access to stored data "at rest," also in bulk quantities; and the third concerns computer hacking, known within GCHQ as "equipment interference" or "network exploitation" techniques. The latter was regarded as active signals intelligence (SIGINT), generating access to data that would otherwise be unavailable. These types mirror the functions of media as defined by Friedrich Kittler: transmission, storage, and processing.[21] We consider each in turn, as each had distinctive legal implications.

INTERCEPTION

A granular account of the techniques and problems of bulk interception of data in transmission is found in a document from September 2011 titled the *HIMR Data Mining Research Problem Book* (hereafter referred to as the Problem Book). HIMR is the Heilbronn Institute for Mathematical Research, which is attached to Bristol University, where mathematicians work on classified research questions for GCHQ.[22] The report explains the process succinctly. The UK government's Joint Intelligence Committee sets intelligence priorities, and GCHQ aims to meet the priorities in End Product Reports (EPR).[23] In the past, it was relatively straightforward to meet the state's requirements. Everyone knew roughly where to start looking for targets because they worked for foreign powers. However, "counterterrorism, and to a lesser extent increased work on serious crime, has changed this landscape dramatically" such that "finding the targets in the first place is now one of the most important problems facing analysts, before they can even begin to assess their plans and intentions."[24]

The difficulty lay in identifying targets that one knows next to nothing about. One option is contact chaining, which requires starting with a clue or "seed" from which a broader associational network might emerge. But GCHQ was interested in developing a much more radical perspective, looking for identifiable modus operandi to indicate terrorist or criminal behaviors that would be present as patterns inscribed within intercepted communication.[25] The document describes the use of two software systems to process bulk data in real time, without any preselected filters, using "big data" techniques to seek patterns of interest. Hadoop was used for analyzing collected data stored in raw form, and Distillery, built using IBM Streams, was used for processing and making sense of real-time interception.[26] Both programs were concerned with the problem that bulk interception produces more data than can be comprehensively processed and analyzed within a useful time frame unless it is filtered according to predetermined criteria. The program's codename was "Tempora," and it was aimed at "slowing down the internet."[27]

Tempora responds to the fact that the internet constantly changes itself through its own operations. Like society, the medium is a transient, mutating entity with no central point of control or single point of failure. It affords no position of total observation, and it generates no unified archive of itself. Because there is no single image of the internet, the internet can only be observed partially within defined temporal limits, and only from within the network itself.[28] This is an effect of the basic architecture. The internet is made possible through the transmission of messages as discrete packets of data. The achievement of the TCP/IP protocol, developed in the 1960s to allow different computer networks to exchange information, was to allow any digital file to be broken down into small packets for transmission using the Transmission Control Protocol (TCP), then assigning to each packet a common destination, known as the Internet Protocol (IP) address.[29] Each packet is then independently routed to the intended IP address by the best available route that the distributed network of servers can identify at that moment. Servers are in principle equivalent and distributed wherever the protocol is installed. At each server, a heuristic assessment of the best next link in the transmission of each incoming packet takes place, based on the addressing data of the packets and the connections available at that moment. In effect, a single message, such as an email or a request to access a website, is transmitted in blasts of discrete packets that each take independent and contingent routes to their destination. The effect is to dissolve the relationship between media and jurisdiction. A message written and read on two devices in one country, even one building, can be routed through foreign servers, particularly if using a cloud-based internet service provider's platform. It is in transit that bulk interception can occur, by constructing a device capable of copying and storing data of potential interest in parallel to the process of transmitting it.[30]

Intercepting data in transit is a more complex task than intercepting analog signals. In a sense, it is closer to postal interception but without the advantage of a central sorting room. The different elements of the content of a message must be gathered across multiple sorting sites and assembled. On the other hand, because each packet contains metadata—communications data necessary for the content of messages to be routed and reassembled, the same "packet inspection" algorithms that route traffic also present the opportunity to map the connections, associations, and networks that are exchanging data and allow files to be reassembled or "sessionized" at physical choke points where data can be captured in bulk quantities.[31]

As of 2011, GCHQ had intercept access to multiple "bearers" of internet traffic worldwide. Each fiber-optic bearer carried around 10 gigabytes per second of data. Britain retained a geographically advantageous position in relation to the global territorial distribution of cables in the age of fiber optics, as most transatlantic communications were routed through the existing US–UK links created by earlier cable-laying operations.[32] From Britain, traffic is distributed onward to Europe, Africa, and South America. Britain controlled a territorial bottleneck in what is, at the application layer, a deterritorialized network. Just as the NSA had unique access to data at rest through the major internet platforms and service providers based on US soil, GCHQ continued to have extraterritorial leverage, enhanced by its integration with global communication companies and their licensing conditions, giving it an outsized role in the global internet surveillance system.[33] In addition to cable interception sites around the world, satellite interception sites continued to operate in England, Cyprus, Kenya, and Oman.

According to the Problem Book, a key aim was to use machine learning techniques to understand the patterns latent within intercepted metadata. Experiments in big data analytics were ongoing at three of the multiple GCHQ interception sites, one in Cornwall, one in Cheltenham, and one in Seeb, Oman, a key interception station for Middle Eastern internet traffic. Around two hundred bearers were intercepted at these sites, more than the system could cover at once, so different probes were selectively brought online for operational needs.[34] The aim was to develop techniques to make vast quantities of data useful in short windows of time. Presumably, if successful, the experimental models would then be distributed to all interception sites.

The basic outline of the interception process is explained in the Problem Book. Most intercepted data packets were immediately discarded at the hardware level in a "massive volume reduction" process. Software then optimized and "sessionized" collected packets, pulling packets together to reconstruct full communications broken down for transmission. The data was then divided into content and communications data databases—the latter defined as "the part of the signal needed to set up the communication" and content as everything else. The latter has "higher legal and policy constraints," meaning it was selectively filtered according to preapproved "selector terms," whereas metadata was "usually unselected—we pull everything we see." A database used for targeting purposes stored details on targets, determining when to retain content so that there would be a valid reason for doing so.[35]

Achieving real-time communication online involves a kind of temporal simulation for the benefit of human users. To simulate a live television broadcast or a two-way telephone call online requires that relevant packets of data be delivered, buffered, assembled, and sequentially executed in microseconds.[36] The digital streaming economy depends on this simulation of continuous signals. The time-binding of intelligence obeys a similar logic. Tempora stored all content packets for three days to be scanned and potentially retained according to selectors, which were distributed by a targeting database called Broad Oak. Different selectors were brought on and off "cover," depending on current operational needs.[37]

All intercepted metadata was stored for thirty days. Around 30 billion metadata "events" were generated each day in 2010, with 50 billion anticipated for 2012 and 100 billion for 2013. After the initial filter, data was backed up to a flat file storage facility called Black Hole. From there it was analyzed, automatically formatted, and distributed to different query-focused databases (QFDs) that allowed analysts to easily interrogate it in different dimensions.[38]

The QFDs are profiling tools that illustrate the surveillance power of bulk metadata. For instance, the QFD named Five Alive collected the basic five elements for "each IP event seen": timestamp, source IP, source port, destination IP, destination port, plus session length and size.[39] Karma Police (after a Radiohead song) collected IP addresses associated with websites to provide a user's browsing history. User IP addresses could be collected and interrogated using Mutant Broth, which contains records of "online presence events" that link human profiles to a machine's IP address, effectively de-anonymizing users through unrelated sources such as password cookies.[40] Then, that person's personal phone number or other identifying accounts or communications data could be run through Social Anthropoid, which analyzes metadata from intercepted communications such as calls, messages, device location data, and other temporal and spatial markers that reveal a user's pattern of life. A further QFD called Samuel Pepys analyzed the content of communication alongside metadata to provide depth to targets—what they were writing, reading, or viewing online.

These examples demonstrate that, in combination, the QFD suite could unmask and give enormous insights into the private communications, lifestyle, and behavior of any of the internet users whose communications happened to be intercepted.[41] Bulk interception has always been premised on the use of inferential reasoning.[42] When discrete data is correlated from different sources, it uncovers a rich environment that can reveal military plans, de-anonymize individuals, or make predictions about classes of unspecified individuals based on shared traits, behaviors, associations, or relations that cannot be categorized and that individuals may not know about themselves. In such an environment, data comes to define what is taken to be true about a subject in an empirical register, regardless of preconceived norms. The target subject emerges from contingent correlations and inferences—provided one has the data and the algorithm to search it.

The search for signature modus operandi required an idea of what suspicious behavior looked like. For instance, buying a separate mobile phone only used to communicate with one other number is not good security because it represents a "closed loop" that leaps out to a mathematician looking at an otherwise complex telephony graph.[43] Anyone who thinks that by frequently changing their phone while calling the same numbers gave them anonymity was working with an analog imagination. Machine learning would present an avenue for finding deeper patterns.[44] Not all targets were human. GCHQ also sought to develop techniques for identifying the communication "signatures" of "infection vectors"—hostile viruses and other implants that sent beacons back to their controllers. If identified, these presented opportunities to counterattack whoever had control of them. As such, the system is structurally indifferent to the distinction between the human and nonhuman prior to the analysis of the data.[45]

One of the tasks set for the mathematicians in 2011 was the improvement of semi-supervised machine learning techniques. GCHQ was at the time experimenting with supervised machine learning techniques to analyze its bulk intercepted data and enjoyed limited success using Random Forest techniques. One problem was that the decisions reached by these systems "cannot be simply and intuitively explained to an analyst," and so they were difficult to trust.[46]

Another problem was that the techniques did not scale well because large datasets were inadequately "truthed." In machine learning, a ground truth is required so that the predictions developed by the learning algorithm about data can be checked against its true values.[47] If the truth of the data is not known, the value of the prediction cannot be assessed. The same problem applied to the use of semi-supervised learning techniques. Only a tiny proportion of GCHQ data could be "truthed" by hand, while policy, law, and the volume of intercepted material meant that there was much more metadata available than content. Content was needed in order to reveal what the metadata patterns actually signified, if anything.[48] One option was "weak labeling," using inaccurate truthing to nevertheless try to develop useful algorithms, building second-order inferences on second-order inferences.[49]

Another research area concerned "graphing" information flows so that significant patterns might be revealed through the timing of communications. Associating related communication events derived from different sources and channels would, for example, allow for the detection of botnets or could de-anonymize users of the encrypted Tor browser, with which users can evade identification of their online browsing patterns.[50] Temporal analysis of communications could theoretically uncover otherwise hidden associations. The document illustrates this by stating that all GCHQ employees must switch off their phones between 9 a.m. and 5 p.m. and leave them outside the building. Converting the gaps in the phones connectivity into events and associating them algorithmically would produce an opportunity to "spot the causality," uncovering who works for a top secret organization and then investigating them further.[51] Graphed analysis of streamed data could also, in theory, lead to "anomaly detection," mapping the spread of certain kinds of ideas and information. This way, the timing of communication became abstracted and converted into a potential source of information.

Bulk interception by NSA and GCHQ depended first on extensive collaboration with "corporate partners," the private telecommunications companies that own and operate the backbone infrastructure of the internet around the world. Interception installations exist quite literally in the shadow of large private data centers, a kind of logical overlay on the processes that enable global networked communication. It also received data from "third-party" governments outside the Five-Eyes alliance that collaborate with NSA or GCHQ in exchange for access to the raw collected intelligence that is produced. Finally, less commonly, it could be conducted clandestinely in hostile locations.[52]

ACQUISITION

Other documents from the Snowden archive suggested GCHQ had extensive access to bulk quantities of communications records and bulk quantities of personal datasets that had not derived from interception power or from the kind of limited access provisions of the Regulation of Investigatory Powers

Act 2000 (RIPA). One possible source was suggested by slides pertaining to a joint NSA-GCHQ program called Muscular, which intercepted data from the private fiber-optic cables of major internet companies, including Yahoo and Google, where unencrypted user data was being transferred between storage facilities within the companies' networks.[53]

But it appeared that GCHQ sources of data were not limited to traditional upstream interception of the internet. Because of its long-standing technical integration and alliance with NSA, GCHQ enjoyed indirect access to the extensive profile data stored on the servers of major internet providers through the so-called Prism program and could use it to build intelligence profiles of targeted individuals and networks.[54] Whereas the NSA relied on the controversial section 702 FISA power to build Prism, and recommended (in internal slides) that analysts use both upstream interception from the fiber-optic infrastructure and the Prism collection system,[55] GCHQ's legal basis for accessing private data "at rest" alongside its interception powers was unclear. Because section 702 FISA protected "US persons" only, there was no obvious reason why GCHQ could not use Prism to profile "internal" targets in the UK, raising fears of a potential mass surveillance loophole in the law. Prism was an enormously revealing tool, as it allowed near real-time observation of targets and their communication networks as they logged into web services, sent emails, made video calls, and exchanged files.[56]

EXPLOITATION

The third source of intelligence disclosed by Snowden concerned cyber operations that actively intervene in other systems, rather than traditionally collecting passive SIGINT.[57] Attacking a device involves actively damaging it, deleting files, or causing other inconveniences. Exploiting it involves gaining covert access to unencrypted data or real-time surveillance of the device in use—for instance, a program called Optic Nerve could intercept webcams.[58] GCHQ was also involved in cyber defense for the UK and in counterattacking hostile actors by detecting their implants and sending malicious data back.[59]

At a network level, exploitation provides opportunities to increase the volume of data available. GCHQ began using computer network exploitation to "exfiltrate" data in the early 1990s and regarded it as a source of long-term data gathering.[60] For instance, GCHQ was revealed to have hacked Belgacom using malware named Regin. Belgacom is a Belgian telecommunications company that operated a roaming service for international travelers—the main target of the attack.[61] Gemalto, a Dutch SIM-card manufacturer, was also targeted, allowing the decryption of intercepted communications from phones using those cards in countries using second-generation mobile networks, such as Afghanistan, where British and US military forces were deployed.[62] These targeted attacks were joined by bulk hacking operations in which malware was widely distributed across targeted networks.

To maximize their potential "attack surfaces," the unstated policy of the agencies undermined internet security for all users. Condemnation from the computer security sector followed. For Susan Landau, the most disturbing revelation was confirmation that the NSA had compromised a cryptographic standard algorithm, Dual EC-DRBG, under a program called Bullrun.[63] The algorithm had long been suspected of containing a backdoor, but because it had been certified by the US National Institute of Standards and Technology (NIST) and promoted by the security company RSA, it was widely used and believed to be credible and trustworthy.[64] The algorithm is supposed to generate random numbers for use in encrypted communication. In fact, the NSA had covertly ensured that it could edit the code, thus allowing the NSA to decrypt any communications or systems using it. In some ways, this continued the NSA's long-standing policy toward encryption for private communications.[65]

Unless one exclusively uses open-source software and understands how it works, user trust in the security of proprietary digital systems depends on reliable symbolic devices. For Landau, the attack damaged trust not only in the NSA but in US-approved standards and the software systems that they underwrite. Landau doubted whether the FISC understood the repercussions of its authorization for trust in US systems and for cybersecurity generally.[66]

All of GCHQ's resources were available to NSA operatives through the XKeyscore platform, a decentralized tool for pulling together stored intercepted data from various sources and databases and making them accessible using a front-end search engine. GCHQ had its own iteration of XKeyscore, but at the same time, GCHQ was interested in contracting with Palantir, a private data analytics firm specializing in the agglomeration and processing of large and differentiated datasets, to use its interface and visualization software.[67] The interface layer not only governs how analysts utilize the data. It was the point at which the law applied to the apparatus.

INTERFACE LEGALITIES

At the time that the Snowden revelations began appearing in the media in 2013, GCHQ's new techniques of experimental communications surveillance was authorized by expansive readings of publicly available legislation. Officially, RIPA was supposed to regulate all communications-related surveillance powers. It would emerge that the broad power to give directions to telecommunications providers (section 94 of the Telecommunications Act 1984) and the general powers to authorize activity under ministerial warrant (the Intelligence Services Act 1994) had been relied on. None of these laws gave any real indication of the purposes that they were being put to, and no oversight body reported on the existence of the capabilities.[68]

Within GCHQ, the legality of operations was taken seriously, and the basic requirements of RIPA warrants and authorizations were designed into standards-based interfaces used to search out targets and obtain intercepted communications. This is explained in a set of leaked legal training slides from GCHQ called "Operational Legalities."[69] An internal interception platform was understood as a technical system that combines the law and the database and that "simultaneously distributes interfaces through their remote coordination and centralizes their integrated control through that same coordination."[70] Interfaces structurally couple the platform with the decentralized agency of its users, who are subjected to its protocols and standards.

The slide presentation makes clear that carrying out "intercept/CNE" (computer network exploitation) without authorization is illegal in the UK.[71] The "principles," stated in another slide, make clear that "we operate within the law; we can demonstrate that we operate within the law; staff have the information they need to be able to comply with the law."[72]

As such, "everything we do" must be authorized, necessary, and proportionate.[73] All operations required that adequate justifications be entered in the system to provide "visibility of operational activities to GCHQ seniors and SoS."[74] With respect to intercepting and accessing external communications, where at least one of the parties to the communication had to be outside the UK, the selection of data was authorized by reference to terms entered on a certificate appended to a section 8(4) warrant issued under RIPA.[75] For internal communications, with all parties in the UK, a targeted RIPA section 8(1) warrant was needed.

The Broad Oak "strategic target knowledge database" stored selectors relating to targets and provided them to front-end processing systems at GCHQ interception sites. Once a selector was entered in the database, the system would search for relevant communications automatically and continually. An example screenshot of a Broad Oak page displays a targeting tab for an email address selector, as indicated in the box that states "type."[76] It is accompanied by a description of the selector. A box containing a "Miranda number" contains a code number that "equates to [an] intelligence requirement,"[77] meaning the current list of intelligence priorities set by the UK's Joint Intelligence Committee. Next to that is a box indicating "JIC Priority/Purpose." By linking each selector to an intelligence priority, it associates the filtering operation with a lawful purpose, so the necessity requirement is satisfied (see figure 7.1).

Below the Miranda number is a textbox labeled "HRA justification," where the analyst must satisfy the proportionality requirement. They must write, in free text, "exactly why you are targeting this individual; don't just repeat the Miranda number but add value."[78] Some positive examples included in the training notes are "wife of Russian Minister, targeted to provide travel details of target" and "employee at Chinese Embassy in London." Indirect targeting is prohibited in relation to communications, but not information about people in the UK, so it is "fine to target a Swedish girl-friend of a person in the UK to find out info about him, as long as you defeat communications between the two of them."[79]

Finally, there is a box labeled "Legal authorization for target," which in the screenshot contains a coded entry and an expiry date. This was necessary only if the communication in question was internal to the UK, meaning they could be targeted only if a RIPA section 8(1) warrant was in

ENVIRONMENTAL INTERCEPTION

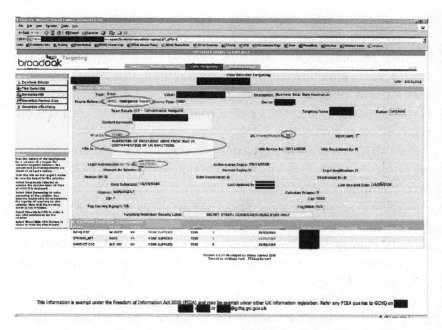

7.1 The Broad Oak selector input page from GCHQ legal training slides. The interface requires analysts to enter justifications and necessity codes for each selector that they wished to target for interception. Later the European Court of Human Rights ruled that greater oversight of selectors was required.

place.[80] If the analyst was uncertain of a target's location, what mattered was their honest belief at the time, while the "main thing is to record why you made your decision" in case it turned out wrong. The law protected people within the UK from unwarranted targeting, while policy protected people in partner states in the UKUSA alliance. GCHQ "must not ask a second party to do something for which we would need a warrant."[81] No one in the US could be targeted without a warrant and no US person outside the US without a court order.[82]

A similar interface labeled UDAQ allowed analysts to engage with the content of intercepted data once processed. All the same fields are present and required. Continued targeting must be "revalidated" every six months, while a target who is no longer justifiably targeted must be "deactivated."[83] Targeting was, however, permitted for the purpose of developing and experimenting to expand capabilities in the future.[84] Each year, a targeting audit was performed on 10 percent of the entries, randomly selected by the commissioner.[85] Provided one adequately responds to the interface prompts, legality would be secured. The law operates through the interface, imposing itself and arranging things in advance so that only formally defined "seed" selectors are used, and these are indexed to lawful purposes. In practice, a tree of connections was supposed to grow from the seed.

For GCHQ, the point of the section 8(4) warrant was not about protecting privacy but rather the efficient collection and deletion of intercepted data. The thousands of individual selector terms appended to warrants were there to narrow the collection to a manageable volume. For all other purposes, the warrants authorized general collection of as much data as could be managed. In practice, analysts could go beyond the legally certificated terms on the section 8(4) interception warrant when inputting selectors, introducing a distinction between the formal entries on the warrant and the actual searches conducted. This slippage between formality and practice was later criticized by the European Court of Human Rights, which ruled in 2021 that all categories of selectors used when analyzing bulk data should be included in the original warrant, that independent authorization should be included in the process, and that any selectors relating to a known individual should be subject to prior internal oversight to ensure the search is necessary and proportionate.[86]

ELUCIDATION

When the disclosures appeared, several nongovernmental organizations (NGOs) sought to challenge the legality of GCHQ's operations, notably Liberty, the UK's leading civil liberties campaign group, and Privacy International, a charity focused on data and privacy. In the summer of 2014, the Rolls Building on Fetter Lane in London served as the venue for a series of public hearings before the Investigatory Powers Tribunal (IPT), the statutory tribunal created by RIPA to investigate complaints of alleged illegality by the agencies empowered by RIPA. The case is reported as *Liberty v. GCHQ*.[87] A group of ten human rights organizations, led by Privacy International and Liberty, challenged the legality of the Tempora interception system and the legality of GCHQ access to the NSA's Prism program.

The government adopted the typical stance of "neither confirm nor deny" (NCND), even though two relevant independent watchdogs, the Intelligence and Security Committee of Parliament (ISC) and the Interception of Communications Commissioner's Office (IOCCO), had confirmed the programs' existence.[88] The tribunal facilitated the hearing with a set of "assumed facts" that referred to the functionality of the programs without using their codenames. Four teams of lawyers spent a week making painstakingly detailed arguments about how the law should apply to the hypothetical programs. It was by then clear that RIPA was deliberately opaque.[89] To understand the scope and magnitude of the powers it authorized and the related safeguards it imposed required carefully piecing together different sections and definitions. Section 8(4) authorized the making of warrants for the collection of external communications in bulk and analyzing them according to selector terms listed in a rolling certificate appended to the section 8(4) warrant. Any communications selected from the bulk intercept according to the certificated terms could be "read, looked at, or listened to" by the agency executing the warrant.[90] The complainants challenged the expansive scope that GCHQ appeared to have developed based on this provision, and argued that the blanket power under section 8(4) to collect data indiscriminately was effectively a general warrant of the kind outlawed in the case of *Entick v. Carrington*.[91]

Much turned on the question of when an intrusion upon privacy occurs. The government argued that the collection of a person's electronic data did not resolve into more than a minimal intrusion on privacy until a human analyst selected it from among billions of terabytes of data and examined it. For overseas communications, this could be done freely if it was for lawful purposes of national security, combatting serious crime, or protecting the UK economy. For those who emerged from the bulk data and were found to be in the UK, RIPA required analysts to obtain special authorization to ensure no arbitrary abuses of privacy, when inspecting the content of their communication. The claimants argued that the capacity for automatic analysis was itself sufficient to make collection of metadata alone highly intrusive and disproportionate and argued that the whole regime was incompatible with the requirements of Article 8 of the European Convention on Human Rights.[92] The tribunal ultimately ruled that bulk interception was adequately described in law and that the safeguards imposed by RIPA were sufficient to make its use compatible with the protections required by Articles 8 and 10 of the European Convention on Human Rights—a view later overturned by the European Court of Human Rights for its lack of sufficient control over selector terms and metadata in the 2021 case of *Big Brother Watch v. UK*.

The second issue in the case was euphemized as "intelligence sharing," but was prompted by leaked evidence of GCHQ access to downstream data stored in the servers of American internet platforms. The claimants argued that if GCHQ had access to data already obtained by the NSA under its Prism program, they could bypass the warrant regime of RIPA and obtain private information without any legal framework in place to constrain them or inform the public of the power, a clear violation of Articles 8 and 10 of the convention. No law governed whether a UK official could access Prism to extract extensive, intrusive data derived from a target's online social media profiles. The government countered that there were sufficient safeguards and powers implied in existing national security law, particularly the Intelligence Services Act 1994, to amount to a coherent framework for the purposes of the convention, and further added that in fact, secret guidance existed "below the waterline" of official secrecy that prevented GCHQ operatives from using foreign sources of data to bypass the rules and duties imposed by the RIPA regime. Nevertheless, on the basis that such intrusive powers needed to be explicitly "in accordance with the law," the IPT ruled in February 2015 that the lack of a clear and accessible legal provision made any such "intelligence sharing" unlawful.

At a special closed hearing that followed, the government's legal team agreed to provide a gist of "arrangements" that existed below the waterline of official secrecy. In essence, the disclosures "signposted" that data shared by foreign allies with GCHQ could be used only where a target was already subject to a RIPA authorization.[93] Based on that disclosure, the tribunal reached a strange and paradoxical conclusion: the situation had been unlawful until the date of the disclosure of the guidance into the public domain. Prior to the disclosure, any such intelligence sharing was unlawful because the rules governing it were not publicly accessible or foreseeable. Disclosure had remedied the unlawfulness of the situation. However, as the relevant disclosure was not published anywhere other than in the IPT's own judgment, the judgment referred to *itself* as the key differential, determinative of its own decision. The implicit meaning was that whatever was going on beyond the waterline could carry on as before, as the tribunal's decision had altered the legal environment that it existed to review. The decision is a text that changed the problem it identified. The paradoxical outcome is that a situation that was found to be illegal was made legal by the process that challenged it.[94] Taking itself as a key inflection point in legal time, the tribunal converted an unlawful past into a lawful future. The European Court of Human Rights, when asked to review this strange process, approved of it, praising the tribunal for its "elucidatory function."[95]

At the second-order level, the effect was surprisingly like the judgment in *Malone v. Metropolitan Police Commissioner* (1979), the case about the legality of telephone tapping by the police. In both situations, a court reached an unprecedented decision that successfully bought political time for the government to adapt and respond to a loss of control over the secrecy of its communication intelligence programs. In both cases, new legislation followed soon after.

Elucidatory events subsequently occurred with respect to computer hacking, known formally as equipment interference (EI) and computer network exploitation (CNE). The legality of such powers was challenged in a case initiated by Privacy International in May 2014.[96] The government responded to all allegations with NCND until February 6, 2015, the day of the tribunal's self-referential judgment in the *Liberty v. GCHQ* case, when the practice was publicly "avowed" in a consultation document published alongside a new draft Equipment Interference Code of Practice.[97] The timing indicated that the *Liberty* case had an obvious effect on governmental strategy. Nevertheless, in its final analysis, the IPT eventually held that hacking had been "in accordance with the law" for the purposes of Article 8 and Article 10 of the European Convention on Human Rights, both before and after it was avowed, on the basis that the "property interference" provisions of the Intelligence Services Act 1994 allowed GCHQ to lawfully undertake operations against property. It declined to address the territoriality of GCHQ's human rights obligations, given that hacking operations appeared to have been launched from within the UK and therefore did not sit neatly within the internal/external distinction that applied to interception powers.

Another case arose in March 2015, when the Intelligence and Security Committee of Parliament, a political oversight body, reported that the UK's intelligence and security services including MI5 and GCHQ had long acquired and used bulk personal datasets (BPD),[98] otherwise known as datasets containing sensitive personal data on millions of individuals, the majority of whom were of no intelligence interest. This was carried out by relying on general statutory powers to acquire information under the Security Service Act 1989 and the Intelligence Services Act 1994.[99] In November 2015, just as the Investigatory Powers bill was presented to Parliament, the government revealed that it had also obtained bulk communications datasets (BCD) from communication service providers under section 94 of the Telecommunications Act 1984.[100]

These disclosures triggered the case of *Privacy International v. Secretary of State for Foreign and Commonwealth Affairs and Others*.[101] As no rules existed in the public domain about the acquisition and use of bulk datasets, the tribunal concluded in its first judgment in October 2016 that both regimes had operated in violation of the law for over ten years—they were effectively unlawful prior to being publicly avowed in March 2015 for BPD and in November 2015 for BCD. It held that the regimes had been compliant since those dates when rules had been made public and that the fundamental technological principle of scanning millions of private records searching for unknown connections and patterns was compatible with human rights law. In its ruling, the tribunal commented on its elucidatory role that "it is important not to identify as the discovery of a failing what is, in fact, the identification of a welcome improvement."[102] In other words, the identification of unlawful secret powers should be regarded as a positive development that contributed to an improved situation rather than cause for concern about the tendency of government to develop mass surveillance regimes.

CLOSING THE GAPS

The legal challenges were not the only response to the Snowden disclosures. Reports were commissioned from the Intelligence and Security Committee of Parliament and the Royal United Services Institute (RUSI).[103] Perhaps most significantly, the independent reviewer of terrorism legislation, Sir David Anderson KC, reviewed the legal framework of investigatory powers generally in 2015 and the specific necessity and utility of bulk data surveillance and hacking techniques in 2016.[104] All argued in favor of the necessity of the powers and made recommendations on how to legally authorize them. These reports served to give independent support to the government's assertion that such powers were necessary and normal aspects of national security practice. Additionally, seven parliamentary reports were commissioned, with over two thousand pages of evidence assessed from civil society and academia by a committee assembled to prepare the legislation. Over a thousand legislative amendments were made during the passage of the Investigatory Powers Act 2016, which eventually passed with bipartisan support.

The underlying concern was to cover gaps in the legal description of the previously secret powers exercised over communication by the British intelligence and security services.[105] This approach not only reversed the centuries-old policy of secrecy and obfuscation but also marked another isomorphism between law and interception in its concern for comprehensive coverage and controlled visibility. Whereas the period between the passage of the telecommunications acts in 1984 and 2013 was characterized by minimalist, deliberately opaque legislation, the post-Snowden approach involved the production of "translucency."[106] The UK's interception powers are now broadly explicated in law, while their operation remains secret. The strategic effect is to immunize the interception apparatus from further legal challenge and political controversy.

The Investigatory Powers Act 2016 begins with "general duties in relation to privacy" that require all public authorities to consider whether less intrusive means could meet their goal. They must also assess whether the information they seek is particularly sensitive, due for example to legal privilege, journalistic confidentiality, and communication between members of Parliament (MPs) and constituents. Additionally, they need to factor in the "public interest in the integrity and security of telecommunications systems and postal services" and to consider "any other aspects of the public interest in the protection of privacy."[107] Unlawfully intercepting or obtaining data otherwise than in accordance with the act is criminalized.

Each power authorized by the act is then described in its own chapter, setting out the conditions and constraints on different categories of warrants and authorizations that can be made by the secretary of state. Together, they provide a detailed legal anatomy of the functional aims that Snowden's leaks disclosed, contained within detailed rules and time limits. The domestic powers are targeted interception and examination warrants; authorizations for acquiring communications data on a targeted basis; powers to give notices requiring the retention of communications data by a service provider; warrants for targeted equipment interference for the purposes of obtaining communications, data, or information; warrants for BCD; and warrants for the acquisition of BPD.

For overseas-related communication, bulk warrants can be issued for bulk interception of communication (including interception carried out overseas) and bulk equipment interference for obtaining communications, data, or information (hacking for other purposes continues to be a matter of "property interference," not covered in the Investigatory Powers Act). The secretary of state can also issue National Security Notices and Technical Capability Notices that require communication providers to take specified steps or make technical changes to facilitate access to communication, but not where these notices would undermine other provisions of the law. All warrants and authorizations must ultimately be indexed to the purposes of national security, serious crime, and the economic well-being of the UK for overseas-related communications. The consistent normative theme is one of proportionality and accountability. All approved applications must be justified such that the intrusion into privacy and the effect on freedom of expression are shown to be "necessary and proportionate" to one of the three overarching statutory purposes.

The ultimate authority to make warrants remains with the office of the secretary of state, the home secretary for domestic agencies, and the foreign secretary for overseas intelligence. Secretarial approval of warrants and notices are now subject to a double-lock, whereby an independent judicial commissioner reviews the secretary's decision to ensure that it is compliant with the law. The commissioners work for the Investigatory Powers Commissioner's Office (IPCO), a body created by the act to unify the oversight work that had been done by three separate surveillance oversight bodies.

Each year, the commissioner must present a report to the prime minister and Parliament on the operation of the powers in the legislation, providing statistical data and narrative accounts of the effectiveness of the intelligence and security agencies in complying with the law and making public recommendations for improvements where necessary. The commissioners fulfill a hybrid role between legal review and accountability and political oversight.[108]

The IPCO reports published so far provide a sense of how the necessity and proportionality assessments required at all stages of the implementation of surveillance powers operate within the agencies. In GCHQ, for instance, these considerations are applied to the selection of communication bearers for bulk interception, the automated filtering of intercepted data, the justifications provided for when entering selectors as search terms and when applying for bulk equipment interference warrants of overseas targets, and so on.[109] The interface legalities identified above have expanded in their complexity and reach, but not in their essential form. In its 2022 report, IPCO comments positively on the quality of the justifications it reviewed and the "mature" systems that it observed. In the agencies that operate bulk datasets, legacy datasets predating the new regime have been progressively phased out of use and purged, while new internal auditing measures have been introduced.[110] The reports are thorough, occasionally critical, always non-adversarial in tone, and attuned to reporting on the implementation of legal and practical developments that have occurred since the act was passed into law in 2016.

For example, in 2021, the European Court of Human Rights found in the case of *Big Brother Watch v. UK* that the RIPA regime for bulk interception was incompatible with the requirements of the convention because it granted too much leeway to analysts when they entered selector terms to search intercepted content, creating a risk of arbitrariness in violation of Article 8. In its judgment, the court described the impact of bulk interception on individuals' rights as "a gradual process" of growing intrusion as the process progresses. The initial interception and retention of data is a minimal but real intrusion, the application of selectors is greater, the human examination of what emerges from the data greater still, and the final intelligence report produced is higher again.[111] Yet bulk interception, in principle, falls within the "margin of appreciation" that the law allows states to pursue their interests, so can be carried out provided there are clear and adequate safeguards in place at all stages. The RIPA regime failed in that respect, as it didn't protect the metadata of targets within the UK and gave analysts too much freedom to arbitrarily search the data.[112] The RIPA regime also fell short for its lack of special protections for journalistic content swept up in bulk interception, violating the Article 10 right to freedom of expression.[113]

Following this case, IPCO reported in 2024 that senior officers in the intelligence services now approve each strong selector term and that IPCO inspected and audited the process while a new process involving the judicial commissioners was being prepared. However, the report emphasizes IPCO's view that only updated legislation would ultimately make the regime compliant, because the Investigatory Powers Act lacks strong safeguards on selector terms.[114]

Also in 2021, the High Court in London found deficiencies in the vetting process for those seeking to work at IPCO after Eric Kind, formerly of Privacy International and an outspoken critic of GCHQ surveillance, was rejected from a position on security grounds. In response to that judgment, a new procedure is being developed with a possible avenue of internal appeal.[115]

In 2023, the IPT issued a determination regarding MI5's mishandling of bulk data stored in a "technical environment" that IPCO reported on publicly in 2019. In 2020, Liberty and Privacy International made a complaint to the IPT alleging that MI5 had failed to disclose its lack of necessary safeguards over that dataset to the home secretary and to judicial commissioners while applying for new warrants, and that the home secretary in turn had failed to investigate the internal deficiencies adequately. The IPT found that these points were true, but its ultimate response was to commend IPCO for its work drawing attention to the issue, and to reject the claimants' suggestion that the issue was evidence of systemic failings that rendered the legal regime "not in accordance with the law" for the purposes of the convention on human rights.[116]

The reflexivity of the 2016 regime is reflected not only in the public reports on internal procedural problems and improvements carried out by IPCO but in the requirement on the secretary of state to review the act after five years and to make their report available to Parliament.[117] On one level, this is a positive change from the years of blanket secrecy and deliberate obfuscation. Yet at the same time, the statutory reflexivity confirms the contingency of the norm, and ensures that law continues to normalize the contingency of power. The law's strategic function in enabling and legitimizing intelligence and security powers—a role that has been implicitly performed for centuries—has adapted to incorporate a normative expectation of transparent self-assessment. So long as this reflexivity is performed, the role of the sovereign at the apex point of surveillance is maintained, and the surveillance capacity embedded in digital networks normalized.

REFLEXIVE LEGALITY

In 2023, in accordance with the Investigatory Powers Act 2016, the home secretary published a five-year review setting out several issues for potential revisions to the law, all of which seek to loosen the strict controls on access to data. Aspects of the legislative regime were reported to be "inhibiting" the UK intelligence services, affecting their operational agility and capability development. In 2016, it was claimed, the complexity of data was not foreseen, nor was the "extent to which cloud and commercially available tools would make powerful analysis of datasets possible," nor the fact that most data can "in theory be resolved to real world identities," bringing more datasets within the definition of bulk personal datasets and thus making more data subject to the strict requirements for a warrant than was anticipated.[118]

The review also proposed changing the procedures by which secret notices regarding data retention and technical modifications to communication systems are issued to communication providers, to make it easier for law enforcement to obtain internet connection records. Further, the review highlighted changes in the interception environment, particularly the impact of encrypted communications. After Snowden, the use of end-to-end encryption is applied by default to most internet traffic, while changes in patterns of communication have blurred the distinction between communication in transit, which is subject to interception, and communications that are stored and can only be accessed by equipment interference. In practice, therefore, agencies tend to apply for both kinds of warrants together. However, as the product of interception cannot be used in criminal evidence while the product of equipment interference can, the legal bifurcation between interception and hacking is "increasingly difficult to distinguish" in practice and has operational consequences that may require revision.[119] The reflexivity of the law can cut both ways, loosening controls on the secret agencies as well as tightening them.

Everything that Snowden disclosed regarding GCHQ and NSA activities has now been assigned a place within the law, updating the loose legislative overlay without interfering with the already functional mass surveillance system. The legislation follows from the structural capacities that had already developed and operationalized through the evolution of media. It has required the reconfiguration of internal processes to bring greater oversight to analytic processes and the creation of new warrant gateways before bulk personal datasets, internet connection records, and bulk communication datasets can be obtained and utilized. But in principle, provided it is deemed necessary and proportionate to the interests of national security, the prevention or detection of serious crime, or the economics interests of the UK overseas, the interception apparatus is fully intact and operational. The execution of its code is the execution of the law.

CONCLUSION

The initial reaction to the Snowden disclosures described it as a mass surveillance system that threatened democracy. But compared to existing mass surveillance regimes, notably in China, the term is inapt and obscures more than it reveals. It is more instructive to consider the evolution of the law against the genealogical backdrop provided in earlier chapters. The interception apparatus that had developed with an obsessive focus on legal secrecy now reports on itself *through* the media and techniques of the legal system. In this way, the potential for interception has become an element in a generalized ecology of political power mediated through ubiquitous digital technologies.

The law too has adapted, as it must do when its environment changes to retain its validity.[120] Snowden made the limits of law's visibility visible and made the question of the line between secrecy and transparency a legal problem. The IPT's improvised findings following the disclosures, now endorsed as a process of necessary "elucidation" by the European Court of Human Rights, presupposes redrawing the line between what is "accessible and foreseeable" to the public and what may legitimately be kept secret. In that moment, the law itself becomes mutable, impermanent, reflexive, and evolutionary in its self-understanding. The key criterion of legitimacy today is not just the content of the law, but its performance of accountability through the mass media. The public is at once the object of the security and intelligence agencies' surveillance power, and at the same time, the hypothecated audience informed by the law that underpins the legitimacy of the surveillance apparatus.

Hence, the law takes public effect through the performance of second-order audit processes, reviewing and reporting on itself to maintain a sense of security, continuity, and stability oriented toward an unknown future. The law does not only regulate the appropriate "balance" of surveillance between security, privacy, and an open public sphere, it communicates its role in maintaining the balance. The legal system is required, by law, to report on itself, to produce an environment in which the law is not only known but is "known to be known."[121]

There is an isomorphic similarity between the legal system's role in describing and regulating the functions of the interception apparatus and the operations of the apparatus itself. The law maps onto the different kinds of data collection available and introduces a pause, a moment of friction in which the analyst, their supervisor, the secretary of state, and the judicial commissioners must perform the consideration of necessity and proportionality. This moment of reason makes the system acceptable. But law does not concern itself with what the system produces. The substantive production of intelligence and how it is operationalized remains a matter of policy, and the law draws a line around it. In the language of the European Court of Human Rights, actions deemed necessary for national security purposes fall within a "margin of appreciation" in which governments act secretly and freely. As such, national security stands over a repository of unseen techniques, capabilities, and purposes that are obliquely, undetectably shaping the world.

To these ends, the promise of intercepting and acquiring data at population scale lies in the capacity to model the social, political, physical, and psychological environment that produces it. Techniques for modeling and mapping the environment within a useful span of time both preempt what one cannot otherwise predict and allow time for its active manipulation. GCHQ and the internet platforms that generate its target data are interested in the psychosocial patterns that stochastically emerge within digitally connected populations.[122]

As such, problems are no longer solely predefined according to existing norms and expectations but instead are elicited from the digital environment. By seeking patterns that might disclose otherwise unknown threats, the interception apparatus is attuned to a technologically mediated ecological risk that lacks any normative preconception. That is not to say that the old intelligence priorities of states, militaries, and known terrorists are forgotten, but they are joined by a new kind of ever-present unknown threat, the "anywhere anytime potential for the proliferation of the abnormal, possessed of a threatening autonomy, which power must paradoxically respect in order to act."[123] Brian Massumi labels this environmental form of politics "ontopower," which presupposes and governs a changing environmental situation rather than focusing on the normative figure of a political "subversive" or the spies and armies of a rival sovereign state.[124] Ontopower both produces and intercepts the environment. It is not limited only to the meaningful dimensions of communication but to its asignifying materiality, patterns, and temporality.

The ecological model of power described here includes the reflexive legal system, with its annual reviews, elucidatory tribunals, and built-in updates. The semantics of interception power, with the secretary of state at its apex, remain the same, but the structure reveals a processual, self-referential, and autopoietic system that is adaptive to its own complexity and contingency.[125]

8

INTERCEPTION AND INTEGRATION

In every media epoch, interception shadows communication. As Michel Serres argued, the parasite must be understood not as an obstacle or interference in an otherwise pure network of information exchange, but as intrinsic to the production of the network itself. Sovereignty over a given system is generated by exploiting the constraints that produce the system.[1] In the postal epoch, the sorting room afforded sovereignty a panoptic view of letters and parcels. The electrical epoch and the transformation of time and space in networks was accompanied by state appropriation, regulation, and a license to declare an emergency and take control of communication. In the twentieth century, the automation of electromechanical teletext enabled unbreakable encryption machines—until the analysts and engineers at Bletchley Park built computing machines that could guess combinations millions of times faster than anyone in history. As Friedrich Kittler demonstrated, new technical standards quickly come to seem natural. The semantics of culture, which operate at the level of the imaginary, change their referents through the precognitive restructuring of the symbolic that technical media perform.[2] In each media epoch, the techniques of interception demonstrate this underlying truth. Interception evolves according to the visibilities that technical media make possible.

This chapter concludes the book by reviewing key changes in the years since the Edward Snowden event. First, it offers a model for understanding media today through the lens of planetary scale computational networks. We consider three dimensions of this model in relation to shifts in the interception apparatus: first, the growing integration of private firms into the intelligence and security systems of Western states; second, the growth of encryption as standard within platforms and devices, narrowing the possibility of intercepting useful data in transit; and third, the concomitant growth in the value of bulk datasets containing personal and communications data. Instead of intercepting data, states must now integrate it at multiple levels and, in the process, redefine the boundary between public power, private entities, and users.

THE EPOCH OF THE STACK

Perhaps the most comprehensive theoretical model of twenty-first century digital media is Benjamin Bratton's figure of the stack.[3] It designates an "accidental megastructure" that goes beyond any idea of computers as machines, platforms as networks, or the internet as a communication medium. The stack is infrastructural, generating and integrating flows of data, information, people, and things. Its standards and parameters determine how the economy, sovereignty, communication, subjects, and the anthropocentric surface of the planet are made legible and understood. The stack was not designed but emerged through its own recursive operations. It sets the stage for governing the era of "planetary computation" and dividing and defining the informational space it produces.

Bratton proposes six layers to navigate in the stack. Each is linked with the others in complex and specific ways in different places, and each is implicated in the transformations now underway. At the bottom is the *earth* layer, where the resources, minerals, fossil fuels, and physical switching of the computational operations needed to run the stack are found.[4] The geopolitics of the stack are being shaped by competition for rare earth metals needed to produce semiconductors.[5] At the same time, the stack transforms the earth, deploying sensors that map and monitor its surface and the changing climate and filtering the geographical referents of states through sensing and distribution networks. The stack is overlaid on spatial geographic referents, which it must code and operationalize in its own digitized terms. Thus, for instance, the legal distinction between internal communication between two devices in the British Islands and external communication involving at least one party outside the British Islands can only be operationalized by the digital address data that accompanies each packet of information. The geographical layer is nothing "real," just one element within the stack.

The *cloud* layer is the computational layer. It includes all the computer hardware, storage and processing centers, and cable connections that materialize and process digital information in the stack. It is divided between rival cloud-processing companies, national security agencies, and all cloud-computational devices through which the cloud is distributed and accessed.[6] It is in the cloud layer that the functions of the state and the market are being redefined and redistributed. States move into the cloud, and in turn the largest monopolistic cloud entities become like states, taking on functions that were formerly the preserve of the bureaucracy, from Google in Western countries to WeChat in China.[7]

The *city* layer is the urban grid through which bodies, commodities, capital, and interfaces flow. It links offices to warehouses to delivery services to food suppliers, transportation systems to passengers, directing traffic, distributing goods, monitoring, recording, and producing a network made up of these heterogenous elements. The idea of a "smart" city is just one expression of a much more complex assemblage of nonhuman agencies that shape human life, in which sensors range from the visual inputs of cameras to the analysis of particulate matter in the air.[8]

The *address* layer is the epistemic order of the stack: it enables things to be indexed and integrated. Everything incorporated into digital reality as such, from human users to hardware and packets of data, must have an address and must in turn be addressable. The stack generates addresses at multiple scales, producing "ubiquitous computing" as a property of things that act the world. Addresses apply not only to telephone numbers, device identifiers, email addresses, geolocation coordinates, and domain name systems, but also to individual packets of data, cryptocurrency tokens, web addresses of user devices, or even the location of an entry in a database. An address is the condition of visibility in the world of networked computation.[9]

Users' desire and attention is captured and oriented to the stack via the *interface* layer.[10] Interfaces make elements of the stack legible to each other. The interface layer is a structural coupling point "between two complex systems that governs the conditions of exchange between those systems."[11] For example, the India Stack, a government project aiming to integrate identity, payments, and presence into a unified architecture, is also the world's largest suite of open application programming interfaces (APIs) built on the Aadhaar biometric identity database.[12] Interfaces are a performative infrastructure for human users, too. Interfaces are distributed onto screens by platforms, setting the terms of what can be imagined, visualized, and communicated. Legally speaking, contracts, service agreements, and consent forms produce a web of legally mediated interfaces through which the "big tech" platform ecosystem is legitimated; the digital economy can be mapped as a series of interfacial agreements and transfer points.

Human bodies and minds are configured for the stack in the *user* layer and connected through interfaces.[13] It is only as users that populations, legal corporate entities, and individuals are addressed, profiled, quantified, predicted, and addicted in the semantic registers of sense. By the same token, subjects are not limited to the user layer. Subjective competencies are distributed throughout the stack. Predictive models of users' desires are constantly generated by algorithmic analysis of data, and users in turn are indexed to the models. Users are objects of governmentality distributed through interfaces that seek to influence, nudge, inform, warn, and target them, depending on the specificities of the situation. Nevertheless, users are the entropic resources that the stack requires as inputs. They provide fresh information for the system—the noise that irritates the production and development of order. Not all users are human. They may be animals, or more frequently machines, some smarter than others, communicating with one another without understanding a thing.[14]

STACK INTEGRATION

Viewed through the lens of the stack, the interception regime has been transformed at each level. As Snowden demonstrated, the state was already moving into the cloud as the Five-Eyes agencies intercepted global cables and communications bearers. Internally, the UKUSA alliance and its distributed cloud computing services allowed data intercepted anywhere on the planet to be interrogated from anywhere else through a search and visualization platform, XKeyscore.[15] Equally, the stack is moving into the state. This is not a metaphor but an epistemic reality, illustrated by the "TreasureMap," as disclosed by Snowden, which was a National Security Agency (NSA) system for mapping and analyzing the internet at a macro level in near real time. For the NSA, the layers were geographical, physical network, logical network, cyber persona, and persona (see figure 8.1).[16] One can theorize and apply the figure of the stack in multiple ways. Below, we review three changes: the growing integration of private intelligence providers, the response to default end-to-end encryption, and the growing reliance on bulk data.

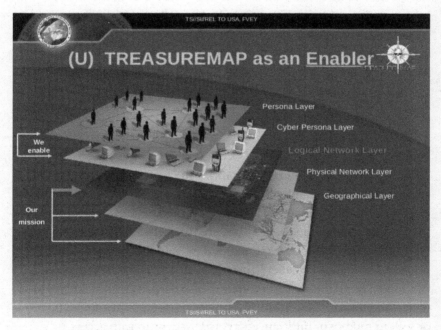

8.1 TreasureMap: the NSA's version of a stack, in an image taken from the Snowden documents. The medium of the internet is inseparable from its layered operations and sociotechnical effects at each level.

PRIVATIZATION

Western intelligence agencies have assigned key functions to outsourced private platforms. In 2021, for instance, the Government Communications Headquarters (GCHQ), the Security Service (MI5), and the Secret Intelligence Service (MI6) signed a contract with Amazon AWS to host data and improve the speed of analytics. The UK's most classified data is now held and analyzed by the private cloud-based platform service. No UK competitor could match Amazon, which already performs the same functions for the US Central Intelligence Agency (CIA).[17] The Snowden documents showed that GCHQ was interested in contracting with Palantir for software to unify its data and make it searchable as early as 2008.[18] The tools of the cloud are multifunctional and can be adapted to interface with very different social and political functions—for example, Palantir today provides "ontological" analytic platforms to Britain's National Health Service and, integrated differently, the Ukrainian military.[19] The private sector is able to work with bulk data gathered at the earth and city layers, where human social life unfolds, to produce insights, distribute them on the cloud, and make them accessible through proprietary interfaces. These are powers that public authorities, constrained by jurisdiction, lack of capital, and constraining frameworks like the Investigatory Powers Act 2016, are unable to produce.[20]

ENCRYPTION

Thinking about the cloud layer clarifies the implications of end-to-end encryption on private platforms. After Snowden, the major commercial platform providers began encrypting communications on and between the devices, software, and storage systems they offered to users by default.[21] Platforms became increasingly like walled gardens, partly to offer users privacy, and partly to defend their proprietary data.[22] This has reduced the utility of traditional interception of data in transit.[23] Increasingly, police, intelligence, and security agencies must try to acquire data at rest or seek to modify or infiltrate encrypted systems to gain access.[24]

The UK government has frequently made statements and proposed policy amendments that would weaken end-to-end encryption. In 2018, GCHQ technical directors publicly proposed a set of "principles" that sought to maintain encryption for "commodity technology" while allowing transparent "exceptional access" regimes for investigatory agencies.[25] The idea is not to compromise encryption at the cloud layer (where data is in transit) but to alter the program without altering the interface layer, which controls what the user knows about their device. In response to receiving a warrant, the platform operator would send an update to the target's device, secretly altering the application so that a third party, the intercepting agency, can extract data stored on the device in plaintext form. The target would continue to communicate on their device normally, with data end-to-end encrypted in transit, not knowing that everything is being secretly copied to the authorities. Dubbed the "ghost protocol," the idea received little political support outside government, not least due to the technical security risks it would present to millions of users, but it illustrated the kind of tactics that have emerged in an era of default encryption.[26]

In its 2023 review of the Investigatory Powers Act 2016, the Home Office reported that in practice, agencies applying for targeted interception warrants now simultaneously seek targeted "equipment interference" warrants. The distinction between data and transit and data at rest is becoming harder to define at the cloud layer.[27] When users communicate through platforms, data is not "sent" as much as copied from one account to another, with copies of all ends of a conversation available on all parties' devices. Accessing data on a device that stores such communication is operationally simpler than intercepting it in transit and attempting to decrypt it.

Anti-encryption tactics were spectacularly illustrated in a series of law enforcement operations against encrypted messaging platforms used (mostly) by criminal networks. In March 2020, the Encrochat network of encrypted phones was infiltrated by French and Dutch authorities, who used a software vulnerability to secret push an update out to around sixty thousand users. Code hidden in the update allowed the authorities to receive data stored on customized Encrochat phones while removing Encrochat's ability to remotely delete data from seized devices. In the UK, the National Crime Agency acquired a Targeted Equipment Interference (TEI) warrant in order to access intercepted data obtained by the French police. On June 12, 2020, Encrochat became aware of the hack and pushed a message to all users, warning they "can no longer guarantee the security of your device." Subsequently, hundreds of arrests were made across Europe, with UK police making over 750 arrests based on intercepted Encrochat messages.[28]

Defendants convicted in the UK on the basis of Encrochat evidence challenged its admissibility on the basis that data had been intercepted in transit, rather than copied while stored, relying on the statutory provision (now contained at section 56 of the Investigatory Powers Act 2016) that excludes intercepted material from being used in legal proceedings. The Court of Appeal rejected this argument, holding that the material had been extracted at rest, not intercepted in transit.[29] Further challenges to the legality of the TEI warrant were rejected by the Investigatory Powers Tribunal in 2023.[30]

In March 2021, European police hacked another encrypted platform favored by criminal networks called Sky, while the US government seized its web domains. The closure of Sky, following from the infiltration of Encrochat, was intended to push criminal users to adopt a platform called Anom.[31] Anom had been built in 2018 by the Australian Federal Police (AFP) to provide organized crime networks with an apparently secure encrypted messaging application and an operating system, ArcaneOS. In reality, it was a trojan horse, copying all messages and data to police servers where the networks it facilitated were mapped and analyzed automatically. In 2019, the FBI joined the operation, funding further promotion and distribution of Anom while accessing data collected on US targets via servers in Lithuania.[32] On June 7, 2021, ten thousand police officers around the world made arrests in "the single largest law enforcement action in history."[33]

If these events demonstrate the efficacy of deception for states, the risks created by deliberately disguising and exploiting security weaknesses have also been illustrated, most notably by Pegasus, a spyware program developed in Israel by NSO Group and sold to governments around the world. Human rights activists, political exiles, lawyers, and investigative journalists around the world have been targeted.[34] In 2022, the High Court in London found that Ghanem Al-Masarir, a political refugee, satirist, and human rights activist from Saudi Arabia, was targeted in the UK by the Kingdom of Saudi Arabia using Pegasus, and gave him permission to sue for damages.[35]

In 2024, in a case brought against the Russian government, the European Court of Human Rights held that any state-imposed obligation to decrypt communications on a given platform that risks weakening end-to-end encryption for all users will always constitute a disproportionate intrusion on the right to private life.[36] Whether this ruling, given against Russia, discourages the UK authorities from their attempts to systemically undermine encryption at the cloud layer remains to be seen.

BULK DATA

A third consequence of the encryption and enclosure of communication and the privatization of functionality is the increasing importance of bulk datasets. This was the principle already underlying the NSA Prism program. In 2013, following Snowden's revelations, the NSA reported that its most significant power—interception—only "touches" 1.6 percent of global internet traffic and examines "less than one part in a million."[37] By contrast, the value of bulk datasets lies not just in the volume of data but in the data's functionality. Former military and intelligence services personnel have developed private firms, often with state financing from the CIA, to develop new tools based on open-source data.[38] For example, in 2015, a US firm called PlanetRisk purchased access to data from "location brokers," intermediaries that collect and agglomerate location data shared through advertising APIs that provide a stream of bulk data, updated daily, for advertisers targeting customers. Bending the terms of service under the cover of "humanitarian" mapping of refugee flows, the company developed a tool called Locomotive for tracking the location of mobile devices globally. The tool was eventually renamed Virtual Intelligence, Surveillance, and Reconnaissance and licensed for use by the US intelligence and military.[39] Anomalous patterns that it uncovered allowed the discovery of Islamic State (ISIS) fighters, the covert locations of US Special Forces, and bodyguards attached to world leaders. By "geofencing" an area of the earth layer, regardless of its formal sovereignty, interfacing with private datasets, and processing the data in the cloud using private computational platforms, the movement patterns and locations of identifiable user-subjects were rendered visible.

The cybersecurity industry is similarly a vast source of intelligence. To combat malware and guard infrastructure, cybersecurity firms and agencies collect and retain connection records in the form of Domain Name System logs that reveal the world's internet traffic. This traffic is mapped across the address layer of the stack, showing which device contacted which server when and for how long. Algorithmic analysis of the data can then reveal patterns indicative of particular threats, which is valuable for network security purposes.[40] When combined with personal datasets and mined for other patterns, this analysis can unveil the inferential connections and associations that GCHQ attempted to develop through its bulk interception Tempora system in 2011.[41]

In the UK and European Union, the principles of the General Data Protection Regulation (GDPR) limit such trade in data to intelligence and security agencies, which may lawfully use it only in accordance with legal frameworks that are compliant with human rights. By contrast, the US has little legal regulation of indiscriminate data surveillance powers derived from private sources, beyond standard contractual clauses. Police at federal, state, and local levels are engaged in data collection and utilization with next to no political or legal oversight.[42] In 2022, the UK–US Data Access Agreement was signed to allow law enforcement access to telecommunications providers in each other's jurisdictions. By 2023, UK law enforcement had made over 10,000 requests to US companies.[43]

LEGAL UPDATES

In 2023, the British government commissioned a review of the first five years of the Investigatory Powers Act by Lord Anderson KC, the former independent reviewer of terrorism legislation whose reports on bulk powers were instrumental in passing the 2016 law. He found that the "world of [the intelligence community] is becoming a mixture of shared systems and services, with specialized tools built on top of them."[44] His report led to legislative reform of the Investigatory Powers Act 2016. First, the act regulates how and when "bulk personal datasets" may be examined and retained by British intelligence or law enforcement agencies. While bulk personal datasets can be acquired without authorization—and many were already held by the time the legislation was passed—before a dataset is used, a warrant must be issued by the secretary of state and approved by a judicial commissioner, following a proportionality assessment compliant with the standards of the European Convention on Human Rights. The bulk personal dataset requirements have now been relaxed to allow the intelligence agencies to unilaterally authorize the use of such datasets where individuals concerned would have "no, or only a low" reasonable expectation of privacy in relation to the data,[45] and to extend the duration of authorizations from six to twelve months for each set.[46] The aim is to enable faster development of better and more flexible artificial intelligence (AI) programs within the intelligence services in line with the commercial sector. The reforms also include a provision for third-party bulk personal dataset warrants. These warrants allow the intelligence and security services to access bulk personal data that is held "electronically by a person other than an intelligence service"—in other words, commercial providers of bulk data.[47]

It seems that the era of interception is giving way to an era of *integration*. The secret collection of communication intercepted or accessed from exploited networks takes effect only through integration with the data-driven systems that, for commercial reasons, produce structured datasets and make them interpretable to users. In this sense, GCHQ and NSA were forerunners, having integrated and shared data through analog and digital networked interfaces long before the open internet was born, but they are now partners in a hybridized public-private national security stack.

The function of the legal system is to enable and smooth the complex and multiplying forms of integrations and divisions now taking place. For *users*, the law gives semantic outline to the operations of the stack. It points to what happens behind the interface in the name of security, without disclosing the details. Law takes effect at the *interface* layer in different ways. It authorizes integration and access to shared data; it embeds the legal requirements of proportionality assessments that users must meet before access is permitted; and it mandates the recording of operations for later audit or for judicial review. Moreover, it mandates the communication and elucidation of these powers so that they are accessible to the public through the distribution of information on screens, including databases of legislation, reports, and case hearings indexed on government websites.

The *address* layer generates the abundance of metadata generated and captured by devices and web services and advertising APIs. It is where the surveillance epiphenomenal to the platform economy finds its rich source of raw material. All transactions and operations are made visible by their addressability.[48] Yet it is also where encryption operates to nullify interception in transit and make access conditional. In the *city* layer, the intelligence services integrate, and the line between the internal and external starts to blur. Data fed in from mobile network infrastructure, Automatic Number Plate Recognition systems, CCTV, and physical surveillance can integrate with the cloud-based processing of data. Machine learning promises to detect threats automatically by recognizing suspicious images or movement patterns or identify a voice.[49] Location data provides a real-time representation of movement in space.

The cloud drives the system forward, producing the intelligence environment as models that map potential threats, preempt risks, and redirect resources. Yet the hardware level matters, too. In 2022, the UK issued legal notices banning the use of Huawei equipment from telecommunications networks in the UK and requiring that it be removed by 2027. The UK passed the National Security Act 2023, marking a pivot away from the focus on international terrorism and back to foreign government agents as a primary national security threat.[50] In 2024, US lawmakers moved to ban TikTok altogether, a popular social media platform owned and operated by a Chinese company.[51]

Where the vertical stack touches the earth, geopolitical divisions matter in new ways. Other integrations and other stacks are possible. In China, the only geopolitical power comparable to the United States, the Communist Party exercises direct control over the economy and the scope of political expression and is seeking to integrate the same architectural features of the stack to those ends. Mass surveillance is facilitated through platforms like Skynet, which integrates CCTV with radio-frequency identification (RFID) chips and mobile phone tracking in cities, and with China's social credit system, which has attracted much Western interest.[52] But it is not digital technology that makes the Chinese political surveillance system powerful; rather, it is "the combination of technology and labour in a system of mass surveillance that can maximize the advantages of both."[53] The geopolitics of the twenty-first century will be defined by rival stacks, different interfacial regimes exercising distinctly different logics of control, power, influence, and resource extraction.[54]

The parasitic question of interception returns as the problem of controlling the location and production of data, if necessary by banning foreign infrastructure and applications. Law once again gives meaning and form to a technical environment that precedes it. Once again, interception shadows communication, but now, law is configured as though it were the code it claims to regulate: contingent, reflexive, open to comments, and constantly evolving through updates and patches.

CONCLUSION

This book has surveyed successive interception assemblages in Britain, from the founding of the postal system to the anticipatory ontologies of planetary computation. The juridical semantics of interception—particularly the organizing device of the warrant—have evolved over time in response to changes in technique and technology. In each media epoch, sovereign power remakes itself, emerging through the strategic codification of communication media. Media, in their design and operation, set the terrain on which power and resistance unfold. Technical standards are grounds for political and legal contestation, but there is nothing predetermined about the assemblages that result.

Law changes more slowly, finding new functions and reflecting new political rationalities. It follows changes in media, viewing them in the rear-view mirror, describing, legitimizing, and attempting to constrain powers that are always already moving ahead. It could not be otherwise, because in each media epoch, law is a discourse mediated by the same technologies and techniques that it imagines itself to master. Law is as much an effect of media standards as interception is. As media develop, promising to become autonomous, they continue to reconfigure the symbolic order that conditions our imagined selves. Media are accelerating. It remains to be seen if law can again catch up.

NOTES

CHAPTER 1

1. Cornelia Vismann and Markus Krajewski, "Computer Juridisms," *Grey Room* 29 (2008): 90–109.

2. Eric Norden, "The Playboy Interview: Marshall McLuhan," *Playboy*, March 1969, https://web.cs.ucdavis.edu/~rogaway/classes/188/spring07/mcluhan.pdf.

3. Friedrich A. Kittler, *Gramophone, Film, Typewriter*, trans. Geoffrey Winthrop-Young (Stanford, CA: Stanford University Press, 1999).

4. Kittler, *Gramophone, Film, Typewriter*, 16.

5. Kittler, *Gramophone, Film, Typewriter*, 3–17;

6. Alan Mathison Turing, "On Computable Numbers, with an Application to the Entscheidungsproblem," *Journal of Math* 58, no. 345–363 (1936): 5.

7. Friedrich Kittler, "Towards an Ontology of Media," *Theory, Culture & Society* 26, no. 2–3 (2009): 23–31.

8. Edward Snowden, *Permanent Record* (London: Macmillan, 2019), 109.

9. Michel Serres, *The Parasite* (Minneapolis: University of Minnesota Press, 2007), 26–27.

10. Alan Rusbridger and Ewen MacAskill, "Edward Snowden Interview—the Edited Transcript," *The Guardian*, July 18, 2014, sec. World News, http://www.theguardian.com/world/2014/jul/18/-sp-edward-snowden-nsa-whistleblower-interview-transcript.

11. Christopher Watkin, *Michel Serres: Figures of Thought* (Edinburgh: Edinburgh University Press, 2020), 300–307.

12. Michel Foucault, *The Birth of Biopolitics*, ed. Arnold I. Davidson, trans. Graham Burchell (Basingstoke: Palgrave Macmillan, 2008), 2.

13. Foucault, *Birth of Biopolitics*, 3.

14. Alain Pottage, "The Materiality of What?," *Journal of Law and Society* 39, no. 1 (March 2012): 167–183.

15. Michel Foucault, "Le Jeu de Michel Foucault," *Dits et Ecrits* 3 (1994): 299; translation and citation by Pottage, "The Materiality of What?," 181.

16. Alain Pottage, "Power as an Art of Contingency: Luhmann, Deleuze, Foucault," *Economy and Society* 27, no. 1 (February 1998): 9.

17. Michel Foucault, *Society Must Be Defended*, trans. David Macey (London: Penguin, 2003), 241.

18. Cornelia Vismann, *Files: Law and Media Technology*, trans. Geoffrey Winthrop-Young (Stanford, CA: Stanford University Press, 2008).

19. John Ferris, *Behind the Enigma: The Authorised History of GCHQ, Britain's Secret Cyber-Intelligence Agency* (London: Bloomsbury Publishing, 2020); Christopher Andrew, *The Defence of the Realm: The Authorized History of MI5* (London: Penguin, 2010); Keith Jeffery, *MI6: The History of the Secret Intelligence Service 1909–1949* (London: Bloomsbury Publishing, 2011).

20. Bernhard Siegert, "Media after Media," in *Media after Kittler*, ed. Eleni Ikoniadou and Scott Wilson (London: Rowman & Littlefield, 2015), 79–91.

21. Vismann, *Files*, 122.

22. Foucault, *Society Must Be Defended*, 243–246.

23. Wolfgang Ernst, *Chronopoetics: The Temporal Being and Operativity of Technological Media* (London: Rowman & Littlefield, 2016).

24. Benjamin H. Bratton, *The Stack: On Software and Sovereignty*, Software Studies (Cambridge, MA: MIT Press, 2015).

CHAPTER 2

1. Saskia Sassen, *Territory, Authority, Rights: From Medieval to Global Assemblages* (Princeton, NJ: Princeton University Press, 2006), 80–81.

2. Samuel Morland, "A Brief Discourse concerning the Nature and Reason of Intelligence," (1695) Add MS 47133 fo. 13–23, Western Manuscripts, British Library.

3. Noel Malcolm, *Reason of State, Propaganda, and the Thirty Years' War: An Unknown Translation by Thomas Hobbes*, (Oxford: Oxford University Press, 2007), 30–31.

4. Malcolm, *Reason of State*, 92.

5. Quentin Skinner, "A Genealogy of the Modern State," *Proceedings of the British Academy* 162 (2009): 327–328.

6. Morland, "Nature and Reason of Intelligence."

7. Skinner, "Genealogy of the Modern State," 339–341.

8. Malcolm, *Reason of State*, 95–97.

9. Michel Foucault, *Security, Territory, Population*, ed. Arnold I. Davidson, trans. Graham Burchell (New York: Palgrave Macmillan, 2007), 274.

10. Alan Marshall, *Intelligence and Espionage in the English Republic C. 1600-60* (Manchester: Manchester University Press, 2023), 177–211.

11. Wildman cited by C. H. Firth, "Thurloe and the Post Office," *English Historical Review* 13 (1898): 531.

12. Wildman cited by Firth, "Thurloe and the Post Office," 533.

13. Cornelia Vismann, *Files: Law and Media Technology*, trans. Geoffrey Winthrop-Young (Stanford, CA: Stanford University Press, 2008), 5–6.

14. Alan Marshall, *Intelligence and Espionage in the Reign of Charles II, 1660–1685* (Cambridge: Cambridge University Press, 2003), 86.

15. James Daybell, "Material Meanings and the Social Signs of Manuscript Letters in Early Modern England," *Literature Compass* 6, no. 3 (2009): 647–667.

16. David Underdown, *Royalist Conspiracy in England, 1649–1660* (New Haven, CT: Yale University Press, 1960), 248, 289.

17. Harold Innis, "The Coming of Paper," *Intermédialités: Histoire et Théorie Des Arts, Des Lettres et Des Techniques/Intermediality: History and Theory of the Arts, Literature and Technologies*, no. 17 (2011): 232–255, https://doi.org/10.7202/1005761ar.

18. Bernhard Siegert, *Relays: Literature as an Epoch of the Postal System*, trans. Kevin Repp (Stanford, CA: Stanford University Press, 1999), 31.

19. Wildman, quoted in Marshall, *Intelligence and Espionage*, 85; see also Underdown, *Royalist Conspiracy in England*, 61.

20. Marshall, *Intelligence and Espionage*, 85.

21. Susan E. Whyman, *The Pen and the People: English Letter Writers 1660–1800* (Oxford: Oxford University Press, 2009), 49.

22. E. J. B. Allen, *Post and Courier Service in the Diplomacy of Early Modern Europe* (The Hague: Martinus Nijhoff, 1972), 3–12.

23. J. C. Hemmeon, *History of the British Post Office* (Cambridge, MA: Harvard University Press, 1912), 4.

24. Rory Cormac and Richard J. Aldrich, *Spying and the Crown: The Secret Relationship between British Intelligence and the Royals* (London: Atlantic Books, 2022), 20.

25. Stephen Alford, *The Watchers: A Secret History of the Reign of Elizabeth I* (London: Penguin, 2013), 17–19.

26. Hemmeon, *History of the British Post Office*, 6.

27. Roger Lockyer, *Tudor and Stuart Britain, 1485–1714* (Harlow: Pearson/Longman, 2005), 145.

28. Lockyer, *Tudor and Stuart Britain*, 226–228.

29. F. H. Cramer, "The Hanseatic League," *Current History* 17 (96) (1949): 88.

30. Hemmeon, *History of the British Post Office*, 190.

31. Allen, *Post and Courier Service*, 2; H. C. Barnard, "The Messageries of the University of Paris," *British Journal of Educational Studies* 4, no. 1 (1955): 49–56.

32. *Report from the Secret Committee on the Post-Office, Together with the Appendix* (C582, 1844), 21.

33. P. O. Beale, *A History of the Post in England from the Romans to the Stuarts* (Brookfield: Ashgate, 1998), 27.

34. Hemmeon, *History of the British Post Office*, 12.

35. Mary Paget, *The King's Messengers, 1199–1377: A Contribution to the History of the Royal Household* (London: Arnold, 1961).

36. Allen, *Post and Courier Service*, 10–20.

37. Hemmeon, *History of the British Post Office*, 1–20; see also William Lewins, *Her Majesty's Mails: A History of the Post Office and an Industrial Account of Its Present Condition* (London: S. Low, Son, and Marston, 1864), 32–34.

38. Hemmeon, *History of the British Post Office*, 13–18; *Report from the Secret Committee on the Post-Office*, 8–9.

39. Whyman, *The Pen and the People*, 48.

40. See, for instance, "House of Commons Journal Volume 2: 10 December 1642," in *Journal of the House of Commons: Volume 2, 1640–1643* (London, 1802), 883–884, accessed April 6, 2024, British History Online, https://www.british-history.ac.uk/commons-jrnl/vol2/pp883-884.

41. Jason Peacey, *Politicians and Pamphleteers: Propaganda during the English Civil Wars and Interregnum* (Aldershot: Ashgate, 2004).

42. Lois Potter, *Secret Rites and Secret Writing: Royalist Literature 1641–1660* (Cambridge: Cambridge University Press, 1989), 39–40.

43. Cited in Potter, *Secret Rites and Secret Writing*, 39.

44. Potter, *Secret Rites and Secret Writing*, 39.

45. Potter, *Secret Rites and Secret Writing*, 60.

46. Lewins, *Her Majesty's Mails*, 33–34.

47. Hemmeon, *History of the British Post Office*, 193–194.

48. J. Wilson Hyde, *The Early History of the Post in Grant and Farm* (London: Adam and Charles Black, 1894), 225–233.

49. Stephen Sedley, *Lions under the Throne: Essays on the History of English Public Law* (Cambridge: Cambridge University Press, 2015), 83–106. Cromwell's Interregnum government saw legislation as a mechanism for remaking the state.

50. "An Act for the Settling of the Postage of England, Scotland and Ireland," (1657) POST 114/1 Postal Museum and Archive, London.

51. Vismann, *Files*, 22.

52. Hyde, *Early History of the Post*, 238.

53. Hyde, *Early History of the Post*, 238.

54. "Thurloe Papers, First Series. Collection of State Letters and Papers Relating to Events at Home and Abroad Chiefly in the Time of the Commonwealth," (1692) Add MS 4155–4159, Western Manuscripts, British Library.

55. Marshall, *Intelligence and Espionage in the Reign of Charles II*, 20–27.

56. Whyman, *The Pen and the People*, 49.

57. Florence Grier Evans, *The Principal Secretary of State: A Survey of the Office from 1558 to 1680* (Manchester: Manchester University Press, 1923), 278–297; Peter Fraser, *The Intelligence of the Secretaries of State and Their Monopoly of Licensed News, 1660–1688* (Cambridge: Cambridge University Press, 1956), 30–31; Whyman, *The Pen and the People*, 50.

58. James Walker, "The Secret Service under Charles II and James II," *Transactions of the Royal Historical Society* 15 (1932): 211.

59. David Kahn, *The Codebreakers: The Comprehensive History of Secret Communication from Ancient Times to the Internet*, 2nd ed. (New York: Scribner, 1996), esp. chap. 4.

60. James Daybell, "Secret Letters," in *The Material Letter in Early Modern England: Manuscript Letters and the Culture and Practices of Letter-Writing, 1512–1635*, ed. James Daybell (London: Palgrave Macmillan, 2012), 148.

61. Friedrich L. Bauer, *Decrypted Secrets: Methods and Maxims of Cryptology*, 3rd ed. (Berlin: Springer, 2002), 12–18.

62. Bauer, *Decrypted Secrets*, 18–24.

63. Bauer, *Decrypted Secrets*, 24.

64. Bauer, *Decrypted Secrets*, 8.

65. Cited by Potter, *Secret Rites and Secret Writing*, 39. See also Bauer, *Decrypted Secrets*, 8.

66. Kahn, *Codebreakers*, 167.

67. John Wallis, "Letter-Book of John Wallis 1651–1701," (1701) Add MS 32499, Western Manuscripts, British Library.

68. Kahn, *Codebreakers*, 161.

69. Potter, *Secret Rites and Secret Writing*, 40.

70. Eva Horn, "Logics of Political Secrecy," *Theory, Culture & Society* 28, no. 7–8 (2011): 103–122.

71. Siegert, *Relays*, 8.

72. Hemmeon, *History of the British Post Office*, 3–15.

73. Kenneth Ellis, *The Post Office in the Eighteenth Century: A Study in Administrative History* (Oxford: Oxford University Press, 1958), 21.

74. Ellis, *The Post Office in the Eighteenth Century*, 6–8.

75. Whyman, *The Pen and the People*, 47–58.

76. Whyman, *The Pen and the People*, 77.

77. Whyman, *The Pen and the People*, 56–57, 106, 128–129.

78. Siegert, *Relays*, 57.

79. Thomas Gardiner, "A General Survey of the Post Office," (1682) Add MS 62091, Western Manuscripts, British Library. Modern spellings have been inserted for ease of reading.

80. On discipline, see Michel Foucault, *Discipline and Punish: The Birth of the Prison*, trans. Alan Sheridan (London: Penguin, 1991), 139–162.

81. Gardiner, "General Survey of the Post Office."

82. Gardiner, "General Survey of the Post Office."

83. Hemmeon, *History of the British Post Office*, 29.

84. Frank Staff, *The Penny Post, 1680–1918* (London: Lutterworth Press, 1964), 35–37.

85. Fraser, *Intelligence of the Secretaries of State*, 128–132.

86. Hemmeon, *History of the British Post Office*, 30.

87. Hemmeon, *History of the British Post Office*, 14.

88. Hemmeon, *History of the British Post Office*, 37.

89. Whyman, *The Pen and the People*, 56–67.

90. Edward Raymond Turner, "The Secrecy of the Post," *English Historical Review* 33, no. 131 (1918): 320–327.

91. *Report from the Secret Committee on the Post-Office*, 9–10.

92. "Warrant," *Oxford English Dictionary* (Oxford: Oxford University Press), continually updated at https://www.oed.com/.

93. John H. Fisher, "Chancery and the Emergence of Standard Written English in the Fifteenth Century," *Speculum* 52, no. 4 (1977): 870–899.

94. Fisher, "Chancery and the Emergence of Standard Written English."

95. Malcolm Richardson, "The Fading Influence of the Medieval Ars Dictaminis in England After 1400," *Rhetorica* 19(2) (2001), 229.

96. G. R. Elton, *The Tudor Revolution in Government* (Cambridge: Cambridge University Press, 1953), 298.

97. Elton, *Tudor Revolution in Government*, 298–303.

98. Robert Jackson, *Sovereignty: The Evolution of an Idea* (Cambridge: Polity, 2007), 2.

99. But see Marshall, *Intelligence and Espionage in the English Republic*, 52–56.

100. Sassen, *Territory, Authority, Rights*, 32–41.

101. Lawrence Goldman, ed., "Coleman [Coleman], Edward (1636–1678), Courtier," in *Oxford Dictionary of National Biography* (Oxford: Oxford University Press, 2009).

102. Marshall, *Intelligence and Espionage in the Reign of Charles II*, 82–83.

103. J. Sommerville, *Politics and Ideology in England 1603–1640* (London: Longman, 1986), 100–101.

104. Sir Daniel Norman Chester, *The English Administrative System 1780–1870* (Oxford: Clarendon Press, 1981), 12.

105. Evans, *Principal Secretary of State*, 142–143.

106. Evans, *Principal Secretary of State*, 284.

107. Martin Loughlin, *Foundations of Public Law* (Oxford: Oxford University Press, 2010), 379–381.

108. Carl Schmitt, *Dialogues on Power and Space* (Malden, MA: Polity, 2015), 34–35.

109. Feisal G. Mohamed, *Sovereignty: Seventeenth-Century England and the Making of the Modern Political Imaginary* (Oxford: Oxford University Press, 2020), 32.

110. Loughlin, *Foundations of Public Law*, 380.

111. Thomas Poole, *Reason of State* (Cambridge: Cambridge University Press, 2015), 21-35.

112. Quentin Skinner, "Conquest and Consent: Thomas Hobbes and the Engagement Controversy," in *The Interregnum: The Quest for Settlement*, ed. G. E. Aylmer (London: Macmillan Press, 1972), 79–98.

113. Skinner, "Genealogy of the Modern State," 348.

114. Mohamed, *Sovereignty*, 34.

115. Skinner, "Genealogy of the Modern State," 351.

116. Michel Foucault, *The Birth of Biopolitics*, ed. Arnold I. Davidson, trans. Graham Burchell (Basingstoke: Palgrave Macmillan, 2008), 8–10.

117. Thomas Hobbes, *Leviathan* (London: Penguin, 2017), part II.

118. Poole, *Reason of State*, 53.

119. Foucault, *Security, Territory, Population*, 278.

CHAPTER 3

1. Michel Foucault, *Discipline and Punish: The Birth of the Prison*, trans. Alan Sheridan (London: Penguin, 1991).

2. See the series beginning "Home Office: Post Office Correspondence 1787–1816," (1816) HO 33/1, The National Archives of the UK (hereafter National Archives).

3. Kenneth Ellis, *The Post Office in the Eighteenth Century: A Study in Administrative History* (Oxford: Oxford University Press, 1958), 62.

4. R. v. Dr. Hensey (1758) 96 E.R. 1212; (1758) 2 Keny. 366; [1758] 1 WLUK 60; (1758) "19 Howell's State Trials," 1341.

5. Lindsay Farmer, "State Trials," in *The New Oxford Companion to Law* (Oxford: Oxford University Press, 2008); Thomas Bayly Howell, ed., *A Complete Collection of State Trials and Proceedings for High Treason and Other Crimes and Misdemeanors: With Notes and Other Illustrations* (London: T. C. Hansard, 1816).

6. "The Pretender" was the exiled son of James II, allied with the French. His father had lost the English throne in 1689 when Parliament overthrew him. The Pretender's supporters in England were the Jacobites, opponents of the ruling Hanoverian dynasty.

7. "19 Howell's State Trials," 1369–1370.

8. (1758) "19 Howell's State Trials," 1370.

9. Michel Foucault, "Governmentality," in *Power*, ed. James D. Faubion, trans. Robert Hurley, vol. 3, *Essential Works of Foucault 1954–1984* (London: Penguin, 2002), 211.

10. Jeremy Black, "Exceptionalism, Structure and Contingency: Britain as a European State, 1688–1815," *Diplomacy & Statecraft* 8, no. 3 (1997): 11–26.

11. Paul S. Fritz, "The Anti-Jacobite Intelligence System of the English Ministers, 1715–1745," *The Historical Journal* 16, no. 2 (1973): 265.

12. Jeremy Black, "Eighteenth Century Intercepted Dispatches," *Journal of the Society of Archivists* 11, no. 4 (October 1990): 138.

13. Ellis, *Post Office in the Eighteenth Century*, 60.

14. Ellis, *Post Office in the Eighteenth Century*, 64.

15. Black, "Eighteenth Century Intercepted Dispatches," 138.

16. Ellis, *Post Office in the Eighteenth Century*, 72–79.

17. Ellis, *Post Office in the Eighteenth Century*, 65.

18. Ellis, *Post Office in the Eighteenth Century*, 81–83.

19. Ellis, *Post Office in the Eighteenth Century*, 69–70.

20. Black, "Eighteenth Century Intercepted Dispatches," 140–141; see Florence Grier Evans, *The Principal Secretary of State: A Survey of the Office from 1558 to 1680* (Manchester: Manchester University Press, 1923), 177.

21. Ellis, *Post Office in the Eighteenth Century*, 75.

22. David Kahn, *The Codebreakers: The Comprehensive History of Secret Communication from Ancient Times to the Internet*, 2nd ed. (New York: Scribner, 1996), 166–169.

23. "Report from Secret Committee of the House of Lords Relative to GPO," (1844) HD 3/16, National Archives; Kahn, *Codebreakers*, 170–171.

24. Ellis, *Post Office in the Eighteenth Century*, 127–131.

25. A. Lang, "The Bishop's Plot," ed. William III Blackwood, *Blackwood's Edinburgh Magazine* 161, no. 975 (January 1897): 90–99.

26. Edward Raymond Turner, "The Secrecy of the Post," *English Historical Review* 33, no. 131 (1918): 321.

27. Kahn, *Codebreakers*, 170.

28. "An Act for Establishing a General Post Office for All Her Majesty's Dominions," (9 Ann.) C A P. X. (11) § (1710), s XL.

29. "Act for Establishing a General Post Office for All Her Majesty's Dominions."

30. Fritz, "The Anti-Jacobite Intelligence System of the English Ministers," 266.

31. Mark A. Thomson, *The Secretaries of State 1681–1782* (Oxford: Clarendon Press, 1932), 154; *Report from the Secret Committee on the Post-Office, Together with the Appendix* (C582, 1844), 8.

32. *Report from the Secret Committee on the Post-Office*, 9.

33. Black, "Eighteenth Century Intercepted Dispatches," 139–141.

34. "Letters and Papers," (1726) SP 35/62 fo. 289, National Archives.

35. *Report from the Secret Committee on the Post-Office*, 12.

NOTES TO CHAPTER 3

36. *Report from the Secret Committee on the Post-Office*, 114.

37. "HO 42/208 Letters and Papers," Correspondence Relating to Post Office, Customs, Excise, Auditors' Office, College of Arms, Lord Chamberlain and the University of Oxford, 1792, 101, National Archives.

38. Frederick Burwick, "The Language of High Treason: Thomas Hardy, John Horne Tooke, and the Edinburgh Seven," *Huntington Library Quarterly* 63, no. 3 (2000): 263–275.

39. Cornelia Vismann, *Files: Law and Media Technology*, trans. Geoffrey Winthrop-Young (Stanford, CA: Stanford University Press, 2008), 6.

40. Walter J. Ong, *Orality and Literacy*, 3rd ed. (Routledge, 2012), 99–101; Elena Esposito, *Artificial Communication* (Cambridge, MA: MIT Press, 2022), 22–23.

41. Adam Tomkins and Paul F. Scott, *Entick v Carrington: 250 Years of the Rule of Law* (Oxford: Hart Publishing, 2015 [1765]), EWHC KB J98; (1765) "19 Howell's State Trials," 1029.

42. Jacob Rowbottom, "The Propaganda Wars and Liberty of the Press," in *Entick v. Carrington: 250 Years of the Rule of Law*, ed. Adam Tomkins and Paul F. Scott (Oxford: Hart Publishing, 2015), 85–107.

43. Rowbottom, "The Propaganda Wars," 89–95.

44. Rowbottom, "The Propaganda Wars," 88.

45. Tom Hickman, "Revisiting Entick v Carrington: Seditious Libel and State Security Laws in Eighteenth-Century England," in *Entick v Carrington: 250 Years of the Rule of Law*, ed. Adam Tomkins and Paul F. Scott (Oxford: Hart Publishing, 2015), 47.

46. Hickman, "Revisiting Entick v Carrington," 82–84.

47. Foucault, "Governmentality," 211.

48. Martin Loughlin, *Foundations of Public Law* (Oxford: Oxford University Press, 2010), 423.

49. Loughlin, *Foundations of Public Law*, 423–24.

50. William Blackstone, *The Oxford Edition of Blackstone's: Commentaries on the Laws of England: Book I: Of the Rights of Persons*, ed. David Lemmings (Oxford: Oxford University Press, 2016), 291.

51. Blackstone, *Commentaries I*, 292.

52. Martin Loughlin, "The State, the Crown and the Law," in *The Nature of the Crown: A Legal and Political Analysis*, ed. Maurice Sunkin and Sebastian Payne (Oxford: Oxford University Press, 1999), 33–76.

53. Friedrich Kittler, "Authorship and Love," *Theory, Culture & Society* 32, no. 3 (2015): 15–47.

54. Ramie Targoff, *John Donne, Body and Soul* (Chicago: University of Chicago Press, 2008), 30–31.

55. Susan E. Whyman, *The Pen and the People: English Letter Writers 1660–1800* (Oxford: Oxford University Press, 2009), 217.

56. Whyman, *The Pen and the People*, 217.

57. Whyman, *The Pen and the People*, 71.

58. Dena Goodman, "Epistolary Property: Michel de Servan and the Plight of Letters on the Eve of the French Revolution," in *Early Modern Conceptions of Property*, ed. John Brewer and Susan Staves (London: Routledge, 1995), 350.

59. Goodman, "Epistolary Property," 353.

60. Goodman, "Epistolary Property," 356.

61. "Censorship Exposed; or Letters Addressed to the R. H. V. Sidmouth and Mrs. Benbow," (1818) HO 33/2/13, National Archives.

62. The comprehensive account is Bernard Porter, *Plots and Paranoia: History of Political Espionage in Britain, 1790–1988* (London: Routledge, 1989), 1–80. The term "police state" was applied with a century of hindsight by constitutional theorist Harold J. Laski, *Parliamentary Government in England*, 1st ed. (London: Allen & Unwin, 1938), 21.

63. Porter, *Plots and Paranoia*, 60–64, 76.

64. David Vincent, *The Culture of Secrecy: Britain 1832–1998* (Oxford: Oxford University Press, 1999), 1–10.

65. Denis Mack Smith, *Mazzini* (New Haven, CT: Yale University Press, 1996), 41.

66. Smith, *Mazzini*, 42.

67. Charles Greville, *The Greville Memoirs, Volume V* (London: Longmans, Green and Co., 1888), 255.

68. Rory Cormac and Richard J. Aldrich, *Spying and the Crown: The Secret Relationship between British Intelligence and the Royals* (London: Atlantic Books, 2022), 59.

69. "Newspaper Cuttings Relating to Letter Opening," (1844/1845) POST 23/7, Postal Museum and Archive, London.

70. *Report from the Secret Committee on the Post-Office*; "Report from Secret Committee of the House of Lords Relative to GPO," (1844) HD 3/16, National Archives.

71. "Post Office—Opening Letters," House of Commons Debates, July 18, 1844.

72. "Post Office—Opening Letters"; Vincent, *Culture of Secrecy*, 6, notes that in his replies to Parliament, Graham implicitly rebuked his fellow MPs for hypocrisy but could not spell it out publicly.

73. Nicholas Wade, "Glomar Explorer: CIA's Salvage Ship a Giant Leap in Ocean Engineering," *Science* 192, no. 4246 (1976): 1313–1315; N. Wade, "Glomar Explorer Said Successful After All," *Science* 194, no. 4270 (1976): 1142. NCND was the reply given to journalists who made Freedom of Information Act requests about the Glomar Explorer, a secret CIA attempt to raise a sunken Soviet nuclear submarine.

74. *Report from the Secret Committee on the Post-Office*, 12.

75. Sir Daniel Norman Chester, *The English Administrative System 1780–1870* (Oxford: Clarendon Press, 1981) 123, 282.

76. *Report from the Secret Committee on the Post-Office*, 9.

77. *Report from the Secret Committee on the Post-Office*, 10.

78. Vismann, *Files*, 81.

79. Michel Foucault, *Security, Territory, Population*, ed. Arnold I. Davidson, trans. Graham Burchell (New York: Palgrave Macmillan, 2007), 353.

80. Foucault, *Security, Territory, Population*, 354.

81. *Report from the Secret Committee on the Post-Office*, 7–11.

82. *Report from the Secret Committee on the Post-Office*, 14.

83. *Report from the Secret Committee on the Post-Office*, 10–11.

84. *Report from the Secret Committee on the Post-Office*, 18–19.

85. *Report from the Secret Committee on the Post-Office*, 14–15.

86. J. M. Beattie, *Crime and the Courts in England, 1660–1800* (Oxford: Clarendon Press, 1986).

87. *Report from the Secret Committee on the Post-Office*, 15.

88. Vismann, *Files*, 120.

89. Cormac and Aldrich, *Spying and the Crown*, 57–68.

90. Vincent, *Culture of Secrecy*.

91. "Newspaper Cuttings Relating to Letter Opening," (1844/1845) POST 23/7 Postal Museum and Archive, London.

92. David Vincent, *I Hope I Don't Intrude: Privacy and Its Dilemmas in Nineteenth-Century Britain* (Oxford: Oxford University Press, 2015), 213–215.

93. *Report from the Secret Committee on the Post-Office*, 3.

94. *Report from the Secret Committee on the Post-Office*, 19.

95. *Report from the Secret Committee on the Post-Office*, 18.

96. *Report from the Secret Committee on the Post-Office*, 19.

97. *Report from the Secret Committee on the Post-Office*.

98. Vincent, *Culture of Secrecy*, 1–25.

99. Ellis, *Post Office in the Eighteenth Century*, 141–42.

100. "Report of the Committee of Privy Councillors Appointed to Inquire into the Interception of Communications (Birkett Report)," para. 136.

101. John Ferris, "Before 'Room 40': The British Empire and Signals Intelligence, 1898–1914," *Journal of Strategic Studies* 12, no. 4 (December 1989): 434.

102. Hill quoted in Porter, *Plots and Paranoia*, 78.

103. "Detection of Lottery Correspondence in the Post; Secretary of State's Warrant of 19 April 1920," (1934) HO 45/25958, National Archives.

104. Porter, *Plots and Paranoia*, 79.

105. Porter, *Plots and Paranoia*, 90.

106. Porter, *Plots and Paranoia*, 112–119; Christopher Andrew, *The Defence of the Realm: The Authorized History of MI5* (London: Penguin, 2010), 5.

107. Michel Foucault, *The Birth of Biopolitics*, ed. Arnold I. Davidson, trans. Graham Burchell (Basingstoke: Palgrave Macmillan, 2008), 12–13.

108. Foucault, *Birth of Biopolitics*, 15.

109. Alain Pottage, "Power as an Art of Contingency: Luhmann, Deleuze, Foucault," *Economy and Society* 27, no. 1 (February 1998).

110. Pottage, "Power as an Art of Contingency," 13.

111. J. C. Hemmeon, *History of the British Post Office* (Cambridge, MA: Harvard University Press, 1912), 61.

112. M. J. Daunton, *Royal Mail: The Post Office Since 1840* (London: Athlone Press, 1985).

113. Hemmeon, *History of the British Post Office*, 172.

114. Bernhard Siegert, *Relays: Literature as an Epoch of the Postal System*, trans. Kevin Repp (Stanford, CA: Stanford University Press, 1999), 100–107.

115. Daunton, *Royal Mail*, 40–43.

116. This description was issued by the mayor's office and the Council of Vienna, 1771, cited in Markus Krajewski, *Paper Machines: About Cards & Catalogs, 1548–1929*, trans. Peter Krapp (Cambridge, MA: MIT Press, 2011), 27.

117. Krajewski, *Paper Machines*, 28.

118. "Draft Report by the Metropolitan Board of Works, Including Post Office Proposals for New Street Names in Central London," (1856) POST 17/120, Postal Museum and Archive, London.

119. Michel Foucault, "Truth and Juridical Forms," in *Power*, ed. James D. Faubion, trans. Robert Hurley, vol. 3, *Essential Works of Foucault 1954–1984* (London: Penguin, 2002), 80–81.

120. Siegert, *Relays*, 108–127.

121. Niklas Luhmann, *Social Systems*, trans. John Bednarz and Dirk Baecker (Stanford, CA: Stanford University Press, 1995).

122. Siegert, *Relays*, 76.

123. John Durham Peters, *Speaking into the Air: A History of the Idea of Communication* (Chicago: University of Chicago, 2000).

124. Vincent, *I Hope I Don't Intrude*, 218.

125. Christopher Moran, *Classified: Secrecy and the State in Modern Britain* (Cambridge: Cambridge University Press, 2012).

126. Moran, *Classified*, 25.

127. One Fleet Street newspaper advertised a rate of £5 for minor news and £100 for "great secrets" (Moran, *Classified*, 33).

128. "Report of the Committee of Privy Councillors Appointed to Inquire into the Interception of Communications (Birkett Report)," paras. 80–81.

129. Jeremy Bentham, "Of Publicity," in *Selected Writings*, ed. Stephen Engelmann (New Haven, CT: Yale University Press, 2011), 298. For further discussion, see Jodi

Dean, *Publicity's Secret: How Technoculture Capitalizes on Democracy* (Ithaca, NY: Cornell University Press, 2002).

130. Bentham, "Of Publicity," 300.

131. Bentham, "Of Publicity," 302.

CHAPTER 4

1. Iwan Rhys Morus, "'The Nervous System of Britain': Space, Time and the Electric Telegraph in the Victorian Age," *British Journal for the History of Science* 33, no. 4 (2000): 456.

2. Iwan Rhys Morus, "The Electric Ariel: Telegraphy and Commercial Culture in Early Victorian England," *Victorian Studies* 39, no. 3 (1996): 339.

3. Wolfgang Ernst, *Chronopoetics: The Temporal Being and Operativity of Technological Media* (London: Rowman & Littlefield, 2016), 175.

4. Ernst, *Chronopoetics*, 174.

5. Morus, "Electric Ariel," 342.

6. Morus, "Electric Ariel," 361–362.

7. Morus, "Nervous System of Britain," 460.

8. Cooke, quoted in Morus, "Nervous System of Britain," 461.

9. Morus, "Electric Ariel," 350.

10. Cooke cited in Morus, "Nervous System of Britain," 461.

11. F. C. Mather, "The Railways, the Electric Telegraph and Public Order during the Chartist Period, 1837–48," *History* 38, no. 132 (1953): 49–51, https://doi.org/10.1111/j.1468-229X.1953.tb00989.x.

12. For discussion, see Paul F. Scott, "The First Interception Provision: Section 4 of the Official Secrets Act 1920," *Journal of Legal History* 43, no. 3 (2022): 325–379.

13. Morus, "Nervous System of Britain," 462.

14. Morus, "Nervous System of Britain," 470.

15. Jean-François Fava-Verde, "Managing Privacy: Cryptography or Private Networks of Communication in the Nineteenth Century," *Technology and Culture* 61, no. 3 (2020): 798–814, https://doi.org/10.1353/tech.2020.0074.

16. Niklas Luhmann, *The Reality of the Mass Media*, trans. Kathleen Cross (Cambridge: Polity, 2000).

17. John Handel, "The Material Politics of Finance: The Ticker Tape and the London Stock Exchange, 1860s–1890s," *Enterprise & Society* 23, no. 3 (September 2022): 857–887, https://doi.org/10.1017/eso.2021.3.

18. Fava-Verde, "Managing Privacy."

19. Alex Preda, "Socio-Technical Agency in Financial Markets: The Case of the Stock Ticker," *Social Studies of Science* 36, no. 5 (2006): 772.

20. For a full exposition of telegraphy's impact on the stock exchange, see Handel, "Material Politics of Finance."

21. Urs Stäheli, *Spectacular Speculation: Thrills, the Economy, and Popular Discourse* (Stanford, CA: Stanford University Press, 2013), 73–81.

22. Preda, "Socio-Technical Agency," 774.

23. Simone Fari, *Victorian Telegraphy before Nationalization* (Basingstoke: Palgrave Macmillan, 2015), 34.

24. Ronald Wenzlhuemer, *Connecting the Nineteenth-Century World* (Cambridge: Cambridge University Press, 2012), 174–175.

25. Morus, "Electric Ariel," 368–372.

26. Electric and International Telegraph Company, *Government and the Telegraphs: Statement of the Case of the Electric and International Telegraph Company against the Government Bill for Acquiring the Telegraphs* (London: E. Wilson, 1868), 78–79 (emphasis in the original), https://catalog.hathitrust.org/Record/006847104; quoted in Fari, *Victorian Telegraphy before Nationalization*, 176.

27. Telegraph Act 1868, section 3.

28. Morus, "Nervous System of Britain," 469.

29. Markus Krajewski, *World Projects: Global Information Before World War I*, trans. Charles Marcrum II (Minneapolis: University of Minnesota Press, 2014), 1–32.

30. The efficacy of military telegraphy in the Civil War is questioned by Roscoe Pound, "The Military Telegraph in the Civil War," *Proceedings of the Massachusetts Historical Society* 66 (1936): 185–203.

31. Brian Hochman, *The Listeners* (Cambridge, MA: Harvard University Press, 2022), 39–42.

32. Hochman, *The Listeners*, 43.

33. *Cornubian and Redruth Times*, November 12, 1869.

34. Fari, *Victorian Telegraphy before Nationalization*, 195.

35. "Strike of Telegraphists 1872, POST 30/215," (1871), BT Archives.

36. "Strike of Telegraphists 1872, POST 30/215," (1871), BT Archives.

37. "Minute to PMG, November 28, 1871," in "Strike of Telegraphists 1872, POST 30/215," (1871), BT Archives.

38. "Minute to PMG, November 28, 1871," in "Strike of Telegraphists 1872, POST 30/215," (1871), BT Archives.

39. It is briefly mentioned by Charles R. Perry, "Frank Ives Scudamore and the Post Office Telegraphs," *Albion: A Quarterly Journal Concerned with British Studies* 12, no. 4 (1980): 350–367. There is no mention in any of the major histories of the Post Office, such as M. J. Daunton, *Royal Mail: The Post Office Since 1840* (London: Athlone Press, 1985); A. M. Ogilvie, "A New History of the Post Office," *The Economic Journal* 23, no. 89 (1913): 137–141; J. C. Hemmeon, *History of the British Post Office* (Cambridge, MA: Harvard University Press, 1912); Duncan Campbell-Smith, *Masters of the Post: The Authorized History of the Royal Mail* (London: Penguin, 2012); Fari, *Victorian Telegraphy before Nationalization*.

40. Wenzlhuemer, *Connecting the Nineteenth-Century World*, 167.

41. "Tapping the Wires," *Blackpool Gazette & Herald*, November 9, 1883; *Manchester Evening News*, November 3, 1883.

42. "Tapping the Wires," *Globe*, November 4, 1885.

43. Hochman, *Listeners*, 19.

44. Friedrich A. Kittler and Michael Metteer, *Discourse Networks 1800/1900* (Stanford, CA: Stanford University Press, 1992), 191–192.

45. Fava-Verde, "Managing Privacy."

46. These features influenced the decision to nationalize telegraphy; see "A Report to the Postmaster General, July 1866, HIC 0197/005/033," (1866), BT Archives.

47. James Gleick, *The Information* (London: Fourth Estate, 2012), 158.

48. Phil Glover, *Protecting National Security: A History of British Communications Investigation Regulation* (Abingdon: Routledge, 2022), 68.

49. This is a point made by Scott, "First Interception Provision."

50. Fava-Verde, "Managing Privacy."

51. Henry James, "In the Cage," in *In the Cage and Other Stories* (London: Penguin, 1972).

52. Henry James, cited by Richard Menke, "Telegraphic Realism: Henry James's *In the Cage*," *PMLA* 115, no. 5 (2000): 975–990, https://doi.org/10.2307/463265.

53. Hans Ulrich Gumbrecht, "Second Order Observation Historicized—An Epistemological Frame Narrative," in *Design of the In/Human* (Stuttgart: Akademie Schloss Solitude, 2010), http://www.design-in-human.de/lectures/gumbrecht.html.

54. Richard J. Noakes, "Telegraphy Is an Occult Art: Cromwell Fleetwood Varley and the Diffusion of Electricity to the Other World," *British Journal for the History of Science* 32, no. 4 (1999): 421–459.

55. Morus, "Nervous System of Britain."

56. This point was developed by Richard Menke; see Menke, "Telegraphic Realism: Henry James's *In the Cage*."

57. "Telegraphs: Interception of Letters in Criminal Case. L.O.O.797 as to Exercise of Power by Secretary of State HO 144/164/A42354," (1886), 1, National Archives.

58. "Out Letters to the General Post Office regarding the Interception of Telegrams and Letters (1887–1899) HO 151/7," National Archives.

59. "Disturbances: Warrant Issued for Production of Telegram Addressed to Anarchist Prisoner at Stafford from the 'United Anarchist Groups, London,' HO 144/242/A53582B," (1892), National Archives.

60. "Telegraphs: Mode of Transmitting Letters Intercepted under Warrant of Secretary of State HO 144/203/A47869," (1887), National Archives.

61. "Home Office Correspondence 1782–1979," National Archives, accessed September 11, 2017, http://www.nationalarchives.gov.uk/help-with-your-research/research-guides/home-office-correspondence-1782-1979/.

62. Jill Pellew, *Home Office: Clerks to Bureaucrats* (East Brunswick, NJ: Fairleigh Dickinson University Press, 1982), 64.

63. "Home Office Correspondence 1782–1979." In the National Archives records, in 1902, there is a six-digit series starting at 100,001 that continued until 1949, when separate series were introduced for each function, each distinguished by letter symbols.

64. Pellew, *Home Office*, 98.

65. Cornelia Vismann, *Files: Law and Media Technology*, trans. Geoffrey Winthrop-Young (Stanford, CA: Stanford University Press, 2008), 298.

66. Alan Delgado, *The Enormous File: Social History of the Office* (London: John Murray Publishers, 1979), 78.

67. "Out Letters to the General Post Office regarding the Interception of Telegrams and Letters (1887–1899) HO 151/7," 7.

68. "Cancellations of Postal Warrants: Practice HO 45/25957," (1933), 25957, National Archives. According to a note in that particular file, however, the file itself was missing until May 1958, when it "turned up in the Private Office after some years of hibernation."

69. Letters from the postmaster general requesting cancellations appear in collections of in-letters from the Post Office in the early nineteenth century; see "Home Office: Post Office Correspondence 1787–1816," (1816) HO 33/1, National Archives; "Home Office: Post Office Correspondence 1823–1837 HO 33/3," (1837), 3, National Archives. Establishing efficient cancellation procedures remained a matter of concern in devising filing protocols. See "Signing Cancellations of Postal Warrants HO 45/25956," (1928), National Archives; "Cancellations of Postal Warrants: Practice HO 45/25957."

70. Pellew, *Home Office*, 24. In addition, women would require a separate working area away from men.

71. Vismann, *Files*, 128–129.

72. "Warrants: Post Office Warrant for Search of Private Correspondence, HO 144/674/100653," (1903), National Archives.

73. Vismann, *Files*, 138.

74. Avital Ronell, *The Telephone Book: Technology, Schizophrenia, Electric Speech* (Lincoln, NE: University of Nebraska Press, 1989), 283–285.

75. Christopher Beauchamp, "Who Invented the Telephone? Lawyers, Patents, and the Judgments of History," *Technology and Culture* 51, no. 4 (2010): 858.

76. Beauchamp, "Who Invented the Telephone?," 863.

77. "Telegraph Act 1868," accessed August 31, 2017, http://www.legislation.gov.uk/ukpga/Vict/31-32/110/contents/enacted.

78. Attorney-General v. Edison Telephone Co of London 6 QBD 244 (1880). The problem was that the US companies involved held the patents for telephone equipment. The GPO might be able to purchase the network, but it could not provide

telephones. As such, a thirty-one-year license arrangement was agreed to, with 10 percent of the profits going to the GPO; see "When a Telephone Conversation Was Actually a Telegram in the Eyes of the Law," *BT.com*, accessed May 25, 2017, http://home.bt.com/tech-gadgets/when-a-telephone-conversation-was-actually-a-telegram-in-the-eyes-of-the-law-11364121187126.

79. Hemmeon, *History of the British Post Office*, 219–236. The city of Hull retained a privately owned network.

80. John Durham Peters, *Speaking into the Air: A History of the Idea of Communication* (Chicago: University of Chicago, 2000), 196.

81. Bernhard Siegert, *Relays: Literature as an Epoch of the Postal System*, trans. Kevin Repp (Stanford, CA: Stanford University Press, 1999), 190.

82. Peters, *Speaking into the Air*, 197.

83. Christopher Andrew, *The Defence of the Realm: The Authorized History of MI5* (London: Penguin, 2010), 134.

84. Marshall McLuhan, *Understanding Media: The Extensions of Man* (Cambridge, MA: MIT Press, 1994), 291.

85. Peters, *Speaking into the Air*.

86. See chapter 5.

87. "Notifications Respecting Censorship and Interruption of Telegraphic Communication in Time of War Issued through the International Telegraph Office," (1900 1870), POST 56/51, Postal Museum and Archive, London.

88. Nicole Starosielski, *The Undersea Network* (Durham, NC: Duke University Press, 2015), 32–33; Arthur C. Clarke, *How the World Was One: Beyond the Global Village* (London: Gollancz, 1992), 103.

89. Fari, *Victorian Telegraphy before Nationalization*, 207.

90. Daniel R. Headrick and Pascal Griset, "Submarine Telegraph Cables: Business and Politics, 1838–1939," *Business History Review* 75, no. 3 (2001): 543–578, https://doi.org/10.2307/3116386.

91. Starosielski, *Undersea Network*, 34.

92. Starosielski, *Undersea Network*, 31.

93. Sandford Fleming, quoted by Simon James Potter, *News and the British World: The Emergence of an Imperial Press System, 1876–1922* (Oxford: Clarendon, 2003), 65–66.

94. Paul M. Kennedy, "Imperial Cable Communications and Strategy, 1870–1914," *English Historical Review* 86, no. 341 (1971): 728–752.

95. Hugh Barty-King, *Girdle Round the Earth: The Story of Cable and Wireless and Its Predecessors to Mark the Group's Jubilee, 1929–1979* (London: Heinemann, 1979), 148.

96. Kennedy, "Imperial Cable Communications," 731–733.

97. "Defence Requirements for Cable Landing Sites,"' (1910), BT Archives.

98. Starosielski, *Undersea Network*, 110–115.

99. Roxana Vatanparast, "David Dudley Field and the Technological Sensibility of International Law Codification," *Denver Journal of International Law and Policy* 52 (2024), https://doi.org/10.2139/ssrn.4628458.

100. Daniel R. Headrick, *The Invisible Weapon: Telecommunications and International Politics, 1851–1945* (New York: Oxford University Press, 1991).

101. Today it is a museum to the telegraphic age and the home of the Cable and Wireless archive.

102. Starosielski, *Undersea Network*, 100.

103. Starosielski, *Undersea Network*, 106; David Souden, *Voices over the Horizon: Tales from Cable and Wireless* (Cambridge: Granta Editions, 1999), 88–112.

104. Starosielski, *Undersea Network*, 95–111; Kennedy, "Imperial Cable Communications."

105. John Ferris, "Before 'Room 40': The British Empire and Signals Intelligence, 1898–1914," *Journal of Strategic Studies* 12, no. 4 (December 1989): 431-457, https://doi.org/10.1080/01402398908437390.

106. BT Archive TCB 175/312.

107. Ferris, "Before 'Room 40.'"

108. "Telegraphic Censorship during the South African War, 1899–1902 and Censorship of Telegrams to and from East and South Africa: Summary of Proceedings, 1902," (1902 1899) POST 56/53, Postal Museum and Archive, London.

109. "Telegraphic Censorship during the South African War," 7.

110. "Telegraphic Censorship during the South African War."

111. "Telegraphic Censorship during the South African War," 8.

112. "Telegraphic Censorship during the South African War," 8.

113. "Telegraphic Censorship during the South African War," 9.

114. Elizabeth Van Heyningen, "A Tool for Modernisation? The Boer Concentration Camps of the South African War, 1900–1902," *South African Journal of Science* 106, no. 5/6 (2010), https://doi.org/10.4102/sajs.v106i5/6.242.

115. Ferris, "Before 'Room 40.'"

116. Ferris, "Before 'Room 40,'" 438–441.

117. Ferris, "Before 'Room 40,'" 446.

118. David Kahn, *The Codebreakers: The Comprehensive History of Secret Communication from Ancient Times to the Internet*, 2nd ed. (New York: Scribner, 1996), 189–214.

119. Sungook Hong, *Wireless: From Marconi's Black-Box to the Audion* (Cambridge, MA: MIT Press, 2001), 2–5.

120. R. F. Pocock and G. R. M. Garratt, *The Origins of Maritime Radio* (London: HMSO, 1972), 3–4.

121. Pocock and Garratt, *Origins of Maritime Radio*, 5–12.

122. Hong, *Wireless*, 22.

123. As Marconi recalled later in life, see Friedrich Kittler, "The Artificial Intelligence of World War: Alan Turing," 183 in *The Truth of the Technological World*, trans. Erik Butler (Stanford, CA: Stanford University Press, 2013), 183

124. Pocock and Garratt, *Origins of Maritime Radio*, 16, 34.

125. Hong, *Wireless*, 89–100. Hong's book deliberately complicates the canonical stories about the invention of wireless technologies, which were from the beginning deployed in competing publicity-oriented demonstrations, disputes, and self-serving dramatizations. Here, we must risk once again reducing the complexity.

126. See the chapter "Tuning, Jamming, and the Maskelyne Affair," in Hong, *Wireless*, 89–118.

127. Hong, *Wireless*, 104.

128. Pocock and Garratt, *Origins of Maritime Radio*, 35–40.

129. Norman Wymer, *From Marconi to Telstar: The Story of Radio* (London: Longman's, 1966), 22–23.

130. Pocock and Garratt, *Origins of Maritime Radio*, 47–50.

131. Hong, *Wireless*, 155.

132. Michel Serres, *The Parasite* (Minneapolis: University of Minnesota Press, 2007), 142.

133. Glover, *Protecting National Security*, 71.

134. Glover, *Protecting National Security*, 71.

135. "Radiotelegram Intercepted: Legislation to Enforce Secrecy POST 30/1904D," 1908, BT Archives.

136. The phrase appears in a memo from 1928, in "Wireless: Interception by Amateurs on Shortwave POST 33/2905D," (1931), BT Archives.

137. Two preliminary conferences were organized by the International Telecommunication Union (ITU) in 1903 and 1906, both in Berlin. For a complete list, see "Complete List of Radio Conferences," *ITU*, accessed April 8, 2017, http://www.itu.int:80/en/history/Pages/CompleteListOfRadioConferences.aspx.

138. *International Radiotelegraph Convention, Signed at London, July 5, 1912* (London: H. M. Stationery Office, 1913), 187–189, see also articles 8 and 9, accessed April 8, 2017, http://search.itu.int/history/HistoryDigitalCollectionDocLibrary/4.37.43.en.100.pdf.

139. Hong, *Wireless*, 118.

140. Hong, *Wireless*, 118.

141. "Radiotelegrams on Board Ships: Censorship Arrangements, Interceptions and Use of Radio-Telegrams by Salvage Vessels, Part 1 POST 30/2097," (1928), BT Archives.

142. "Marconi-Bellini-Tosi Apparatus for Directive Wireless Telegraphy POST 30/3139," (1914), BT Archives; "Reports on Directed Wireless Telegraphy Systems Including the Belini-Tosi System TCB 274/10," (1915), BT Archives.

143. "Minutes of 23rd Meeting (Home Defence; Possibility of Invasion; Use by Private Persons of Wireless Telegraph Stations in War-Time; Importance of Joint Naval and Military Manoeuvres) CAB 38/3/72," (1903), National Archives.

144. "Suppression of Experimental and Private Business Wireless Stations during the First World War, Part 1 POST 30/3501," (1914), BT Archives.

145. Headrick, *Invisible Weapon*, 145.

146. Headrick, *Invisible Weapon*, 158.

147. For a comprehensive account of the code systems used in the First World War, see Kahn, *Codebreakers*, 266–350.

148. Kahn, *Codebreakers*, 270.

149. John Ferris, *Behind the Enigma: The Authorised History of GCHQ, Britain's Secret Cyber-Intelligence Agency* (London: Bloomsbury Publishing, 2020), 24.

150. Ferris, *Behind the Enigma*, 32, 268.

151. David Vincent, *I Hope I Don't Intrude: Privacy and Its Dilemmas in Nineteenth-Century Britain* (Oxford: Oxford University Press, 2015), 224.

CHAPTER 5

1. Christopher Andrew, *The Defence of the Realm: The Authorized History of MI5* (London: Penguin, 2010), 3–25.

2. Andrew, *Defence of the Realm*, 36–37.

3. "Investigation of Espionage 1914–1919," (1919) KV 1/48, National Archives.

4. Andrew, *Defence of the Realm*, 37–39.

5. "Special Duties: General Post Office Investigation Branch," (1919) MEPO 2/1500, National Archives.

6. Nicholas Hiley, "Counter-Espionage and Security in Great Britain during the First World War," *English Historical Review* CI, no. CCCC (July 1986): 637.

7. "Report on Postal Censorship during the Great War," (1919) POST 56/57, Postal Museum and Archive, London.

8. "Report on Postal Censorship during the Great War," 9–10.

9. Daniel R. Headrick, *The Invisible Weapon: Telecommunications and International Politics, 1851–1945* (Oxford: Oxford University Press, 1991), 141.

10. "Report on Postal Censorship during the Great War," 3.

11. "Memoranda and Correspondence between the War Office and the Postmaster General Regarding Special Censorship Warrants," (1916–1937) POST 56/61, Postal Museum and Archive, London.

12. Hiley, "Counter-Espionage and Security in Great Britain," 341–344.

13. "Report on Postal Censorship during the Great War," 77; see also John Ferris, *Behind the Enigma: The Authorised History of GCHQ, Britain's Secret Cyber-Intelligence Agency* (London: Bloomsbury Publishing, 2020), 665.

14. "Report on Postal Censorship during the Great War," 315.

15. "Report on Postal Censorship during the Great War," 310–315.

16. "Report on Postal Censorship during the Great War," 310–314.

17. "Report on Postal Censorship during the Great War," 317.

18. "Report on Postal Censorship during the Great War," 317–318.

19. Hiley, "Counter-Espionage and Security in Great Britain," 646–647.

20. "Report on Postal Censorship during the Great War," 337.

21. Hiley, "Counter-Espionage and Security in Great Britain," 641.

22. "Report on Postal Censorship during the Great War," 301–307.

23. Raphael Tuck & Sons produced popular designed postcards.

24. "Investigation of Espionage 1914–1919," 163. It should be noted that British attempts to infiltrate information past German censors do not feature in this report.

25. David Kahn, *The Codebreakers: The Comprehensive History of Secret Communication from Ancient Times to the Internet*, 2nd ed. (New York: Scribner, 1996), 353, 524; Peter Wright, *Spycatcher* (New York: Viking, 1987), 119.

26. Kahn, *Codebreakers*, 525–526.

27. Nigel West, *British Security Coordination: The Secret History of British Intelligence in the Americas 1940–1945* (London: Little Brown, 1998), 353–354, 362.

28. Hiley, "Counter-Espionage and Security in Great Britain," 645.

29. Hiley, "Counter-Espionage and Security in Great Britain," 647.

30. "WAR: Anti-Conscription Campaigns by Various Bodies," (1916–17) HO 45/10801/307402, National Archives; see also Hiley, "Counter-Espionage and Security in Great Britain," 651.

31. Hiley, "Counter-Espionage and Security in Great Britain," 653.

32. Hiley, "Counter-Espionage and Security in Great Britain," 660–661.

33. Martin Loughlin, *Public Law and Political Theory* (Oxford: Oxford University Press, 1992), 63–104.

34. Loughlin, *Public Law and Political Theory*, 102–104.

35. A. V. Dicey, *The Law of the Constitution*, ed. J. W. F. Allison (Oxford: Oxford University Press, 2013).

36. Loughlin, *Public Law and Political Theory*, 146.

37. Loughlin, *Public Law and Political Theory*, 149–153.

38. Michel Foucault, *The Birth of Biopolitics*, ed. Arnold I. Davidson, trans. Graham Burchell (Basingstoke: Palgrave Macmillan, 2008), 63–65.

39. Loughlin, *Public Law and Political Theory*, 162.

40. Harold J. Laski, "The Responsibility of the State in England. To Roscoe Pound," *Harvard Law Review* 32, no. 5 (1919): 447, https://doi.org/10.2307/1327923.

41. Laski, "Responsibility of the State in England," 450.

42. Laski, "Responsibility of the State in England," 460.

43. Laski, "Responsibility of the State in England," 458.

44. Laski, "Responsibility of the State in England," 459.

45. Laski, "Responsibility of the State in England," 471–72.

46. Laski, "Responsibility of the State in England," 472.

47. "Memo of December 15, 1943," in "Discussions Held in 1943 on the Future of the Security Service," (1942–1943) KV 4/448, National Archives.

48. Keith Ewing, Joan Mahoney, and Andrew Moretta, *MI5, the Cold War, and the Rule of Law* (Oxford: Oxford University Press, 2020), 93.

49. Ewing, Mahoney, and Moretta, *MI5, the Cold War*, 94.

50. Andrew, *Defence of the Realm*, 323.

51. Andrew, *Defence of the Realm*, 323.

52. Andrew, *Defence of the Realm*, 525–528; Ewing, Mahoney, and Moretta, *MI5, the Cold War*, 225.

53. Andrew, *Defence of the Realm*, 321–322.

54. This material included novels. See "PUBLICATIONS: Interception in Mail of Copies of Poetry Book Pansies by D. H. Lawrence," (1929) HO 144/20642, National Archives; "PUBLICATIONS: Indecent Wares from Abroad: Warrants for the Detention of Illegal Postal Packets," (1911–1923) HO 144/1837, National Archives; "Detection of Lottery Correspondence in the Post," (1920–1934) HO 45/25958, 259, National Archives.

55. "Interception of Letters in Criminal Case," (1886) HO 144/164/A42354, 164, National Archives.

56. Post Office Act 1908, section 56, http://www.legislation.gov.uk/ukpga/1908/48/section/56/enacted.

57. "Detection of Lottery Correspondence in the Post," 259.

58. "Precedents in Common Law for Opening Letters in the Post," (1935) HO 45/25961, National Archives.

59. "Constitutional Authority to Stop Letters in the Post," (1935) HO 45/25962, National Archives.

60. "Cases of Leakage of Information about Interception of Mail 1926–1932," (1932) KV 4/221, National Archives.

61. "'John Bull' Article on Working of Postal Warrants," (1935) HO 45/25960, National Archives.

62. David A. Mindell, *Between Human and Machine* (Baltimore: Johns Hopkins University Press, 2002), 107–109, https://doi.org/10.56021/9780801868955.

63. Mindell, *Between Human and Machine*, 112.

64. Mindell, *Between Human and Machine*, 134–137.

65. Patrick Fitzgerald and Mark Leopold, *Stranger on the Line: The Secret History of Phone Tapping* (London: The Bodley Head, 1987), 59–61.

66. Andrew, *Defence of the Realm*, 134.

67. Fitzgerald and Leopold, *Stranger on the Line*, 63–64.

68. Andrew, *Defence of the Realm*, 135, fn108.

69. Fitzgerald and Leopold, *Stranger on the Line*, 64.

70. Fitzgerald and Leopold, *Stranger on the Line*, 64–65.

71. Fitzgerald and Leopold, *Stranger on the Line*, 62–64.

72. Fitzgerald and Leopold, *Stranger on the Line*, 68–74.

73. Richard Aldrich, *GCHQ* (London: Harper Press, 2011), 147.

74. Wright, *Spycatcher*, 44–47.

75. Fitzgerald and Leopold, *Stranger on the Line*, 206, 222–24.

76. Duncan Campbell, "Big Buzby Is Watching You," *New Statesman*, February 1, 1980, 159.

77. Aldrich, *GCHQ*, 499, in general terms, the scale of communications intelligence used by the security services in Northern Ireland is relatively under-researched.

78. "Report of the Committee of Privy Councillors Appointed to Inquire into the Interception of Communications" (Birkett Report)," (Cmnd 283, 1957), paras. 40–52.

79. Ewing, Mahoney, and Moretta, *MI5, the Cold War*, 27.

80. "Warrants: Listening-in to and Recording of Telephone Conversations under Written Authority of Home Secretary," (1937) HO 144/20619, National Archives.

81. "Warrants: Listening-in to and Recording of Telephone Conversations."

82. "Policy and Procedure for the Imposition of Home Office Warrants for the Interception of Mail and Telephone Communications in the UK 1939–1945," (1944) KV 4/222, National Archives.

83. "Policy and Procedure for the Imposition of Home Office Warrants."

84. Cornelia Vismann, *Files: Law and Media Technology*, trans. Geoffrey Winthrop-Young (Stanford, CA: Stanford University Press, 2008), 138–140.

85. "The Findlater Stewart report and Prime Minister's directive to the Director General of the Security Service (MI5)" (1946) CAB 301/31, National Archives; Ewing, Mahoney, and Moretta, *MI5, the Cold War*, 103–104.

86. Ewing, Mahoney, and Moretta, *MI5, the Cold War*, 27–28; Wright, *Spycatcher*, 46.

87. Wright, *Spycatcher*, 46.

88. Ewing, Mahoney, and Moretta, *MI5, the Cold War*, 104–10.

89. Carl Schmitt, *Dialogues on Power and Space*, 1st ed. (Malden, MA: Polity, 2015), 35.

90. Ewing, Mahoney, and Moretta, *MI5, the Cold War*, 111–112.

91. Campbell, "Big Buzby Is Watching You," 160.

92. Wright, *Spycatcher*, 45; Andrew, *Defence of the Realm*, 334, 549.

93. Wright, *Spycatcher*, 72–73.

94. Andrew, *Defence of the Realm*, 336.

95. Ewing, Mahoney, and Moretta, *MI5, the Cold War*, 207–11; Andrew, *Defence of the Realm*, 336.

96. Fitzgerald and Leopold, *Stranger on the Line*, 116.

97. "Report of the Committee of Privy Councillors Appointed to Inquire into the Interception of Communications (Birkett Report)."

98. "Birkett Report," para. 8

99. "Birkett Report," para. 21.

100. "Birkett Report," paras 21–26. See also Sir William Anson, *The Law and Custom of the Constitution, Volume 2: The Crown, Part 2* (Oxford: Clarendon Press, 4th Ed. 1909), 22.

101. "Birkett Report," para. 30.

102. "Birkett Report," paras. 44–49.

103. "Birkett Report," para. 51.

104. "Birkett Report," para. 52.

105. "Birkett Report," paras. 129–131.

106. "Birkett Report," paras. 64–66.

107. "Birkett Report," para. 67.

108. "Birkett Report," para. 78.

109. "Birkett Report," paras. 80–81.

110. "Birkett Report," para. 84.

111. "Birkett Report," para. 74.

112. The rejection of judicial approval was a "big prize" for the government, according to Ewing, Mahoney, and Moretta, *MI5, the Cold War*, 118–119.

113. "Birkett Report," para. 177.

114. Fitzgerald and Leopold, *Stranger on the Line*, 124.

115. Fitzgerald and Leopold, *Stranger on the Line*, 125.

116. "Interception of Postal and Telephone Communications: Interception Working Party Correspondence," (1979) HO 325/536, National Archives.

117. Phil Glover, *Protecting National Security: A History of British Communications Investigation Regulation* (Abingdon: Routledge, 2022), 96.

118. Ewing, Mahoney, and Moretta, *MI5, the Cold War*, 112–14.

119. "Birkett Report," para. 79.

120. Ewing, Mahoney, and Moretta, *MI5, the Cold War*, 115–16.

121. Harold J. Laski, *Parliamentary Government in England*, 1st ed. (London: Allen & Unwin, 1938), 13.

122. Laski, *Parliamentary Government in England*.

123. Laurence Lustgarten and Ian Leigh, *In from the Cold: National Security and Parliamentary Democracy* (Oxford: Oxford University Press, 1994).

124. For an elaboration of the argument, see Ewan Smith, review of "Keith Ewing, Joan Mahoney, and Andrew Moretta, *MI5, the Cold War and the Rule of Law*," *Modern Law Review* 86, no. 1 (2023): 297–302, https://doi.org/10.1111/1468-2230.12737.

125. David Williams, *Not in the Public Interest: The Problem of Security in Democracy* (London: Hutchinson, 1965), 134–136.

126. E. P. Thompson, "The Secret State," *Race & Class* 20, no. 3 (January 1979): 219–242, https://doi.org/10.1177/030639687902000301.

127. Duncan Campbell and Mark Hosenball, "The Eavesdroppers," *Time Out*, May 1976, http://www.duncancampbell.org/menu/journalism/Eavesdroppers.pdf.

128. R v. Secretary of State for the Home Department, ex parte Hosenball [1977] 1 WLR 766; [1977] 3 All ER 452.

129. Rhodri Jeffreys-Jones, *In Spies We Trust: The Story of Western Intelligence* (Oxford: Oxford University Press, 2015), 154.

130. Jeffreys-Jones, *In Spies We Trust*, 154.

131. Jeffreys-Jones, *In Spies We Trust*, 156–165.

132. Christopher Moran, *Classified: Secrecy and the State in Modern Britain* (Cambridge: Cambridge University Press, 2012), 323.

133. Malone v. Metropolitan Police Commissioner [1979], 344.

134. The facts as recounted in Parliament, House of Commons Debates, March 12, 1985, vol. 75, col. 238.

135. *Malone*, 348 H.

136. *Malone*, 351 F.

137. Fitzgerald and Leopold, *Stranger on the Line*, 135.

138. *Malone*, 349 H.

139. J. Lambert, "Executive Authority to Tap Telephones," *Modern Law Review* 43, no. 1 (1980): 59–65.

140. *Malone*, 366–367.

141. *Malone*, 380 G.

142. *Malone*, 383 H–384 B.

143. The European Convention of Human Rights became domestically applicable in UK courts after 2000 under the Human Rights Act 1998.

144. Malone v. United Kingdom [1985] 7 EHRR 14, at [79].

145. Bernard Keenan, "The Evolution of Elucidation: The Snowden Cases before the Investigatory Powers Tribunal," *Modern Law Review* 85, no. 4 (2022): 906–937.

146. Peter Goodrich, "Freedom of the Phone," *Liverpool Law Review* 3, no. 2 (1981): 91–98.

147. "Interception of Postal and Telephone Communications: Interception Working Party Correspondence."

148. Interception of Communications Act 1985, s2(1).

149. Keenan, "Evolution of Elucidation."

150. Aldrich, *GCHQ*, 385.

151. Fitzgerald and Leopold, *Stranger on the Line*, 154.

152. Samuel Moyn, *Last Utopia: Human Rights in History* (Cambridge, MA: Harvard University Press, 2010).

153. William Davies, "Neoliberalism: A Bibliographic Review," *Theory, Culture & Society* 31, no. 7–8 (December 2014): 309–317, https://doi.org/10.1177/0263276414546383.

154. Foucault, *Birth of Biopolitics*, 168–179.

155. "Privatisation," *BT Archives* (November 2013), accessed April 12, 2024, https://www.bt.com/bt-plc/assets/documents/about-bt/our-history/bt-archives/information-sheets-and-timelines/privatisation.pdf.

156. Glover, *Protecting National Security*, 117.

157. F. A. Hayek, *Law, Legislation and Liberty: A New Statement of the Liberal Principles of Justice and Political Economy* (London: Routledge & Kegan Paul, 1982), I: 94–123.

158. Hayek, *Law, Legislation and Liberty*, I: 134.

159. Hayek, *Law, Legislation and Liberty*, III: 54–57.

160. Hayek, *Law, Legislation and Liberty*, I: 124–44.

161. Foucault, *Birth of Biopolitics*, 328–329; Wendy Brown, *Undoing the Demos* (New York: Zone Books, 2015), 115–150.

162. Michel Serres, *The Parasite* (Minneapolis: University of Minnesota Press, 2007).

163. Andrew, *Defence of the Realm*, 551; Fitzgerald and Leopold, *Stranger on the Line*, 41.

164. See, for instance, Samuel Moyn, "A Powerless Companion: Human Rights in the Age of Neoliberalism," *Law and Contemporary Problems* 77, no. 4 (2014): 147–169; Susan Marks, "Four Human Rights Myths," in *Human Rights* (Cheltenham: Edward Elgar Publishing, 2013), 217–235.

CHAPTER 6

1. Alan Mathison Turing, "On Computable Numbers, with an Application to the Entscheidungsproblem," *Journal of Math* 58, no. 345–363 (1936).

2. Harold Adams Innis, *Empire and Communications*, 2nd ed. (Toronto: University of Toronto Press, 1972).

3. Stuart Elden, "Land, Terrain, Territory," *Progress in Human Geography* 34, no. 6 (December 2010): 799–817, https://doi.org/10.1177/0309132510362603.

4. R. F. Pocock and G. R. M. Garratt, *The Origins of Maritime Radio* (London: HMSO, 1972).

5. John Ferris, *Behind the Enigma: The Authorised History of GCHQ, Britain's Secret Cyber-Intelligence Agency* (London: Bloomsbury Publishing, 2020), 268.

6. Aimé Césaire and Joan Pinkham, *Discourse on Colonialism* (New York: New York University Press, 2000), 35–46; Michel Foucault, *Society Must Be Defended*, trans. David Macey (London: Penguin, 2003), 103.

7. "Report on Postal Censorship during the Great War," (1919) POST 56/57, 1, Postal Museum and Archive, London.

8. "Official Secrets Bill: Note on Clause 4," (1920) HO 144/20992, National Archives. I owe this observation to Paul Scott.

9. Daniel R. Headrick, *The Invisible Weapon: Telecommunications and International Politics, 1851–1945* (Oxford: Oxford University Press, 1991), 145.

10. Headrick, *Invisible Weapon*, 147.

11. Headrick, *Invisible Weapon*, 168–169; David Paull Nickels, *Under the Wire: How the Telegraph Changed Diplomacy* (Cambridge, MA: Harvard University Press, 2003), 148–152.

12. Ferris, *Behind the Enigma*, 36–37.

13. Ferris, *Behind the Enigma*, 58–60.

14. Ferris, *Behind the Enigma*, 51–53.

15. Ferris, *Behind the Enigma*, 51–53.

16. Ferris, *Behind the Enigma*, 9, 36–37.

17. Ferris, *Behind the Enigma*, 31, 268.

18. Ferris, *Behind the Enigma*, 67.

19. Michael Herman, *Intelligence Power in Peace and War* (Cambridge: Cambridge University Press, 1996), 69.

20. Herman, *Intelligence Power*, 83–84.

21. Friedrich A. Kittler, *Gramophone, Film, Typewriter*, trans. Geoffrey Winthrop-Young (Stanford, CA: Stanford University Press, 1999), 256.

22. Alfred Price, *Instruments of Darkness: The History of Electronic Warfare 1939–1945* (Barnsley: Frontline Books, 2017), 24–26.

23. See, generally, Price, *Instruments of Darkness*; Headrick, *Invisible Weapon*, 248–250.

24. Ferris, *Behind the Enigma*, 141.

25. "Sedition, Warrants," (1920–1921) HO 144/1684/400430, National Archives.

26. Paul F. Scott, "The First Interception Provision: Section 4 of the Official Secrets Act 1920," *Journal of Legal History* 43, no. 3 (2022): 325–379.

27. James Bamford, *The Puzzle Palace: A Report on America's Most Secret Agency* (New York: Penguin, 1983), 415–416.

28. Official Secrets Act 1920, section 4.

29. A. G. Denniston, "The Government Code and Cypher School between the Wars," *Intelligence and National Security*, 1, no. 1 (1986): 65.

30. Ferris, *Behind the Enigma*, 66–68.

31. Ferris, *Behind the Enigma*, 66–68.

32. See "Monomarks: System of Identification: Instructions to the Commissioner's Office and the Position under the Official Secrets Act 1920," (1978) MEPO 2/9582, National Archives.

33. Cornelia Vismann, *Files: Law and Media Technology*, trans. Geoffrey Winthrop-Young (Stanford, CA: Stanford University Press, 2008), 82.

34. A. G. Denniston, "The Government Code and Cypher School between the Wars," *Intelligence and National Security* 1, no. 1 (1986): 48–49.

35. Denniston, "The Government Code and Cypher School between the Wars," 48–53.

36. Ferris, *Behind the Enigma*, 77, 99–104.

37. Denniston, "The Government Code and Cypher School between the Wars," 64–66.

38. Christopher Moran, *Classified: Secrecy and the State in Modern Britain* (Cambridge: Cambridge University Press, 2012), 136–176.

39. Ferris, *Behind the Enigma*, 31.

40. "Wireless: Interception of Transmissions by Amateurs on Short Wave," (1925–1931) POST 33/2905D, Postal Museum and Archive.

41. Headrick, *Invisible Weapon*, 203–206.

42. David Souden, *Voices over the Horizon: Tales from Cable and Wireless* (Cambridge: Granta Editions, 1999), 132–154.

43. In 2013, a PhD candidate at the University of Exeter was awarded a doctorate based on research at the Cable and Wireless archive in Porthcurno, Cornwall. During the course of his research, he discovered entries in the archive stamped "Top Secret." He contacted the Ministry of Defence and was subsequently informed that many of the entries should not be open and must be removed from the archive. He was invited to participate in the process of redacting and excising the archive. See Benjamin David Oldcorn, "On the Wire: The Strategic and Tactical Role of Cable and Wireless during the Second World War" (PhD thesis, University of Exeter, 2013), 61–70, https://ore.exeter.ac.uk/repository/handle/10871/14642.

44. Ferris, *Behind the Enigma*, 84–99.

45. Ferris, *Behind the Enigma*, 99–104, 163–168.

46. Cable and Wireless stationed workers on Ascension Island and Direction Island, an uninhabited part of the Cocos; see Souden, *Voices over the Horizon*, 113–130.

47. James Gleick, *The Information* (London: Fourth Estate, 2012), 202.

48. R. N. Renton, *Telegraphy* (London: Pitman Publishing, 1976), 1–10.

49. "GC&CS Erection of Wireless Interception Stations and Staffing," (1939) FO 366/1059, National Archives.

50. "GC&CS Erection of Wireless Interception Stations."

51. "Wireless: Interception of Transmissions by Amateurs on Short Wave."

52. Ferris, *Behind the Enigma*, 80.

53. Ferris, *Behind the Enigma*, 95.

54. "Letter from F. Riley to Personnel Department, 14 June 1939," Interception Service (1938) FO 366/2381, National Archives.

55. Ferris, *Behind the Enigma*, 80.

56. David Kahn, *The Codebreakers: The Comprehensive History of Secret Communication from Ancient Times to the Internet*, 2nd ed. (New York: Scribner, 1996), 394–396.

57. Kahn, *Codebreakers*, 403.

58. Kahn, *Codebreakers*, 400–402.

59. Richard Aldrich, *GCHQ* (London: Harper Press, 2011), 19–21.

60. Kahn, *Codebreakers*, 415–34.

61. Ferris, *Behind the Enigma*, 107–13.

62. Ferris, *Behind the Enigma*, 184–86.

63. Ferris, *Behind the Enigma*, 219.

64. Ferris, *Behind the Enigma*, 181.

65. Ferris, *Behind the Enigma*, 221.

66. Turing, "On Computable Numbers."

67. "Kittler on the NSA," *Theory, Culture & Society* (blog), February 12, 2014, http://www.theoryculturesociety.org/kittler-on-the-nsa/.

68. Kittler, *Gramophone, Film, Typewriter*, 263.

69. Bamford, *Puzzle Palace*, 488–489.

70. Bamford, *Puzzle Palace*, 498–499.

71. Ferris, *Behind the Enigma*, 269–271.

72. Ferris, *Behind the Enigma*, 231–233, 326–349.

73. Aldrich, *GCHQ*, 93–95.

74. Ferris, *Behind the Enigma*, 349.

75. Aldrich, *GCHQ*, 89.

76. Ferris, *Behind the Enigma*, 348.

77. Aldrich, *GCHQ*, 101.

78. Ferris, *Behind the Enigma*, 370.

79. Ferris, *Behind the Enigma*, 305.

80. Ferris, *Behind the Enigma*, 364.

81. Aldrich, *GCHQ*, 100.

82. Nasia Hadjigeorgiou, "Decolonizing Cyprus 60 Years after Independence: An Assessment of the Legality of the Sovereign Base Areas," *European Journal of International Law* 33, no. 4 (November 2022): 1125–1152, https://doi.org/10.1093/ejil/chac062.

83. Aldrich, *GCHQ*, 154–156, 329–339.

84. Nicole Starosielski, *The Undersea Network* (Durham, NC: Duke University Press, 2015), 42.

85. Starosielski, *Undersea Network*, 113.

86. Starosielski, *Undersea Network*, 70.

87. Claude E. Shannon, "Communication Theory of Secrecy Systems," *Bell System Technical Journal* 28, no. 4 (October 1949): 656–715.

88. Ferris, *Behind the Enigma*, 522–25.

89. Aldrich, *GCHQ*, 416–436; Ferris, *Behind the Enigma*, 465–479.

90. As explained with respect to the NSA by Thomas R. Johnson, *American Cryptology during the Cold War, 1945–1989, Book III: Retrenchment and Reform, 1972–1980* (Washington, DC: National Security Agency, Center for Cryptologic History, 1998), 83-84, https://www.nsa.gov/news-features/declassified-documents/cryptologic-histories/assets/files/cold_war_iii.pdf. This document was excised and declassified in 2007.

91. Wireless Telegraphy Act 1949, section 5.

92. Phil Glover, *Protecting National Security: A History of British Communications Investigation Regulation* (Abingdon: Routledge, 2022), 75.

93. James Bamford, *The Shadow Factory: The Ultra-Secret NSA from 9/11 to the Eavesdropping on America* (New York: Doubleday, 2008), 216.

94. Bamford, *Puzzle Palace*, 490.

95. Bamford, *Puzzle Palace*, 501–502.

96. Renton, *Telegraphy*, 322.

97. Renton, *Telegraphy*, 320–322.

98. Bamford, *Puzzle Palace*, 312.

99. Johnson, *American Cryptology III*, 83–84.

100. Johnson, *American Cryptology III*, 84-85.

101. An early NSA explanatory paper gives an insight into how hard it was to work with early computing hardware; see J. A. Meyer, "Computers: The Wailing Wall," *NSA Technical Journal* 1, no. 3 (1956): 69–90.

102. Edward T. Engstrom, "Science and Cryptology," *NSA Technical Journal* 3, no. 3 (July 1958): 2–3 (declassified 2008).

103. "Report of the Second Computer Study Group," *NSA Technical Journal* 19, no. 1 (1974): 21–63.

104. Howard H. Campaigne, "Lightning," *NSA Technical Journal* 4, no. 3 (July 1959): 63–67 (declassified 2012).

105. Miles A. Merkel, "A 'Word Spotter,'" *NSA Technical Journal* 4, no. 4 (1959): 91–100 (declassified 2011).

106. Joseph Eachus et al., "Growing Up with Computers at NSA," *NSA Technical Journal*, no. Special Issue (1972): 12 (declassified 2012).

107. Eachus et al., "Growing Up with Computers at NSA," 12–13.
108. Bamford, *Puzzle Palace*, 137–139.
109. Ferris, *Behind the Enigma*, 360–364.
110. Stuart Hampshire, quoted in Ferris, *Behind the Enigma*, 302.
111. Hampshire, quoted in Ferris, *Behind the Enigma*, 300.
112. Ferris, *Behind the Enigma*, 300–304.
113. Ferris, *Behind the Enigma*, 430–431.
114. Ferris, *Behind the Enigma*, 434–435.
115. Ferris, *Behind the Enigma*, 480–483.
116. Ferris, *Behind the Enigma*, 488.
117. Johnson, *American Cryptology III*, 373.
118. Johnson, *American Cryptology III*, 169.
119. Eachus et al., "Growing Up with Computers at NSA," 13.
120. Cornelia Vismann and Markus Krajewski, "Computer Juridisms," *Grey Room* 29 (2008): 95.
121. Friedrich A. Kittler, "Protected Mode," in *Literature, Media, Information Systems*, ed. John Johnston (Amsterdam: G+B Arts, 1997), 156–168.
122. Eachus et al., "Growing Up with Computers at NSA," 14.
123. Eachus et al., "Growing Up with Computers at NSA," 14.
124. The internet has many genealogies. See, for instance, Roy Rosenzweig, "Wizards, Bureaucrats, Warriors, and Hackers: Writing the History of the Internet," *American Historical Review* 103, no. 5 (1998): 1530–15052; Tung-Hui Hu, *A Prehistory of the Cloud* (Cambridge, MA: MIT Press, 2015).
125. NSA, "The PLATFORM Network Evolution," *Cryptologic Quarterly* (1989), https://www.nsa.gov/news-features/declassified-documents/cryptologic-quarterly/assets/files/The_PLATFORM_Network_Evolution.pdf.
126. Johnson, *American Cryptology III*, 155.
127. The mechanism and protocol were first described in the classic paper by Paul Baran, *On Distributed Communications Networks* (Santa Monica, CA: The RAND Corporation, 1962), https://www.rand.org/content/dam/rand/pubs/papers/2005/P2626.pdf. For an excellent introduction, see Florian Sprenger, *The Politics of Micro-Decisions*, trans. Valentine A. Pakis (Lüneburg: Hybrid Publishing Lab, 2015), 34–53, http://meson.press/books/the-politics-of-micro-decisions/.
128. Hu, *Prehistory of the Cloud*, 15.
129. Stephen C. Pascall and David J. Withers, *Commercial Satellite Communication* (Oxford: Focal Press, 1997), 7.
130. Bamford, *Puzzle Palace*, 420.
131. Aldrich, *GCHQ*, 342.
132. Pascall and Withers, *Commercial Satellite Communication*, 147–149.

133. Ferris, *Behind the Enigma*, 484.

134. Bamford, *Puzzle Palace*, 488–500.

135. Duncan Campbell, "Inside Echelon: The History, Structure, and Function of the Global Surveillance System Known as Echelon," in *CTRL [SPACE]: Rhetorics of Surveillance from Bentham to Big Brother*, ed. Thomas Levin, Ursula Forhne, and Peter Weibel (Cambridge, MA: MIT Press, 2002), 159-169.

136. Pascall and Withers, *Commercial Satellite Communication*, 4–5.

137. Aldrich, *GCHQ*, 427–461; Bamford, *Puzzle Palace*, 419–420.

138. Aldrich, *GCHQ*, 501.

139. Aldrich, *GCHQ*, 343.

140. Campbell, "Inside Echelon," 164.

141. Patrick Fitzgerald and Mark Leopold, *Stranger on the Line: The Secret History of Phone Tapping* (London: The Bodley Head, 1987), 97–98.

142. "Kittler on the NSA."

143. Aldrich, *GCHQ*, 343–44.

144. Hugh Lanning and Richard Norton-Taylor, *A Conflict of Loyalties: GCHQ 1984–1991* (Cheltenham: New Clarion, 1991), 69.

145. Post Office Act 1969, section 1.

146. Post Office Act 1969, section 2.

147. Bamford, *Puzzle Palace*.

148. Duncan Campbell and Mark Hosenball, "The Eavesdroppers," *Time Out*, May 1976; Rhodri Jeffreys-Jones, *In Spies We Trust: The Story of Western Intelligence* (Oxford: Oxford University Press, 2015).

149. Ferris, *Behind the Enigma*, 672–674.

150. K. D. Ewing, "Prerogative—Judicial Review—National Security," *Cambridge Law Journal* 44, no. 1 (March 1985): 1–3, https://doi.org/10.1017/S0008197300114278.

151. Ferris, *Behind the Enigma*, 687–690.

152. Cornelia Vismann and Markus Krajewski, "Computer Juridisms," *Grey Room* 29 (2008): 90–109.

153. Campbell, "Inside Echelon."

154. Cited in Campbell, "Inside Echelon," 164–165.

155. Bamford, *Shadow Factory*, 217. Of the territorial reach of the UKUSA network, GCHQ's director, Sir Leonard Hooper, wrote, "Between us, we have ensured that the blankets and sheets are more tightly tucked around the bed in which our two sets of people lie and, like you, I like it that way."

156. Richard Lamont, "The Capenhurst Phone-Tap Tower," accessed April 15, 2024, https://www.lamont.me.uk/capenhurst/followup.html.

157. Liberty and Others v. the United Kingdom, No. 58243/00 (ECtHR 1 July 2008).

CHAPTER 7

1. Edward Snowden, *Permanent Record* (London: Macmillan, 2019), 215–217.
2. Snowden, *Permanent Record*, 221–222.
3. Snowden, *Permanent Record*, 172–178.
4. "Report on the President's Surveillance Program" (hereafter "Report on the PSP"), Offices of the Inspectors General of the DOD, DOJ, CIA, NSA, ODNI, July 2009, 399–400, https://oig.justice.gov/reports/2015/PSP-09-18-15-full.pdf.
5. "Report on the PSP," 390–391.
6. "Report on the PSP," 267–270.
7. Foreign Intelligence Surveillance Act, section 702.
8. "The National Security Agency: Missions, Authorities, Oversight and Partnerships," National Security Agency, August 9, 2013, 4, https://irp.fas.org/nsa/nsa-story.pdf.
9. Barry Friedman and Danielle Citron, "Indiscriminate Data Surveillance," *Virginia Law Review* 110, no. 6 (2024): 1351.
10. "Report on the PSP."
11. Snowden, *Permanent Record*, 177.
12. Snowden, *Permanent Record*, 177–178.
13. Friedman and Citron, "Indiscriminate Data Surveillance."
14. Snowden, *Permanent Record*, 44 Snowden was inspired by Barlow's Cyberlibertarian Declaration of the Independence of Cyberspace, 107.
15. Alexander R. Galloway, *Protocol: How Control Exists after Decentralization* (Cambridge, MA: MIT Press, 2006).
16. Alan Rusbridger and Ewen MacAskill, "Edward Snowden Interview—the Edited Transcript," *The Guardian*, July 18, 2014, sec. World News, http://www.theguardian.com/world/2014/jul/18/-sp-edward-snowden-nsa-whistleblower-interview-transcript.
17. Snowden, *Permanent Record*, 3.
18. Snowden, *Permanent Record*, 109.
19. Cornelia Vismann and Markus Krajewski, "Computer Juridisms," *Grey Room* 29 (2008); Lawrence Lessig, *Code 2.0*, CC Online (New York: Basic Books, 2006), http://codev2.cc/download+remix/Lessig-Codev2.pdf.
20. Snowden, *Permanent Record*, 239.
21. Friedrich Kittler, "The History of Communication Media," in *ZERO—The Art of Being Everywhere* (Graz: Steirische Kulturinitiative, 1993), 66–81.
22. *HIMR Data Mining Research Problem Book*, September 20, 2011, https://www.maths.ed.ac.uk/~tl/docs/Problem-Book-Redacted.pdf.
23. *HIMR Data Mining Research Problem Book*, 9.

24. *HIMR Data Mining Research Problem Book*, 11.

25. *HIMR Data Mining Research Problem Book*, 12.

26. *HIMR Data Mining Research Problem Book*, 8.

27. "GCHQ Report on the Technical Abilities of TEMPORA," Electronic Frontier Foundation, June 18, 2014, https://www.eff.org/document/20140618-der-spiegel-gchq-report-technical-abilities-tempora.

28. Wolfgang Ernst, *Chronopoetics: The Temporal Being and Operativity of Technological Media* (London: Rowman & Littlefield, 2016), 190.

29. Vinton G. Cerf and Robert E. Icahn, "A Protocol for Packet Network Intercommunication," *ACM SIGCOMM Computer Communication Review* 35, no. 2 (2005): 71–82.

30. Florian Sprenger, *The Politics of Micro-Decisions*, trans. Valentine A. Pakis (Lüneburg: Hybrid Publishing Lab, 2015).

31. This point was made as early as 1992; see John Perry Barlow, "Decrypting the Puzzle Palace," *Communications of the ACM* 35, no. 7 (July 1992): 25–31, https://doi.org/10.1145/129902.129910.

32. Nicole Starosielski, *The Undersea Network* (Durham, NC: Duke University Press, 2015).

33. "Cable Master List," Snowden Archive, accessed April 7, 2024, https://grid.glendon.yorku.ca/items/show/202; "Partner Cables," accessed April 7, 2024, https://grid.glendon.yorku.ca/items/show/297. Both lists were created by the GCHQ and published by Süddeutsche Zeitung. See also Ewen MacAskill et al., "GCHQ Taps Fibre-Optic Cables for Secret Access to World's Communications," *The Guardian*, June 21, 2013, sec. UK News, https://www.theguardian.com/uk/2013/jun/21/gchq-cables-secret-world-communications-nsa.

34. *HIMR Data Mining Research Problem Book*, 9–10.

35. *HIMR Data Mining Research Problem Book*, 10.

36. Ernst, *Chronopoetics*, 194.

37. *HIMR Data Mining Research Problem Book*, 10.

38. "QFDs and Blackhole," Electronic Frontier Foundation, March 2009, https://www.eff.org/files/2015/10/12/20150925-intercept-qfd_blackhole_technology_behind_inoc.pdf.

39. *HIMR Data Mining Research Problem Book*, 11.

40. "QFDs and Blackhole."

41. "GCHQ Profiling: An Appendix," *The Intercept*, September 25, 2015, https://theintercept.com/gchq-appendix/.

42. Ethem Alpaydin, *Machine Learning: The New AI* (Cambridge, MA: MIT Press, 2016), 13–14.

43. *HIMR Data Mining Research Problem Book*, 12.

44. *HIMR Data Mining Research Problem Book*, 12.

45. *HIMR Data Mining Research Problem Book*, 14–15.

46. *HIMR Data Mining Research Problem Book*, 17.

47. Alpaydin, *Machine Learning*.

48. *HIMR Data Mining Research Problem Book*, 17–18.

49. *HIMR Data Mining Research Problem Book*, 21.

50. *HIMR Data Mining Research Problem Book*, 27.

51. *HIMR Data Mining Research Problem Book*, 29.

52. Glenn Greenwald, *No Place to Hide: Edward Snowden, the NSA & the Surveillance State* (London: Penguin Books 2015), 102–107, 118–132.

53. Charlie Savage, Claire Cain Miller, and Nicole Perlroth, "N.S.A. Said to Tap Google and Yahoo Abroad," *New York Times*, October 31, 2013, sec. Technology, https://www.nytimes.com/2013/10/31/technology/nsa-is-mining-google-and-yahoo-abroad.html.

54. James Ball, "NSA's Prism Surveillance Program: How It Works and What It Can Do," *The Guardian*, June 8, 2013, sec. US News, https://www.theguardian.com/world/2013/jun/08/nsa-prism-server-collection-facebook-google.

55. "NSA Prism Program Slides," *The Guardian*, November 1, 2013, http://www.theguardian.com/world/interactive/2013/nov/01/prism-slides-nsa-document.

56. Greenwald, *No Place to Hide*, 110–112.

57. *HIMR Data Mining Research Problem Book*, 9, 12.

58. Spencer Ackerman and James Ball, "Optic Nerve: Millions of Yahoo Webcam Images Intercepted by GCHQ," *The Guardian*, February 28, 2014, sec. US News, https://www.theguardian.com/world/2014/feb/27/gchq-nsa-webcam-images-internet-yahoo.

59. *HIMR Data Mining Research Problem Book*, 12.

60. *HIMR Data Mining Research Problem Book*, 13.

61. Daniel Boffey, "British Spies 'Hacked into Belgian Telecoms Firm on Ministers' Orders," *The Guardian*, September 21, 2018, sec. UK News, https://www.theguardian.com/uk-news/2018/sep/21/british-spies-hacked-into-belgacom-on-ministers-orders-claims-report.

62. "Gemalto Presents the Findings of Its Investigations into the Alleged Hacking of SIM Card Encryption Keys by Britain's Government Communications Headquarters (GCHQ) and the U.S. National Security Agency (NSA)," *Thales Group*, February 25, 2015, https://www.thalesgroup.com/en/markets/digital-identity-and-security/press-release/gemalto-presents-the-findings-of-its-investigations-into-the-alleged-hacking-of-sim-card-encryption-keys.

63. "Documents Reveal N.S.A. Campaign against Encryption," *New York Times*, accessed April 13, 2024, https://www.nytimes.com/interactive/2013/09/05/us/documents-reveal-nsa-campaign-against-encryption.html.

64. Susan Landau, "Highlights from Making Sense of Snowden, Part II: What's Significant in the NSA Revelations," *IEEE Security Privacy* 12, no. 1 (January 2014):

63; see also Susan Landau, "Making Sense from Snowden: What's Significant in the NSA Surveillance Revelations," *IEEE Security Privacy* 11, no. 4 (July 2013): 54–63; Whitfield Diffie and Susan Landau, *Privacy on the Line: The Politics of Wiretapping and Encryption*, updated (Cambridge, MA: MIT Press, 2007).

65. Barlow, "Decrypting the Puzzle Palace."

66. Landau, "Highlights from Making Sense of Snowden, Part II," 63.

67. Sam Biddle, "How Peter Thiel's Palantir Helped the NSA Spy on the Whole World," *The Intercept*, February 22, 2017, https://theintercept.com/2017/02/22/how-peter-thiels-palantir-helped-the-nsa-spy-on-the-whole-world/.

68. Phil Glover, *Protecting National Security: A History of British Communications Investigation Regulation* (Abingdon: Routledge, 2022), 167.

69. "Operational Legalities: GCHQ PowerPoint Presentation," Electronic Frontier Foundation, NSA Primary Sources, June 22, 2015, https://www.eff.org/document/20150622-intercept-operational-legalities-gchq-powerpoint-presentation.

70. Benjamin H. Bratton, *The Stack: On Software and Sovereignty*, Software Studies (Cambridge, MA: MIT Press, 2015), 42.

71. "Operational Legalities," 10.

72. "Operational Legalities," 22.

73. "Operational Legalities," 23.

74. "Operational Legalities," 88.

75. "Operational Legalities," 103.

76. "Operational Legalities," 28.

77. "Operational Legalities," 30.

78. "Operational Legalities," 31.

79. "Operational Legalities," 109.

80. "Operational Legalities," 106.

81. "Operational Legalities," 138.

82. "Operational Legalities," 139.

83. "Operational Legalities," 32–33.

84. "Operational Legalities," 129.

85. "Operational Legalities," 38.

86. Big Brother Watch and Others v. the United Kingdom, No. 58170/13, 62322/14, 24960/15 (ECtHR [GC] 25 May 2021).

87. Liberty v. GGHQ [2015] 3 All ER 212, [2015] 2 WLUK 215. Note that this reference is to the second and most consequential of three decisions of the IPT in the case.

88. Bernard Keenan, "The Evolution of Elucidation: The Snowden Cases before the Investigatory Powers Tribunal," *Modern Law Review* 85, no. 4 (2022): 925, https://doi.org/10.1111/1468-2230.12713.

89. Glover, *Protecting National Security*, 181.

90. RIPA, section 8(4) and section 16(1),(2); see Glover, *Protecting National Security*, 166–167.

91. See Chapter 3.

92. See Chapter 5.

93. Keenan, "Evolution of Elucidation," 925–930.

94. B. Keenan, "Going 'Below the Waterline': The Paradoxical Regulation of Secret Surveillance in the UK," *LSE Law Policy Briefing Series*, no. 9 (2015).

95. Keenan, "Evolution of Elucidation."

96. Privacy International v. Secretary of State for Foreign and Commonwealth Affairs [2016] 2 WLUK 351.

97. "Consultation: Equipment Interference and Interception of Communications Codes of Practice," Home Office, February 6, 2015, https://assets.publishing.service.gov.uk/government/uploads/system/uploads/attachment_data/file/401867/Consultation_on_the_draft_Codes_of_Practice_on_Interception_and_Equipmen....pdf.

98. Intelligence and Security Committee of Parliament, *Privacy and Security: A Modern and Transparent Legal Framework*, HC 1075, March 12, 2015.

99. Privacy International v. Secretary of State for Foreign and Commonwealth Affairs [2017] 3 All E.R. 647, [2016] HRLR 21, at [5]-[8]. This was the first of four legal judgments in the case.

100. Privacy International v. Secretary of State for Foreign and Commonwealth Affairs [2017], at [14].

101. Privacy International v. Secretary of State for Foreign and Commonwealth Affairs [2018] 4 All E.R. 275. This was the last in a series of four open judgments on the law, all prior to a final determination.

102. Privacy International v. Secretary of State for Foreign and Commonwealth Affairs [2018], at [6].

103. Intelligence and Security Committee of Parliament, "Report on the Draft Investigatory Powers Bill," HC 795, February 9, 2016, https://isc.independent.gov.uk/wp-content/uploads/2021/01/20160209_ISC_Rpt_IPBillweb.pdf; see also "A Democratic Licence to Operate: Report of the Independent Surveillance Review," April 5, 2024, https://rusi.org.

104. David Anderson, "A Question of Trust: Report of the Investigatory Powers Teview," Stationery Office, 2015.

105. Glover, *Protecting National Security*, 242.

106. John Ferris, *Behind the Enigma: The Authorised History of GCHQ, Britain's Secret Cyber-Intelligence Agency* (London: Bloomsbury Publishing, 2020), 698.

107. Investigatory Powers Act 2016, section 2.

108. Paul F. Scott, "Hybrid Institutions in the National Security Constitution: The Case of the Commissioners," *Legal Studies* 39, no. 3 (September 2019): 432–454, https://doi.org/10.1017/lst.2018.44.

109. Sir Brian Leveson, "Annual Report of the Investigatory Powers Commissioner 2022," *IPCO*, March 26, 2024.

110. Leveson, "Investigatory Powers Commissioner 2022," 46–47.

111. Big Brother Watch and Others v. the United Kingdom, paragraph 225.

112. Big Brother Watch and Others v. the United Kingdom, paragraphs 339, 425.

113. Big Brother Watch and Others v. the United Kingdom, paragraphs 458, 509.

114. Leveson, "Investigatory Powers Commissioner 2022," 16.

115. Leveson, "Investigatory Powers Commissioner 2022," 16.

116. Liberty and Privacy International v. Security Service and Secretary of State for the Home Department [2023] UKIPTrib_1.

117. Investigatory Powers Act 2016, section 260.

118. "Home Office Report on the Operation of the Investigatory Powers Act 2016 (Accessible Version)," *GOV.UK*, 14–15, accessed April 7, 2024, https://www.gov.uk/government/publications/report-on-the-operation-of-the-investigatory-powers-act-2016/home-office-report-on-the-operation-of-the-investigatory-powers-act-2016-accessible-version.

119. "Operation of the Investigatory Powers Act 2016," 17–19.

120. Niklas Luhmann, *Law as a Social System*, trans. Klaus A. Ziegert, ed. Fatima Kastner, Richard Nobles, David Schiff, and Rosamund Ziegert (Oxford: Oxford University Press, 2004), 451.

121. Niklas Luhmann, *The Reality of the Mass Media*, trans. Kathleen Cross (Cambridge: Polity, 2000).

122. "Psychology, A New Kind of SIGDEV: GCHQ PowerPoint Presentation," Electronic Frontier Foundation, NSA Primary Sources, February 18, 2014, https://www.eff.org/document/20140218-intercept-gchq-sigdev.

123. Brian Massumi, *Ontopower: War, Powers, and the State of Perception* (Durham, NC: Duke University Press, 2015), 26.

124. Foucault outlined the concept in a discussion of neoliberal rationality's "regulation of environmental effects"; see Michel Foucault, *The Birth of Biopolitics*, ed. Arnold I. Davidson, trans. Graham Burchell (Basingstoke: Palgrave Macmillan, 2008), 261.

125. This resonates with social systems theory, as proposed by Niklas Luhmann, *Theory of Society*, trans. Rhodes Barrett (Stanford, CA: Stanford University Press, 2012), 1:28-49; see also Erich Hörl, "Introduction to General Ecology," in *General Ecology: The New Ecological Paradigm*, ed. James Edward Burton, trans. Nils F. Schott (London: Bloomsbury Academic, 2017).

CHAPTER 8

1. Michel Serres, *The Parasite* (Minneapolis: University of Minnesota Press, 2007), 26–27.

2. Friedrich A. Kittler, "Protected Mode," in *The Truth of the Technological World*, trans. Erik Butler (Stanford, CA: Stanford University Press, 2013), 209–218.

3. Benjamin H. Bratton, *The Stack: On Software and Sovereignty*, Software Studies (Cambridge, MA: MIT Press, 2015).

4. Bratton, *The Stack*, 75–107.

5. Chris Miller, *Chip War: The Fight for the World's Most Critical Technology*, 1st ed. (London: Simon & Schuster UK, 2023).

6. Bratton, *The Stack*, 109–145.

7. Bratton, *The Stack*, 120–121.

8. Bratton, *The Stack*, 147–189.

9. Bratton, *The Stack*, 191–217.

10. Bratton, *The Stack*, 219.

11. Bratton, *The Stack*, 220.

12. Kavita Dattani, "'Governtrepreneurism' for Good Governance: The Case of Aadhaar and the India Stack," *Area* 52, no. 2 (2020): 411–419, https://doi.org/10.1111/area.12579. See also "India Stack," accessed April 14, 2024, https://indiastack.org/.

13. Bratton, *The Stack*, 251.

14. Bratton, *The Stack*, 279.

15. "XKeyScore—NSA Presentation," Snowden Doc Search, February 25, 2008, https://www.eff.org/document/2013-07-31-guard-xkeyscore-training-slides.

16. "NSA/CSS Threat Operations Center, TREASURE MAP: Bad Guys Are Everywhere, Good Guys Are Somewhere! Undated. TS//SI//REL TO USA, FVEY," National Security Archive, accessed May 8, 2024, https://nsarchive.gwu.edu/document/22626-document-01-nsa-css-threat-operations-center.

17. Helen Warrell and Nic Fildes, "Amazon Strikes Deal with UK Spy Agencies to Host Top-Secret Material," *Financial Times*, October 25, 2021, https://www.ft.com/content/74782def-1046-4ea5-b796-0802cfb90260.

18. Sam Biddle, "How Peter Thiel's Palantir Helped the NSA Spy on the Whole World," *The Intercept*, February 22, 2017.

19. "How Palantir Is Shaping the Future of Warfare," *Time*, July 10, 2023, https://time.com/6293398/palantir-future-of-warfare-ukraine/; Stephen Armstrong, "Palantir Gets £480m Contract to Run NHS Data Platform," *BMJ* 383 (2023): 2752, https://doi.org/10.1136/bmj.p2752.

20. David Anderson, "Independent Review of the Investigatory Powers Act 2016," Home Office, June 30, 2023, 17–18, https://www.gov.uk/government/publications/independent-review-of-the-investigatory-powers-act-2016--2.

21. Robin Simcox, "Surveillance after Snowden: Effective Espionage in an Age of Transparency," Henry Jackson Society, May 26, 2015, 63, https://henryjacksonsociety.org/wp-content/uploads/2015/06/Surveillance-After-Snowden-16.6.15.pdf.

22. Devlin Barrett, Danny Yadron, and Daisuke Wakabayashi, "Apple and Others Encrypt Phones, Fueling Government Standoff," *Wall Street Journal*, November 19, 2014, sec. US, http://online.wsj.com/articles/apple-and-others-encrypt-phones-fueling-government-standoff-1416367801; Craig Timberg and Jia Lynn Yang, "Google Is

Encrypting Search Globally. That's Bad for the NSA and China's Censors," *Washington Post*, December 6, 2021, https://www.washingtonpost.com/news/the-switch/wp/2014/03/12/google-is-encrypting-search-worldwide-thats-bad-for-the-nsa-and-china/.

23. Anderson, "Independent Review of the Investigatory Powers Act 2016," 8.

24. Ian Walden, "'The Sky is Falling!'—Responses to the 'Going Dark' Problem," *Computer Law & Security Review* 34, no. 4 (2018): 901–907.

25. Ian Levy and Crispin Robinson, "Principles for a More Informed Exceptional Access Debate," *Lawfare* (blog), November 29, 2018, https://www.lawfaremedia.org/article/principles-more-informed-exceptional-access-debate.

26. Sharon B. Franklin and Andi W. Thompson, "Open Letter to GCHQ on the Threats Posed by the Ghost Proposal," *Lawfare* (blog), accessed April 14, 2024, https://www.lawfaremedia.org/article/open-letter-gchq-threats-posed-ghost-proposal; Mallory Knodel, "To the UK: An Encrypted System That Detects Content Isn't End-to-End Encrypted," *Center for Democracy and Technology* (blog), May 25, 2022, https://cdt.org/insights/to-the-uk-an-encrypted-system-that-detects-content-isnt-end-to-end-encrypted/.

27. "Home Office Report on the Operation of the Investigatory Powers Act 2016 (Accessible Version)," *GOV.UK*, 14–15, accessed April 7, 2024, https://www.gov.uk/government/publications/report-on-the-operation-of-the-investigatory-powers-act-2016/home-office-report-on-the-operation-of-the-investigatory-powers-act-2016-accessible-version. 18–19.

28. Joseph Cox, *Dark Wire* (New York: PublicAffairs, 2024), 145–146.

29. R v. A, B, D and C [2021] EWCA Crim 128; see also *R v. Atkinson and others* [2021] EWCA 1447.

30. SF and Ors v. NCA [2023] UKIPTrib 3.

31. Cox, *Dark Wire*, 237–240.

32. Cox, *Dark Wire*, 85–101.

33. Cox, *Dark Wire*, 287.

34. See "The Pegasus project," *The Guardian*, https://www.theguardian.com/news/series/pegasus-project; "Digital Violence: How the NSO Group Enables State Terror," *Forensic Architecture*, https://digitalviolence.org/.

35. Ghanem Al-Masarir v. Kingdom of Saudi Arabia [2022] EWHC 2199 (QB).

36. Podchasov v. Russia, No. 33696/19 (ECtHR February 13, 2024).

37. "The National Security Agency: Missions, Authorities, Oversight and Partnerships," National Security Agency, August 9, 2013, 4–6.

38. Lee Fang, "The CIA Is Investing in Firms That Mine Your Tweets and Instagram Photos," *The Intercept*, April 14, 2016, https://theintercept.com/2016/04/14/in-undisclosed-cia-investments-social-media-mining-looms-large/.

39. Byron Tau, *Means of Control: How the Hidden Alliance of Tech and Government Is Creating a New American Surveillance State* (New York: Crown Publishing, 2024), 144–156.

40. Guanghua Yan et al., "Discovering Suspicious APT Behaviors by Analyzing DNS Activities," *Sensors* 20, no. 3 (January 2020): 731, https://doi.org/10.3390/s20030731.

41. "HIMR Data Mining Research Problem Book," September 20, 2011.

42. Barry Friedman and Danielle Citron, "Indiscriminate Data Surveillance," *Virginia Law Review* (forthcoming), Virginia Public Law and Legal Theory Research Paper No. 2024-22, February 26, 2024.

43. Tom Tugendhat, "UK-US Data Access Agreement: First Year of Use," House of Commons, Home Office, December 19, 2023, https://questions-statements.parliament.uk/written-statements/detail/2023-12-19/hcws152.

44. Anderson, "Independent Review of the Investigatory Powers Act 2016," 11.

45. Investigatory Powers (Amendment) Act 2024, section 2.

46. Anderson, "Independent Review of the Investigatory Powers Act 2016," 16–43.

47. Investigatory Powers (Amendment) Act 2024, section 5.

48. Shoshana Zuboff, *The Age of Surveillance Capitalism: The Fight for a Human Future at the New Frontier of Power* (London: Profile Books, 2019); Nick Srnicek, *Platform Capitalism* (Cambridge: Polity, 2016).

49. Anderson, "Independent Review of the Investigatory Powers Act 2016," 20.

50. Paul F. Scott, "'State Threats,' Security, and Democracy: The National Security Act 2023," *Legal Studies* 44, no. 2 (2024): 260–276.

51. Bernd Debusmann, Matt Murphy, and Natalie Sherman "US House Passes Bill That Could Ban TikTok Nationwide," *BBC News*, March 13, 2024, sec. US and Canada, https://www.bbc.com/news/world-us-canada-68556540.

52. Fan Liang et al., "Constructing a Data-Driven Society: China's Social Credit System as a State Surveillance Infrastructure," *Policy & Internet* 10, no. 4 (2018): 415–453, https://doi.org/10.1002/poi3.183.

53. Minxin Pei, *The Sentinel State: Surveillance and the Survival of Dictatorship in China* (Cambridge, MA: Harvard University Press, 2024), 215.

54. Bratton, *The Stack*, 112.

INDEX

Note: page numbers followed by *f* indicate figures, illustrations, and photographs.

Aadhaar biometric identity database, 206
ABC trial, 130–131
Absolute prerogative, 34
Accountability, 197, 201
Act for Settling the Post (1657), 22
Act of Settlement (1701), 40
Addington, Henry (Viscount Sidmouth), 54
Address system, 65–66
Administrative bureaucracy, 11, 60–61
Afghanistan, 186
AI. *See* Artificial intelligence (AI), 213
Al-Masarir, Ghanem, 210
All-Red cables, 152
Alphabetic writing, 4
Alphanumerical systems, 83–84
Amazon AWS, 208
American Civil War (1861–1865), 76
Anderson, David, 195, 212
Anne, Queen of Great Britain, 40
Anomaly detection, 184
Anom platform, 210

Anson, William, 125
Anti-encryption tactics, 209
Apparatus (*dispositifs*), 8, 38
Application programming interfaces (APIs), 206, 213
Arcana imperii (mysteries of state), 11, 22, 34, 38, 52
ArcaneOS, 210
Archives, 10
Aristotelian morality, 18
ARPANET network, 165
Artificial intelligence (AI), 213, 215
Ascension Island, 90
Asquith, Herbert Henry, 85*f*
AT&T engineers, 154–155
Atomic Energy Commission, 163
Atterbury, Bishop, 44
Attorney-General v. Edison Telephone Co of London Ltd (1880), 88, 125
Aubrey, Crispin, 130, 169
Australia, 158, 172, 174
Australian Federal Police (AFP), 210
Authoritarianism, 136

Automatic Number Plate Recognition (ANPR), 214

Babington Plot (1586), 20
Bamford, James, 168
Banks, 74
Baran, Paul, 247n127
Barbarism of interception, 21
Bar Council, 124
Battle of Naseby (1645), 22
Baudot code, 153
Belgacom, 186
Bell, Alexander Graham, 87, 89
Bellini-Tosi directive device, 101–102
Benbow, William, 54, 55f, 63
Bentham, Jeremy, 38, 64, 68–69
Berry, John, 130, 169
Big Brother Watch and Others v. the United Kingdom (2021), 192, 197
Big data, 179, 181
Big tech, 206
Bill of Rights (1689), 125
Biopolitics, 9, 12, 38, 95
Biopower, 64
Birkett, Norman, 68, 124, 135
Birkett Committee, 117, 131f, 132
Birkett Report, 124–130, 138
Black Chambers of European states, 37, 41, 62
"Blacker" system, 165
Black Hole (storage facility), 182
Blackmail, 129
Blackstone, William, 52
Blencowe, William, 43
Bode, John, 43
Boer War (1899–1902), 62, 93–95, 143
Bolshevik revolution (Russia), 111, 147
Bombes, 156
Booth, Frederick, 89, 117
Borneo, 90
Botero, Giovanni, 16–17
Bratton, Benjamin, 14, 204
Bribery, 20

British Communications Service, 152
British constitution, 129. *See also* Unwritten constitution
British Empire, 90–91, 97, 143–144, 152, 159
British Telecom, 10, 137, 169
British–US Communication Intelligence Agreement (UKUSA), 158–159, 162, 166, 168, 173, 189, 207, 248n155
Broadcasting, concept of, 97
Broad Oak (database), 182, 188, 189f
Browsing history, 182
BRUSA Agreement (1943), 158
Bulk communications datasets (BCD), 194, 196
Bulk data, 207–208, 211–212
Bulk interception, 212
Bulk personal datasets (BPD), 194, 196, 212–213
Bullrun program, 186
Bureaucracy. *See* Administrative bureaucracy
Bush, George W., 175

Cable and Wireless (C&W), 151–152, 244n43
Cable censorship, 93–96
Cablemen, 92–93
Cables (Landing Rights) Committee of the Board of Trade, 91
Cable vetting, 150
Calahan, Edward, 74
Campbell, Duncan, 11, 130, 132, 168–169
Canada, 158, 172, 174
Cancellation practices, 84, 232n69
Capitalism, 14, 129, 138
Carlton, Newcomb, 147
Carlyle, Thomas, 56
CCTV, 214
Censorship, 72, 106–111, 114–115, 142. *See also* Cable censorship
super-censorship, 110
war and, 143–144

INDEX

Central Intelligence Agency (CIA), 132, 162, 208, 211, 226n73
Central Telegraph Office (London), 94
Césaire, Aimé, 143
Chancery clerks, 31
Charities, 190
Charles I, king of England, 16–17, 21–22
Charles II, king of England, 17, 23, 25, 31–32, 45
Chartist movement, 59, 63
  strikes and riots (1842–1843), 54
China, 200, 205, 214
  political surveillance, 214
  social credit system, 214
Christian morality, 18
Church Committee hearings (1970s), 168, 175
Churchill, Winston, 106
CIA. *See* Central Intelligence Agency (CIA)
Ciphers, 11, 22
Civil service unions, 169
Civil War. *See* English Civil War
Codebreaking, 11, 93, 95–96, 146
Coding, 25
Cold War, 118, 158, 160, 170
Coleman, Edward, 33, 45
Colonialism, 90–91, 95, 143, 159. *See also* British Empire; Decolonization
Colossus Mark II, 156–157
COMINT (communications intelligence), 145–150
Committee of Imperial Defence, 106
Committee on Telegraphic Communication with India, 91
Commodity technology, 209
Common Council of London, 22
Communication
  abstract function of, 67
  meaning and sense of, 1
Communications intelligence, 145–147
Communism, 115–116, 122, 128, 131*f*

Communist Party, 214
Community, 7
Competent Military Authority, 108
Computer hacking. *See* Hacking
Computer network exploitation (CNE), 187, 193
Computer power, 162–164
Computing communications, 160–162
Confidential clerks, 73, 82–83
Confidentiality, 80, 133
Conservative Party (UK), 128
Constitutional theory, 106, 226n62
Contingency, 9
Convention for the Protection of Submarine Telegraph Cables (1884), 92
Cooke, William Fothergill, 72–73
Copies, 83–87
Corbiere, Anthony, 44
Corporate partners, 184
Corruption. *See* Political corruption
Counter-Espionage Bureau (MO5), 106
Counterterrorism, 175, 179. *See also* Terrorism
Court-martial, 107
Coventry, Henry, 32–34
Covert listening devices, 123
Cribs, 43, 156
Cribtology, 156
Crimean War (1855), 89
Cromwell, Oliver, 17–18, 22, 220n49
Cromwell, Thomas, 32
Crooked sub-postmasters, 115
Cryptography, 5, 24–25, 95–96, 155
Cryptology, 25, 159
Culture crises, 4
Cumming, Mansfield, 106
Customs work, 135
Cybernetics, 81
Cybersecurity, 186, 211–212
Cyprus, 130, 159, 166, 181
Cryptanalysis, 95, 142

Daily Express, 150
Daily Worker, The, 115
Damages, 210
D-Notice system, 150
Data. *See also* Bulk data
  acquisition, 13
  analytics, 208
  bulk interception of, 173, 179–180, 182, 190, 195–198
  collection, 13
  downstreaming, 192
  exfiltration of, 186
  malicious, 185
  mining, 13
  protection, 139
  visualization software, 187
Databases, 181, 188, 213
de Trevisa, John
  Polychronicon Ranulphi Higden (1387), 31
Deciphering Branch, 42–44, 62
Deciphering process, 25, 62, 95, 146
Decolonization, 91, 159
Defence of the realm, 114, 123, 129
Defence of the Realm Act (1914), 101–102, 107, 110
Defense Advanced Research Projects Agency (DARPA), 165
Democracy, parliamentary, 129
Denniston, Alastair, 150
Department of Defense (US), 165
Department of Justice (US), 175
Depersonalized voice, 88
Dicey, A. V., 111–113, 137
Dictaphone recorders, 117
Dictionary program, 167
Diego Garcia Island, 159
Digby, George, 21
Digital streaming economy, 181
Diplomatic post, 41–42
Direction finding techniques (RDF or D/F), 101–102
Disclosure, 192–193

Dispositif (apparatus), 8, 38
Distillery, 179
Distribution networks, 164–165
Dividing the ether, 98–102
Divine right to rule, 17, 32
Dockwra, William, 29
Domain Name System logs, 212
Donne, John, 53
Dorislaus, Isaac, 18
Dual EC-DRBG (algorithm), 186
Duncombe, Thomas, 56–57

Eastern Telegraph Company, 91
Easter Rising (1916), 110
Echelon, 170–171
Ecological power, 202
Economic depression, 54
Economic well-being, 135
Edison, Thomas, 88
Edison Telephone Company, 88
Electrical epoch, 1, 12, 203
Electrical interception, 71–103
Electrical telegraphy, 12, 72–75
Electric Code Machine, 155
Electric Telegraph Company, 73–75
Electromagnetic code-wheel systems, 155
Electromagnetic switching, 153
Electromagnetic waves, 96–97
Electromechanical encryption machines, 152
Electromechanical teletext, 1
ELINT (electronic intelligence), 146
Elizabeth I, queen of England, 20
Emergency powers, 73
Emergency transmissions, 100–101. *See also* Morse code
Empire. *See* British Empire
Empire Cables, 90–91
Enciphering, 25
Encrochat network, 209–210
Encryption, 1, 13, 208–211. *See also* End-to-end encryption

INDEX

End Product Reports (EPR), 178
End-to-end encryption, 200, 207, 209, 211
English Civil War, 15, 19–24, 26, 43
Enigma machine (*Geheimschrijfmachine*), 152–153, 155–157
Enlightenment era 54
Entick v. Carrington (1765), 50–52 191
Entscheidungsproblem, 157
Environmental effects, regulation of, 254n124
Environmental interception, 173–202
Environmental power, 174
Epistolary subjectivity, 53–56
Equipment interference (EI), 178, 193
Ernst, Wolfgang, 72
Espionage, 12, 23, 120, 126
   economic, 135, 147
   German, 106, 110
   government networks, 54, 63
   letter, 61
   Soviet, 169
   US, 132, 173, 175
Espionage Act (US), 173
European Convention on Human Rights, 133–136, 171, 197–199, 213
   freedom of expression (Art 10), 3, 192–193, 198
   private and family life, right to (Art 8), 3, 192–193, 197
European Court of Human Rights, 2, 134, 169, 171, 189f, 190, 193, 197–198, 201–202, 211
Ewing, Keith, 10
Expression, freedom of. *See* Freedom of expression
Extel, 74
External communications, 135
Extraordinary emergency, 175

Family life. *See* Private and family life, right to
Fascism, 128

FBI. *See* Federal Bureau of Investigation (FBI)
Federal Bureau of Investigation (FBI), 162, 175, 176, 210
Ferris, John, 10, 95, 142, 158
Feudalism, 32
Fiber optics, 180, 185
Field, Cyrus, 91
Field, David, 91
Files, 83–87
Film, 4
First World War. *See* World War I
Fists, 156
Fitzgerald, Peter, 11
Five Alive (QFD), 182
Five-Eyes alliance, 174, 184, 207
Fletcher, Reginald, 119
Flowers, Tommy, 13
Foreign intelligence information, 176
Foreign Intelligence Surveillance Act (1978) (FISA), 168, 175
   Amendments Act (2008), s 702, 176, 185
Foreign Intelligence Surveillance Court (FISC), 175, 186
Foreign languages, 89
Foreign security and intelligence agencies, 113
Foreseeability, 134, 136, 201
Foucault, Michel, 7–9, 18, 38, 58–59, 63–64, 68, 112, 254n124
France, 95
Franking privileges, 30, 64–65
Frank Leslie's Illustrated Newspaper, 76
Fraud (wiretap), 78
Freedom of expression, 3, 196, 198
Freedom of information requests, 168
Freedom of thought, 54
French Revolution (1789–1799), 48

Galloway, Alexander, 177
Gambling, 74, 78, 115
Gardiner, Thomas, 27–29

Gemalto, 186
Genealogical methodology, 3, 7–10
General Data Protection Regulation (GDPR), 212
General Letter Office, 18
General Post Office (GPO)
 communist publications, 115
 date stamps, 28
 engineers, 117
 epistolary communication, 26–27
 establishment, 22
 financial administration of, 26
 function of, 25
 histories of, 12, 16, 18, 29, 31, 36, 77
 Home Office Warrants, 144
 letter interception, 41
 licenses, 98–100
 London Gazette, distribution of, 30
 memoranda, 151
 police apparatus, 37
 postal surveillance, 38
 purpose of, 22–23
 satellites, 166
 stamp system, 29
 telegraphic communication, 75, 82–83
 telephone tapping, 116
General Strike (1926), 149
Geofencing, 211
George I, king of England, 40
George VI, king of England, 72
Germany
 espionage, 106, 110
 governments, 94
 naval transmissions, 102
 spies, 106, 136
 World War I, 107, 110–111, 144–145
 World War II, 146, 152, 156
Ghost protocol, 209
Gibraltar, 102
Global computational networks, 5, 14
Globalization, 93
Global telecommunications, 141
Globe, 78

Glomar Explorer, 226n73
Glorious Revolution (1688), 17, 40, 52
Glover, Phil, 10, 128–129
Google, 185, 205
Gordon Riots (1780), 54
Governmentality, 38, 112
 postal, 40, 51–52
Government Code and Cipher School (GC&CS), 145–147, 149–150, 152, 154–155
Government Communications Headquarters (GCHQ), 10, 124, 130, 136–137, 142, 158–159, 161, 163–170, 174, 208, 213
 Snowden and, 178–187, 200, 202, 248n155
GPO. *See* General Post Office (GPO)
Graham, James, 56–57, 62
Graphing information flows, 184
Great Fire of London, 19
Greenwald, Glenn, 178
Greenwich Mean Time (GMT), 73–75
Greville, Charles, 56
Gutta-percha, 90

Habeas Corpus Suspension Act (1817), 54
Hacking, 13, 123, 173, 178, 195, 200
 bulk operations, 186
Hadoop, 179
Hagelin M-209 machine, 155
Hampshire, Stuart, 163
Handwriting, 4, 19, 84, 117
Harcourt, William, 116
Hardy, Thomas, 48
Harvest Computer, 162–163
Hayek, Friedrich, 137–138
Hebern Electric Code Machine, 155
Heilbronn Institute for Mathematical Research, 178
Henrietta Maria (wife of Charles I), 21
Henry VIII, king of England, 32
Hertz, Heinrich, 96, 101
Hertzian waves, 96

INDEX

Hill, Billy, 124
Hill, Rowland, 62, 64–65
Historical investigation, 132
History
  human, 4
  intelligence services, 10
  interception, 1, 7
  legal, 1–2
  media, 5
  postal system, 12, 15–16
  Post Office, 230n39
HMS Defiance, 96
HMS Diana, 97
Hobbes, Thomas, 34–35, 52
Home Office Warrants (HOW), 144
Hong, Sungook, 235n125
Hong Kong, 154, 159, 166, 178
Hooper, Leonard, 248n155
Horne Tooke, John, 48, 49f
Hosenball, Mark, 130, 168
Howell, James, 21
Huawei, 214
Humanism, 3–4
Human perception, 3
Human rights law, 133–134
  activists, 210
  Convention rights. *See* European Convention on Human Rights
  importance of, 2
  international law, 136, 138–139
  legal compliance, 212
  organizations, 190
  transnational instruments, 105

IBM, 162–164
IBM Streams, 179
ILC communications traffic, 164
ILC Control Party, 161
ILC traffic, 167
Imaginary level, 3–4
Immoral literature, 115
Imperial Communications Advisory Committee, 151
Imperialism, 90, 172
In camera trials (1980s), 136
Indecent material, 114–115
Index cards, 108, 111, 152, 164
India, 90–91, 95, 154
India Stack, 206
Indonesia (Sumatra), 90
Infection vectors, 183
Information
  duty not to misuse, 100
  right to receive, 100
  science, 4, 13
  theory, 6, 116–117
Informers, 113
Inland Letter Office, 26
Innis, Harold, 141
Instrumentalism, 18
Integration, 203–215
Intelligence
  gathering, 142
  interception and 10, 16–19
  sharing, 192
Intelligence and Security Committee of Parliament (ISC), 191, 195
Intelligence Services Act (1994), 170, 187, 192, 194
INTELSAT satellites, 165
Interception of Communications Act 1985 (IOCA), 2, 135–137, 169–170
Interception of Communications Commissioner's Office (IOCCO), 191
Interception of Communications Tribunal (ICT), 136
International cable switching centers, 167
International Licensed Carriers (ILCs), 158
International maritime law, 91–92
International Telecommunication Union (ITU), 235n137
International Telegraph Bureau (Berne), 90, 94–95

International Telegraph Convention (1875), 90, 93
International Telegraph Union, 90
Internet
  cloud-based service providers, 180, 208, 214
  digital networks, 5
  genealogies of, 247n124
  global traffic, 180, 200, 211–212
  rise of, 2
  turn (1996), 142
Internet Protocol (IP), 179–180
Interpersonal communication, 5
Interregnum, 15, 220n49
Interrogation techniques, 113
Investigatory Powers Act (2016), 3, 194–196, 198–199, 208–210, 212
Investigatory Powers Commissioner's Office (IPCO), 197–199
Investigatory Powers Tribunal (IPT), 171, 190, 193, 198, 201, 210
Invisible ink, 24, 110
Iraq, 90
Ireland, 102. *See also* Northern Ireland
  bombing campaigns, 63
  civil unrest, 147
  nationalism, 59
  republicanism, 110, 119
Islamic State (ISIS), 211
Israel, 210
ITT (cable company), 161

Jackson, Henry, 96
Jacobite rebellion (1745), 40–41, 48, 223n6
James, Henry
  In the Cage (1898), 80–81
James Francis Edward Stuart, 40
James II, king of England, 16–17, 33, 40, 223n6
Japan, 97
John Bull 116
Joint Intelligence Committee (JIC), 188
Journalism, 11, 132
Judicial review, 106, 130, 169, 213

Keill, John, 43
Kell, Vernon, 106, 110–111, 119–120, 121*f*
Kenya, 181
KGB (Soviet Union), 169
Kind, Eric, 198
King's Cabinet Opened, The, 22
Kittler, Friedrich, 3–4, 157, 178, 203
Knickebein-Verfahren system, 146
Knowledge, 18

Labor movements, 54
Labour Party (UK), 128
Lacan, Jacques, 3
Lamont, Richard, 171
Landau, Susan, 186
Languages, 89, 156
Laski, Harold, 112–113, 129, 138, 226n62
  Crown, critique of the, 111–113
Lawson, Neil, 131*f*
Legalization, 168–170
Legal updates, 212–215
Legislative turn, 135–138
Legitimacy, 201
Leopold, Mark, 11
Letter Office, 21
Letters, 2
  feminine nature of, 75
  interception, 12, 16–17, 20
  "letter check" requests, 123
  private, 26
  surveillance of, 11
Leviathan, state as, 34–36
Libel. *See* Seditious libel
Liberalism, 63–64, 136–137
Liberal technology of communication, 38
Liberty, 38
Liberty (campaign group), 171, 190, 198

INDEX

Liberty v. GCHQ (2015), 190, 193
Lightning project, 162
Listening watch, 100
Lists, 50
Literacy
  epistolary, 53
  technical, 177
Lithuania, 210
Location brokers, 211
Location data, 214
Locomotive (tracking tool), 211
London Gazette, 23, 30
London Stock Exchange (LSE), 74–75
Long packets, 42
Lorenz SZ40/42, 156
Lottery competitions, 62–63, 114–115

Machiavelli, Niccolò, 18
  Prince, The (1532), 16
Machine learning (ML), 181, 183, 214
Macmillan, Harold, 124
Magna Carta (1215), 21
Magnetic audiotape recorders, 117
Mahoney, Joan, 10
Malaya, 90
Malone, James, 132–134
Malone v. Metropolitan Police Commissioner (1979), 132–137, 169, 193
Malta, 154
Malware, 186, 211
Manchester Chamber of Commerce, 77
Marconi, Guglielmo, 96–98, 102, 147, 166, 235n123
Margin of appreciation doctrine, 202
Maritime communication. *See* Submarine telegraphy
Marrinan, Patrick, 124
Mary, Queen of Scots, 20
Mary II, queen of England, 17, 40
Maskelyne, Nevil, 97
Massive volume reduction, 181
Mass surveillance, 7, 194, 200, 214
Massumi, Brian, 202

Materiality of interception, 10–11, 48, 67, 71–72, 80, 86, 101–102, 143, 202
Mathematics, 157
Matthews, Thomas, 39
Maxwell, James Clerk, 96
Maxwell-Fyfe Directive (1952), 114
Mazzini, Giuseppe, 56–61, 67, 105
McLuhan, Marshall, 3, 89
Mechanical cryptanalysis, 155–157
Mechanical transmission, 153–155
Media theory, 3–7
Medieval government, 20, 31
Megarry, Mr., 132–133, 137
Members of Parliament (MPs), 30, 45, 116, 195
Merchant Posts and Strangers' Posts, 20
Metadata, 119, 170, 175, 177, 180–183, 191–192, 198, 213
Meter check printer (MCP), 119
Metering, 119
Metropolitan Police Special Branch, 63
Mexico, 144
MI5. *See* Security Service (MI5)
MI6. *See* Secret Intelligence Service (MI6)
Microdots, 110
Microphones, secret, 113
Microwaves, 166–167, 171
Middle East, 154
MILNET network, 165
Minaret, 162
Ministry of Defence (UK), 171
Miranda number, 188
Mirror of Life, 89
Mobile networks, 186
Mobile phones, 183
  encrypted, 209
  location tracking, 211, 214
Modernity, 8–9
Monarchy, Restoration of, 15
Mondial House, 167
Monoalphabetic transformation system, 25

Morality, 18, 63
Moretta, Andrew, 10
Morland, Samuel, 5, 16–20, 23–24, 34, 108
Morse code, 72, 79, 96–97, 100–102, 110, 153
Muscular program, 185
Mutant Broth, 182
Mutual Weapons Development Program, 163

National Archives (UK), 10, 48, 84, 129, 232n63
National Crime Agency (NCA), 209
National Health Service (NHS), 208
National Institute of Standards and Technology (NIST), 186
Nationalization, 75–76, 87–88
National Security Act UK (2023), 214
National Security Agency (NSA), 3, 7, 13, 246n90, 246n101
  environmental interception, 173–178, 180, 184, 186
  integration, 207, 211, 213
  radio epoch, 159, 161–166, 170
  telephone tapping, 132
National Security Notices, 196
national security orders, 169
Neither confirm nor deny (NCND), 57, 191, 193, 226n73
Neoliberalism, 106, 137–138, 254n124
Network exploitation, 178
Newspapers, 30, 74, 115
New York Stock Exchange (NYSE), 74–75
New York Times, 176
New Zealand, 158, 172, 174
NGOs. *See* Nongovernmental organizations (NGOs)
Noise pollution, 97–98
Nomos, concept of, 137–138
Nongovernmental organizations (NGOs), 190

Northern Ireland
  communications intelligence, scale of, 239n77
  Troubles conflict (1968–1998), 119, 169
NSA. *See* National Security Agency (NSA)
NSA Technical Journal, 162
NSO Group, 210
Nuncii et cursores, 20

Obama, Barack, 176
Official Secrets Act (1889), 67, 108, 130
Official Secrets Act (1920), 169
  ss. 4–5 147, 149
Oman, 181
One-Time Pad (OTP), 155
Ontopower, 202
Open reception, 98
Open-source data, 168, 186, 211
Operational closure, concept of, 66
Operational Legalities, 187
Operation Shamrock, 161, 168
Optic Nerve program, 185
Orange Free State, 93–94
Overseas territories, 159
Oversight bodies, 106, 187, 194, 197
Over-the-horizon observation, 102
Overwriting, 84

Packet inspection algorithms, 180
Packet-switching, 165
Paine, Thomas, 48, 49f
Pakistan (Karachi), 90
Palantir (data analytics firm), 187, 208
Paramilitaries, 119
Parasitic interception, 6–7, 203, 215
Parliamentary sovereignty doctrine, 111
Patents, Designs and Trade Marks Act (1883), 97
Pegasus program, 210

Penny post system, 29, 65
Peterloo Massacre, 54
Phonographs, 4, 110
Photography, 108, 110, 119
Physics, 96
Pianola device, 144–145
Planetary computation, 14, 204, 215
PlanetRisk (US firm), 211
Platform network, 165
Poitras, Laura, 178
Pole Star system, 164
Police
　powers, 36
　state, 12, 15, 52, 226n62
　suppression, strategies of, 54
　wiretapping, 12
　work, 135
Political activism, 136
Political corruption, 54
Political crime, 54
Political freedom, 54
Pornography, 63, 115
Porter, Bernard, 226n62
Positive international law, 51, 91
Postal epoch, 1–2, 5, 8, 15–16, 203
Postal Museum and Archive (London), 10
Postal system
　apparatus, 25–30
　governmentality, 51–52
　historical development, 2, 12
　illegal networks, 11
　institutionalization of, 26–28
　materiality, 66–67
　professionalization of, 26–28
　sorting work/desks, 28–29
　surveillance apparatus, 11, 38–41
　technology, 63–68
Postcards, 79
Postmen (messengers), 106
Post Office (Protection) Act (1884), 99
Post Office (Revenues) Act (1710), 58
Post Office Act (1908)

s. 56(2), 114
Post Office Act (1969), 169
　s. 11, 167
　s. 11(3), 167–168
　s. 11(6), 168
Post Office Engineering Union, 128
　ss. 40–41, 44
Power
　absolute, 36
　administrative, 11
　categories of, 8
　coercive, 35
　communication, 1
　ecological model, 202
　environmental, 13, 174
　exceptional, 36
　law and, 7
　medieval, 31–32
　military, 13
　ontopower, 202
　political, 17
　as *potentia*, 52
　as *potestas*, 52
　production of, 1
　reflexive, 69
　semantics of, 202
　sovereign, 5–7, 16, 33–35, 59, 215
　surveillance, scope of, 12–13
　writing and, 19
President's Surveillance Program (PSP), 175–176
Pretender, the, 223n6
Prideaux, Edmund, 22
Prime, Geoffrey, 169
Prism program, 185, 191–192, 211
Prisoners of war (POWs), 110, 147
Privacy, 9
　abuses of, 191–192
　data, 2
　private communication, right to, 54
　right to, 2–3, 15, 134
　writing, 19
Privacy International, 190, 193, 198

Privacy International v. Secretary of State for Foreign and Commonwealth Affairs (2016), 194
Private life, right to, 134, 211
Privatization, 13, 208
Probable cause, 51, 176
Problem Book, 178, 181
Programmers, 164
Propaganda, 21
Property
 damage, 123
 interference, 194, 196
 private, 51, 129
Proportionality, 136, 212–213
Protectorate government (1649–1660), 17–18
Public interest, 196
Publicity, 37–69, 115–116
Public law, 2, 10, 106, 136
Public power, 52
Puzzle Palace, The, 168

Quantum computing, 215
Query-focused databases (QFDs), 182

Radio epoch, 5, 13, 141–172, 176
Radio-frequency identification (RFID), 214
Radio Security Service, 102
Radio signals, 2
Ragion di stato, 16–17
Raison d'état, 2, 11, 15
Random Forest, 183
Random noise, 160
Rationality, 12, 16, 51, 63–64, 71, 215, 254n124
 economic, 136, 138
RCA (cable company), 161
Real, 4
Reasonable grounds for suspicion, 51
Reason of state, 15–16, 33–36, 51
Reformism, 37, 64, 83
Reform movements, 54–56

Refugees, 210–211
Regin (malware), 186
Regulation of Investigatory Powers Act 2000 (RIPA), 2, 136, 170, 184–185, 187, 190–192, 197–198
 s. 8(1) warrant, 188
 s. 8(4) warrant, 188, 190–191
Repeater amplifiers, 116
Representation of the People Act (1867), 64
Republic of letters (*Republic de lettres*), 53
Risk, 9
Room 40 codebreakers, 144
Royal Navy, 91, 96–98, 102, 142, 154
Royal prerogative, 2, 37
Royal Society, 43
Royal Ulster Constabulary (RUC), 119
Royal United Services Institute (RUSI), 195
Royal writs, 20
RSA (security company), 186
Rule of law, 130–134, 139
 ordinary law, 111–112
Russia, 111, 144, 173, 211. *See also* Soviet Union
 language, 118
 naval radio operators, 97
 Soviet, 115, 147, 148f, 157–158
 telegrams, 95
R. v. Doctor Hensey (1758), 39

Samuel Pepys (QFD), 182
Satellite interception, 142, 165–168
Saudi Arabia, 210
Schmitt, Carl, 33–34
Scientific American, 87
Scott, Paul F., 10
Scott, Russell, 120, 121f
Scriveners, 83
Scudamore, Frank Ives, 77
Sea communication. *See* Submarine telegraphy
Sealed Knot conspiracy, 19

Seal opening, 18
Second World War. *See* World War II
Secrecy, 2, 5, 115–116
  absolute, 10
  declarations of, 99
  essential state component, 69
  governmental, 67
  language, 94
  management, 67
  official, 12
  policy, as, 61–63
  political, 19
  privacy and, 7
  selling secrets, criminalization of, 67
Secret Committee, 45
Secret Committees of Parliament, 56–61
Secret Intelligence Service (MI6), 106, 152, 170, 208
Secret Office, 41–44
Secret Service Bureau, 106
Secret writing. *See* Cryptography
Security Service Act (1989), 114, 194
Security Service (MI5), 12
  electrical interception, 89
  environmental interception, 194, 198
  integration, 208
  publicity, 68
  telephone tapping, 105–106, 108–109, 111, 113–114, 117, 122–123, 138–139
Security work, 135
Seditious libel, 50–51
Selectors, 162
September 11, 2001 attacks, 174–175
Serious crime, 126, 135, 191, 196, 200
Serres, Michael 6, 203
Servan, Michel de, 53–54
Security Service Act (1989), 123
Sexual assault, 169
Sexual morality, 63
Shannon, Claude, 160

Ship-to-ship communication, 99–100
Shortwave, 150–152, 167
Siegert, Bernhard, 66
Siemens T-52 *Geheimschreiber* (Cryptwriter), 156
SIGINT (signals intelligence), 145–147, 158, 163–165, 178, 185
Signal jamming, 97
Signals intelligence, 102
SIM-card manufacturers, 186
Skynet platform, 214
Sky platform, 210
Slavery, 76
Smart cities, 205
Smartphones, 4. *See also* Mobile phones
Smith, Adam, 52
Snowden, Edward, 3, 5, 7, 13, 169, 171, 173–202, 204, 206, 211
  acquisition, 184–185
  elucidation, 190–194
  exploitation, 185–187
  gap closures, 195–199
  SGCHQ and, 178–187, 208
  interception, 178–184
  interface legalities, 187–190
  reflexive legality, 199–200
Social Anthropoid, 182
Social class, 66, 68–69
Socialism, 138
Social media, 214
Software languages, 165
South African Republic, 93–94
Sovereign interests, 34
Sovereign power, 5–7, 16, 33–35, 59, 215
Sovereignty, 203, 211. *See also* Power
  absolute, 11, 15, 17
  classical, 9
  interception and, 15–36
  knowledge and, 18
  parliamentary, 17, 111
  political, 6–7
  territorial, 15–16

Soviet Union, 147, 148f
  collapse of, 174
  economic development, 160
Special Branch (UK), 113
Special Facilities (SF), 123
Special Forces (US), 211
Spyware, 210
Stack, the
  address layer, 205, 212–214
  city layer, 205, 214
  cloud layer, 205, 208–209, 211
  concept, 14
  earth layer, 204–205, 211
  epoch of the, 204–206
  integration, 206–207
  interface layer, 206, 213
  rival, 214
  user layer, 206
  vertical, 214
Stamps, 66–67
Starosielski, Nicole, 159
State
  apparatus, 8
  categories of, 8
  police (see Police: state)
  practices, 8
  reason of (see Reason of state)
  security, 67
  territorial, 17, 32
Statistics, 18, 25, 30, 59, 153–154
Steganography
  censorship and, 110
  linguistic, 24
  postal, 110
  technical, 24
Stellar Wind report, 174, 177
Stewart, Findlater, 122
St. Helena, 90, 95
Stock exchanges. See London Stock Exchange (LSE); New York Stock Exchange (NYSE)
  telegraphy, impact on, 229n20

Strowger automatic telephone exchange, 116
Stuart dynasty, 17
Studeman, William, 170
Subcommittee on Competition, 151
Submarine telegraphy, 89–93, 226n73
  British imperial control, 90
  threats to undersea cables, 91
Subversives, 129
Supercomputers, 162, 164
Surveillance, mass. See Mass surveillance
Symbolic order, 4
Syntony, 97
Systems theory, 66, 202

Tacitus, 16, 18
Tapping, 12, 14
Tapping the line, 76–78
Targeted Equipment Interference (TEI), 209–210
Taxation, 22
TCP/IP (internet communications protocols), 165, 179
Technical Capability Notices, 196
Technical literacy, 7
Techniques, interception, 11
Technology standards, 5
Technoscientific techniques, 123
Telecommunications Act (1984), 195
  s. 94, 137, 169, 187, 194
Telecommunications Act (2013), 195
Telegrams, 2, 4
  acquisition of, 78–81
  definition of, 75
  masculine nature of, 75
  nationalization of, 75
Telegraph Act (1863), 73, 75
  Punishment for disclosing or intercepting Messages (s. 20), 80
  telephones as telegraphs (s. 3), 88
  warrants and licensing arrangements (s. 52), 144

INDEX

Telegraphy. *See also* Electrical telegraphy; Submarine telegraphy
  era, 5
  nationalization of, 231n46
  warrants, 81–83
  wireless, 12
Telekryption machines, 155
Telephone interception, 2, 12. *See also* Tapping
  warrants, 119–123
Telephone patents, 232–233n78
Telephone tapping, 116–119
Telephony, 12, 87–89. *See also* Tapping the line
  Bell telephone, 87
  depersonalization, 88
  female operators, 88
  legal definition of, 87
  nationalization of, 88
  tapping, 89, 105–139
Teletype
  equipment, 164
  principle, 154
Television, 165–166
Tempora program, 179, 181–182, 190–191, 212
Territoriality, 141–142, 171, 194
Terrorism, 169. *See also* Counterterrorism; September 11, 2001 attacks; War on terror
  legislation, 195, 212, 214
  suspects, business records of, 177
Thatcher, Margaret, 137, 169
Thesis, concept of, 137
Thirty Years' War (1618–1648), 16
Thompson, William (Lord Kelvin), 87
Thurloe, John, 18–19, 23
TikTok, 214
Time Out, 130, 168–169
Times, The, 56, 128
Todd, Anthony, 42–43
Tor (browser), 184
Total interception, 143–145

Totalitarianism, 136, 138
Tractor (magnetic tape handling system), 163
Trades Union Congress (TUC), 128
Traffic analysis, 146
Transcription techniques, 117–118
Translucency, 195
Transmission Control Protocol (TCP), 179
TreasureMap, 207, 207f
Trespass, 51, 53, 123
Tuck, Raphael, 110
Turing, Alan, 4, 13, 141, 157, 160
Turing Machine, 157
Twin Star system, 164
Typewriters, 1, 4, 86, 108
Typex machines, 155

UHF transmission, 166
Ukraine, 208
UKUSA. *See* British–US Communication Intelligence Agreement (UKUSA)
UK–US Data Access Agreement (2022), 212
Ultra program, 156, 159
Undersea cables. *See* Submarine telegraphy, 91
Union of Soviet Socialist Republics (USSR). *See* Soviet Union
United States (US), 13
  cable-laying operations, 180
  civil war (*see* American Civil War (1861–1865))
  Congress, 168
  Constitution, 129, 177
  counterterrorism, 175
  cryptology, 159
  Five-Eyes alliance, 174
  Navy, 97
  post-war alliance, 172
  telegraph network, 74
  telephony, 87–88

United States (US) (*continued*)
   UK alliance, 157–159 (*see also* British–US Communication Intelligence Agreement (UKUSA))
   USA PATRIOT Act, *s.* 215, 175, 177
UNIVAC 1101 (computer), 162–163
UNIVAC 1103A (computer), 163
Universal discrete machine, 4, 13, 141, 157
Universal suffrage, 54
Unwritten constitution, 2, 52, 111
US. *See* United States (US)
Users, 164
Utilitarianism, 37, 59, 64

VHF transmission, 166
Vigenère system, 25
Virtual Intelligence, Surveillance, and Reconnaissance, 211
Vismann, Cornelia, 10–11, 18
Voice recognition, 214
Voluntary interceptors, 102
Voting rights. *See* Universal suffrage

Walker, Gordon, 128
Wallis, John, 25, 43
Walpole, Robert, 45
Walsingham, Francis, 20
War, 5, 78
   censorship and, 143–144
   undersea cable network, effect on, 92
War Office, 93–94, 108
War on terror, 174
Warrants, 2, 6, 30–34
   COMINT and, 147–150
   definitions of, 31
   general, 51
   legislation, 44–50
   prohibition on general, 50–51
   radio epoch, 147–150
   telegraphic, 81–83
   telephone interception, 119–123
   two-sided (1726), 46–47*f*

War Trade Intelligence Department (WTID), 145
Watchdogs, 191
Watergate scandal, 168
Wavelength settings, 100
Weak labelling, 183–184
Webcams, 185
WeChat, 205
Western Union, 74, 87, 147, 161
Wheatstone, Charles, 72
Whigs, 29
Whistleblowers, 3, 178
Whyman, Susan, 53
Wildman, John, 18
Willes, Edward, 43–44
William III, king of England, 40
Williamson, Joseph, 33
Wilson, Woodrow, 144
Wireless interception, 142–143
Wireless messaging, 96–98
Wireless technologies, 235n125
Wireless Telegraph and Signal Company, 96
Wireless Telegraphy Act (1904), *s.* 5, 98–99, 151
Wireless Telegraphy Act (1949), 161
Wiretap fraud, 78
Wiretapping, 10, 12–13
Witherings, Thomas, 21
Women
   confidential information, 80–81
   female typists, 86
Word spotters, 162–163
Workers Weekly, 115
World War I, 12–13
   blanket censorship, 142
   censorship regime, 72, 106
   code systems, 236n147
   handwritten conversations, 117
   market transactions, 160
   radio for military power, 141
   telephone tapping, 89

wireless apparatus, 101–102
World War II, 4, 13
  Bletchley Park codebreakers, 1, 5, 13, 141, 154, 157, 160, 203
  mobile telephone censorship units, 120
  night bombing, 146
  official intelligence accounts, 132
  post-war records, 10
  pre-war archives, 10
  radio for military power, 141

Wright, Peter, 123
Writing, secret. *See* Cryptography
Wrongdoing, 113

XKeyscore platform, 186–187, 207

Yahoo, 185
Yoo, John, 175
Y stations, 154

Zimmerman telegram, 144–145